THE Chrysanthemum *and the* Sword

THE Chrysanthemum *and the* Sword

Patterns of Japanese Culture

by

RUTH
BENEDICT

A MERIDIAN BOOK

NEW AMERICAN LIBRARY

NEW YORK AND SCARBOROUGH, ONTARIO

Library of Congress Catalog Card Number: 67-26538
ISBN 0-452-00561-2
Reprinted by arrangement with
Houghton Mifflin & Company

MERIDIAN TRADEMARK REG. U.S. PAT. OFF. AND FOREIGN COUNTRIES
REGISTERED TRADEMARK—MARCA REGISTRADA
HECHO EN WESTFORD, MASS., U.S.A.

SIGNET, SIGNET CLASSIC, MENTOR, ONYX, PLUME, MERIDIAN and
NAL BOOKS are published *in the United States* by
NAL PENGUIN INC.,
1633 Broadway, New York, New York 10019,
in Canada by The New American Library of Canada Limited,
81 Mack Avenue, Scarborough, Ontario M1L 1M8.

First Printing/World Publishing Company, 1967
First Printing/New American Library, May 1974

9 10 11 12 13 14 15 16 17
PRINTED IN THE UNITED STATES OF AMERICA

Acknowledgements

JAPANESE MEN AND WOMEN who had been born or educated in Japan and who were living in the United States during the war years were placed in a most difficult position. They were distrusted by many Americans. I take special pleasure, therefore, in testifying to their help and kindness during the time when I was gathering the material for this book. My thanks are due them in very special measure. I am especially grateful to my wartime colleague, Robert Hashima. Born in this country, brought up in Japan, he chose to return to the United States in 1941. He was interned in a War Relocation Camp, and I met him when he came to Washington to work in the war agencies of the United States.

My thanks are also due to the Office of War Information, which gave me the assignment on which I report in this book, and especially to Professor George E. Taylor, Deputy Director for the Far East, and to Commander Alexander H. Leighton, MC–USNR, who headed the Foreign Morale Analysis Division.

I wish to thank also those who have read this book in whole or in part: Commander Leighton, Professor Clyde Kluckhohn and Dr. Nathan Leites, all of whom were in the Office of War Information during the time I was working on Japan and who assisted in many ways; Professor Conrad Arensberg, Dr. Margaret Mead, Gregory Bateson and E. H. Norman. I am grateful to all of them for suggestions and help.

RUTH BENEDICT

THE AUTHOR wishes to thank the publishers who have given her permission to quote from their publications: D. Appleton-Century Company, Inc., for permission to quote from *Behind the Face of Japan*, by Upton Close; Edward Arnold and Company for permission to quote from *Japanese Buddhism*, by Sir Charles Eliot; The John Day Company, Inc., for permission to quote from *My Narrow Isle*, by Sumie Mishima; J. M. Dent and Sons, Ltd., for permission to quote from *Life and Thought of Japan*, by Yoshisabura Okakura; Doubleday and Company for permission to quote from *A Daughter of the Samurai*, by Etsu Inagaki Sugimoto; Penguin Books, Inc., and the *Infantry Journal* for permission to quote from an article by Colonel Harold Doud in *How the Jap Army Fights*; Jarrolds Publishers (London), Ltd., for permission to quote from *True Face of Japan*, by K. Nohara; The Macmillan Company for permission to quote from *Buddhist Sects of Japan*, by E. Oberlin Steinilber, and from *Japan: An Attempt at Interpretation*, by Lafcadio Hearn; Rinehart and Company, Inc., for permission to quote from *Japanese Nation*, by John F. Embree; and The University of Chicago Press for permission to quote from *Suye Mura*, by John F. Embree.

CONTENTS

I

Assignment: Japan

THE JAPANESE were the most alien enemy the United States had ever fought in an all-out struggle. In no other war with a major foe had it been necessary to take into account such exceedingly different habits of acting and thinking. Like Czarist Russia before us in 1905, we were fighting a nation fully armed and trained which did not belong to the Western cultural tradition. Conventions of war which Western nations had come to accept as facts of human nature obviously did not exist for the Japanese. It made the war in the Pacific more than a series of landings on island beaches, more than an unsurpassed problem of logistics. It made it a major problem in the nature of the enemy. We had to understand their behavior in order to cope with it.

The difficulties were great. During the past seventy-five years since Japan's closed doors were opened, the Japanese have been described in the most fantastic series of 'but also's' ever used for any nation of the world. When a serious observer is writing about peoples other than the Japanese and says they are unprecedentedly polite, he is not likely to add, 'But also insolent and overbearing.' When he says people of some nation are incomparably rigid in their behavior, he does not add, 'But also they adapt themselves readily to extreme innovations.' When he says a people are submissive, he does not explain too that they are not easily amenable to control from above. When he says they are loyal and generous, he does not declare, 'But also treacherous and spiteful.' When he says they are genuinely brave, he does not expatiate on their timidity. When he says they act out of concern for others' opinions, he does not then go on to tell that they have a truly terrifying conscience. When he describes robot-like discipline in their Army, he does not continue by describing the way the soldiers in that Army take the bit in their own teeth even to the point of insubordination. When he describes a people who devote themselves with passion to Western learning, he does not also enlarge on their fervid conservatism. When he writes a book on a nation with a popular cult of aestheticism which gives high honor to actors and to artists and lavishes art upon the cultivation of chrysanthemums, that book does not ordinarily have to be supplemented by another which is devoted to the cult of the sword and the top prestige of the warrior.

All these contradictions, however, are the warp and woof of books on Japan. They are true. Both the sword and the chrysanthemum are a part of the picture. The Japanese are, to the highest degree, both aggressive and unaggressive, both militaristic and aesthetic, both insolent and polite, rigid and adaptable, submissive and resentful of being pushed around, loyal and treacherous, brave and timid, conservative and hospitable to new ways. They are terribly concerned about what other people will think of their behavior, and they are also overcome by guilt when other people know nothing of their misstep. Their soldiers are disciplined to the hilt but are also insubordinate.

When it became so important for America to understand Japan, these contradictions and many others equally blatant could not be waved aside. Crises were facing us in quick succession. What would the Japanese do? Was capitulation possible without invasion? Should we bomb the Emperor's palace? What could we expect of Japanese prisoners of war? What should we say in our propaganda to Japanese troops and to the Japanese homeland which could save the lives of Americans and lessen Japanese determination to fight to the last man? There were violent disagreements among those who knew the Japanese best. When peace came, were the Japanese a people who would require perpetual martial law to keep them in order? Would our army have to prepare to fight desperate bitter-enders in every mountain fastness of Japan? Would there have to be a revolution in Japan after the order of the French Revolution or the Russian Revolution before international peace was possible? Who would lead it? Was the alternative the eradication of the Japanese? It made a great deal of difference what our judgments were.

In June, 1944, I was assigned to the study of Japan. I was asked to use all the techniques I could as a cultural anthropologist to spell out what the Japanese were like. During that early summer our great offensive against Japan had just begun to show itself in its true magnitude. People in the United States were still saying that the war with Japan would last three years, perhaps ten years, more. In Japan they talked of its lasting one hundred years. Americans, they said, had had local victories, but New Guinea and the Solomons were thousands of miles away from their home islands. Their official communiqués had hardly admitted naval defeats and the Japanese people still regarded themselves as victors.

In June, however, the situation began to change. The second front was opened in Europe and the military priority which the High Command had for two years and a half given to the European theater paid off. The end of the war against Germany was in sight. And in the Pacific our forces landed on Saipan, a great operation forecasting eventual Japanese defeat. From then on our soldiers were to face the Japanese army at constantly closer quarters. And we knew well, from the fighting in New Guinea, on Guadalcanal, in Burma, on Attu and Tarawa and Biak, that we were pitted against a formidable foe.

In June, 1944, therefore, it was important to answer a multitude of questions about our enemy, Japan. Whether the issue was military or diplomatic, whether it was raised by questions of high policy or of leaflets to be dropped behind the Japanese front lines, every insight was important. In the all-out war Japan was fighting we had to know, not just the aims and motives of those in power in Tokyo, not just the long history of Japan, not just economic and military statistics; we had to know what their government could count on from the people. We had to try to understand Japanese habits of thought and emotion and the patterns into which these habits fell. We had to know the sanctions behind these actions and opinions. We had to put aside for the moment the premises on which we act as Americans and to keep ourselves as far as possible from leaping to the easy conclusion that what we would do in a given situation was what they would do.

My assignment was difficult. America and Japan were at war and it is easy in wartime to condemn wholesale, but far harder to try to see how your enemy looks at life through his own eyes. Yet it had to be done. The question was how the Japanese would behave, not how we would behave if we were in their place. I had to try to use Japanese behavior in war as an asset in understanding them, not as a liability. I had to look at the way they conducted the war itself and see it not for the moment as a military problem but as a cultural problem. In warfare as well as in peace, the Japanese acted in character. What special indications of their way of life and thinking did they give in the way they handled warfare? Their leaders' ways of whipping up war spirit, of reassuring the bewildered, of utilizing their soldiers in the field—all these things showed what they themselves regarded as the strengths on which they could capitalize. I had to follow the details of the war to see how the Japanese revealed themselves in it step by step.

The fact that our two nations were at war inevitably meant, however, a serious disadvantage. It meant that I had to forego the most important technique of the cultural anthropologist: a field trip. I could not go to Japan and live in their homes and watch the strains and stresses of daily life, see with my own eyes which were crucial and which were not. I could not watch them in the complicated business of arriving at a decision. I could not see their children being brought up. The one anthropologist's field study of a Japanese village, John Embree's *Suye Mura*, was invaluable, but many of the questions about Japan with which we were faced in 1944 were not raised when that study was written.

As a cultural anthropologist, in spite of these major difficulties, I had confidence in certain techniques and postulates which could be used. At least I did not have to forego the anthropologist's great reliance upon face-to-face contact with the people he is studying. There were plenty of Japanese in this country who had been reared in Japan and I could ask them about the concrete facts of their own experiences, find out how they judged them, fill in from their descriptions many gaps in our knowledge which as an anthropologist I believed were essential in understanding any culture. Other social scientists who were studying Japan were using libraries, analyzing past events or statistics, following developments in the written or spoken word of Japanese propaganda. I had confidence that many of these answers they sought were embedded in the rules and values of Japanese culture and could be found more satisfactorily by exploring that culture with people who had really lived it.

This did not mean that I did not read and that I was not constantly indebted to Westerners who had lived in Japan. The vast literature on the Japanese and the great number of good Occidental observers who have lived in Japan gave me an advantage which no anthropologist has when he goes to the Amazon headwaters or the New Guinea highlands to study a non-literate tribe. Having no written language such tribes have committed no self-revelations to paper. Comments by Westerners are few and superficial. Nobody knows their past history. The field worker must discover without any help from previous students the way their economic life works, how stratified their society is, what is uppermost in their religious life. In studying Japan, I was the heir of many students. Descriptions of small details of life were tucked away in antiquarian papers. Men and women from Europe and America had set down their vivid experiences, and the Japanese themselves had written really extraordinary self-revelations. Unlike many Oriental people they have a great impulse to write themselves out. They wrote about the trivia of their lives as well as about their programs of world expansion. They were amazingly frank. Of course they did not present the whole picture. No people does. A Japanese who writes about Japan passes over really crucial things which are as familiar to him and as invisible as the air he breathes. So do Americans when they write about America. But just the same the Japanese loved self-revelation.

I read this literature as Darwin says he read when he was working out his theories on the origin of species, noting what I had not the means to understand. What would I need to know to understand the juxtaposition of ideas in a speech in the Diet? What could lie back of their violent condemnation of some act that seemed venial and their easy acceptance of one that seemed outrageous? I read, asking the ever-present question: What is 'wrong with this picture'? What would I need to know to understand it?

I went to movies, too, which had been written and produced in Japan—propaganda movies, historical movies,

movies of contemporary life in Tokyo and in the farm villages. I went over them afterward with Japanese who had seen some of these same movies in Japan and who in any case saw the hero and the heroine and the villain as Japanese see them, not as I saw them. When I was at sea, it was clear that they were not. The plots, the motivations were not as I saw them, but they made sense in terms of the way the movie was constructed. As with the novels, there was much more difference than met the eye between what they meant to me and what they meant to the Japanese-reared. Some of these Japanese were quick to come to the defense of Japanese conventions and some hated everything Japanese. It is hard to say from which group I learned most. In the intimate picture they gave of how one regulates one's life in Japan they agreed, whether they accepted it gladly or rejected it with bitterness.

In so far as the anthropologist goes for his material and his insights directly to the people of the culture he is studying, he is doing what all the ablest Western observers have done who have lived in Japan. If this were all an anthropologist had to offer, he could not hope to add to the valuable studies which foreign residents have made of the Japanese. The cultural anthropologist, however, has certain qualifications as a result of his training which appeared to make it worth his while to try to add his own contribution in a field rich in students and observers.

The anthropologist knows many cultures of Asia and the Pacific. There are many social arrangements and habits of life in Japan which have close parallels even in the primitive tribes of the Pacific islands. Some of these parallels are in

Malaysia, some in New Guinea, some in Polynesia. It is interesting, of course, to speculate on whether these show some ancient migrations or contacts, but this problem of possible historical relationship was not the reason why knowledge of these cultural similarities was valuable to me. It was rather that I knew in these simpler cultures how these institutions worked and could get clues to Japanese life from the likeness or the difference I found. I knew, too, something about Siam and Burma and China on the mainland of Asia, and I could therefore compare Japan with other nations which are a part of its great cultural heritage. Anthropologists had shown over and over in their studies of primitive people how valuable such cultural comparisons can be. A tribe may share ninety per cent of its formal observances with its neighbors and yet it may have revamped them to fit a way of life and a set of values which it does not share with any surrounding peoples. In the process it may have had to reject some fundamental arrangements which, however small in proportion to the whole, turn its future course of development in a unique direction. Nothing is more helpful to an anthropologist than to study contrasts he finds between peoples who on the whole share many traits.

Anthropologists also have had to accustom themselves to maximum differences between their own culture and another and their techniques have to be sharpened for this particular problem. They know from experience that there are great differences in the situations which men in different cultures have to meet and in the way in which different tribes and nations define the meanings of these situations. In some Arctic village or tropical desert they were faced with tribal arrangements of kinship responsibility or financial exchange which in their moments of most unleashed imagination they could not have invented. They have had to investigate, not only the details of kinship or exchange, but what the consequences of these arrangements were in the tribe's behavior and how each generation was conditioned from childhood to carry on as their ancestors had done before them.

This professional concern with differences and their conditioning and their consequences could well be used in the study of Japan. No one is unaware of the deep-rooted cultural differences between the United States and Japan. We have even a folklore about the Japanese which says that whatever we do they do the opposite. Such a conviction of difference is dangerous only if a student rests content with saying simply that these differences are so fantastic that it is impossible to understand such people. The anthropologist has good proof in his experience that even bizarre behavior does not prevent one's understanding it. More than any other social scientist he has professionally used differences as an asset rather than a liability. There is nothing that has made him pay such sharp attention to institutions and peoples as the fact that they were phenomenally strange. There was nothing he could take for granted in his tribe's way of living and it made him look not just at a few selected facts, but at everything. In studies of Western nations one who is untrained in studies of comparative cultures overlooks whole areas of behavior. He takes so much for granted that he does not explore the range of trivial habits in daily living and all those accepted verdicts on homely matters, which, thrown large on the national screen, have more to do with that nation's future than treaties signed by diplomats.

The anthropologist has had to develop techniques for studying the commonplace because those things that are commonplaces in the tribe he was studying were so different from their counterparts in his own home country. When he tried to understand the extreme maliciousness of some tribe or the extreme timidity of another, when he tried to plot out the way they would act and feel in a given situation, he found he had to draw heavily on observations and details that are not often noted about civilized nations. He had good reason to believe they were essential and he knew the kind of research that would unearth them.

It was worth trying in the case of Japan. For it is only when one has noted the intensely human commonplaces of any people's existence that one appreciates at its full importance the anthropologist's premise that human behavior in any primitive tribe or in any nation in the forefront of civilization is *learned* in daily living. No matter how bizarre his act or his opinion, the way a man feels and thinks has some relation to his experience. The more baffled I was at some bit of behavior, the more I therefore assumed that there existed somewhere in Japanese life some ordinary conditioning of such strangeness. If the search took me into trivial details of daily intercourse, so much the better. That was where people learned.

As a cultural anthropologist also I started from the premise that the most isolated bits of behavior have some systematic relation to each other. I took seriously the way hundreds of details fall into over-all patterns. A human society must make for itself some design for living. It approves certain ways of meeting situations, certain ways of sizing them up. People in that society regard these solutions as foundations of the universe. They integrate them, no matter what the difficulties. Men who have accepted a system of values by which to live cannot without courting inefficiency and chaos keep for long a fenced-off portion of their lives where they think and behave according to a contrary set of values. They try to bring about more conformity. They provide themselves with some common rationale and some common motivations. Some degree of consistency is necessary or the whole scheme falls to pieces.

Economic behavior, family arrangements, religious rites and political objectives therefore become geared into one another. Changes in one area may occur more rapidly than in others and subject these other areas to great stress, but the stress itself arises from the need for consistency. In preliterate societies committed to the pursuit of power over others, the will to power is expressed in their religious practices no less than in their economic transactions and in their relations with other tribes. In civilized nations which have old written scriptures, the Church necessarily retains the phrases of past centuries, as tribes without written language do not, but it abdicates authority in those fields which would interfere with increasing public approval of economic and political power. The words remain but the meaning is altered. Religious dogmas, economic practices and politics do not stay dammed up in neat separate little ponds but they overflow their supposed boundaries and their waters mingle inextricably one with the other. Because this is always true, the more a student has seemingly scattered his investigation among facts of economics and sex and religion and the care of the baby, the better he can follow what is happening in the society he studies. He can draw up his hypotheses and get his data in any area of life with profit. He can learn to see the demands any nation makes, whether they are phrased in political, economic, or moral terms, as expressions of habits and ways of thinking which are learned in their social experience. This volume therefore is not a book specifically about Japanese religion or economic life or politics or the family. It examines Japanese assumptions about the conduct of life. It describes these assumptions as they have manifested themselves whatever the activity in hand. It is about what makes Japan a nation of Japanese.

One of the handicaps of the twentieth century is that we still have the vaguest and most biased notions, not only of what makes Japan a nation of Japanese, but of what makes the United States a nation of Americans, France a nation of Frenchmen, and Russia a nation of Russians. Lacking this knowledge, each country misunderstands the other. We fear irreconcilable differences when the trouble is only between Tweedledum and Tweedledee, and we talk about common purposes when one nation by virtue of its whole experience and system of values has in mind a quite different course of action from the one we meant. We do not give ourselves a chance to find out what their habits and values are. If we did, we might discover that a course of action is not necessarily vicious because it is not the one we know.

It is not possible to depend entirely upon what each nation says of its own habits of thought and action. Writers in every nation have tried to give an account of themselves. But it is not easy. The lenses through which any nation looks at life are not the ones another nation uses. It is hard to be conscious of the eyes through which one looks. Any country takes them for granted, and the tricks of focusing and of perspective which give to any people its national view of life seem to that people the god-given arrangement of the landscape. In any matter of spectacles, we do not expect the man who wears them to know the formula for the lenses, and neither can we expect nations to analyze their own outlook upon the world. When we want to know about spectacles, we train an oculist and expect him to be able to write out the formula for any lenses we bring him. Some day no doubt we shall recognize that it is the job of the social scientist to do this for the nations of the contemporary world.

The job requires both a certain tough-mindedness and a certain generosity. It requires a tough-mindedness which people of good will have sometimes condemned. These protagonists of One World have staked their hopes on convincing people of every corner of the earth that all the differences between East and West, black and white, Christian and Mohammedan, are superficial and that all mankind is really like-minded. This view is sometimes called the brotherhood of man. I do not know why believing in the brotherhood of man should mean that one cannot say that the Japanese have their own version of the conduct of life and that Americans have theirs. It sometimes seems as if the tender-minded could not base a doctrine of good will upon anything less than a world of peoples each of which is a print from the same negative. But to demand such uniformity as a condition of respecting another nation is as neurotic as to demand it of one's wife or one's children. The tough-minded are content that differences should exist. They respect differences. Their goal is a world made safe for differences, where the United States may be American to the hilt without threatening the peace of the world, and France may be France, and Japan may be Japan on the same conditions. To forbid the ripening of any of these attitudes toward life by outside interference seems wanton to any student who is not himself convinced that differences need be a Damocles' sword hanging over the world. Nor need he fear that by taking such a position he is helping to freeze the world into the status quo. Encouraging cultural differences would not mean a static world. England did not lose her Englishness because an Age of Elizabeth was followed by an Age of Queen Anne and a Victorian Era. It was just because the English were so much themselves that different standards and different national moods could assert themselves in different generations.

Systematic study of national differences requires a certain generosity as well as tough-mindedness. The study of comparative religions has flourished only when men were secure enough in their own convictions to be unusually generous. They might be Jesuits or Arabic savants or unbelievers, but they could not be zealots. The study of comparative cultures too cannot flourish when men are so defensive about their own way of life that it appears to them to be by definition the sole solution in the world. Such men will never know the added love of their own culture which comes from a knowledge of other ways of life. They cut themselves off from a pleasant and enriching experience. Being so defensive, they have no alternative but to demand that other nations adopt their own particular solutions. As Americans they urge our favorite tenets on all nations. And other nations can no more adopt our ways of life on demand than we could learn to do our calculations in units of 12's instead of 10's, or stand on one foot in repose like certain East African natives.

This book, then, is about habits that are expected and taken for granted in Japan. It is about those situations when any Japanese can count on courtesy and those situations when he cannot, about when he feels shame, when he feels embarrassment, what he requires of himself. The ideal authority for any statement in this book would be the proverbial man in the street. It would be anybody. That does not mean that this anybody would in his own person have been placed in each particular circumstance. It does mean that anybody would recognize that that was how it was under those conditions. The goal of such a study as this is to describe deeply entrenched attitudes of thought and behavior. Even when it falls short, this was nevertheless the ideal.

In such a study one quickly reaches the point where the testimony of great numbers of additional informants provides no further validation. Who bows to whom and when, for instance, needs no statistical study of all Japan; the approved and customary circumstances can be reported by almost any one and after a few confirmations it is not necessary to get the same information from a million Japanese.

The student who is trying to uncover the assumptions upon which Japan builds its way of life has a far harder task than statistical validation. The great demand upon him is to report how these accepted practices and judgments become the lenses through which the Japanese see existence. He has to state the way in which their assumptions affect the focus and perspective in which they view life. He has to try to make this intelligible to Americans who see existence in very different focus. In this task of analysis the court of authority is not necessarily Tanaka San, the Japanese 'anybody.' For Tanaka San does not make his assumptions explicit, and interpretations written for Americans will undoubtedly seem to him unduly labored.

American studies of societies have not often been planned to study the premises on which civilized cultures are built. Most studies assume that these premises are self-evident. Sociologists and psychologists are preoccupied with the 'scatter' of opinion and behavior, and the stock technique is statistical. They subject to statistical analysis masses of census material, great numbers of answers to questionnaires or to interviewers' questions, psychological measurements and the like, and attempt to derive the independence or interdependence of certain factors. In the field of public opinion, the valuable technique of polling the country by using a scientifically selected sample of the population has been highly perfected in the United States. It is possible to discover how many people support or oppose a certain candidate for public office or a certain policy. Supporters and opponents can be classified as rural or urban, low income or high income, Republicans or Democrats. In a country with universal suffrage, where laws are actually drafted and enacted by the people's representatives, such findings have practical importance.

Americans can poll Americans and understand the findings, but they can do this because of a prior step which is so obvious that no one mentions it: they know and take for granted the conduct of life in the United States. The results of polling tell more about what we already know. In trying to understand another country, systematic qualitative study of the habits and assumptions of its people is essential before a poll can serve to good advantage. By careful sampling, a poll can discover how many people are for or against government. But what does that tell us about them unless we know what their notions are about the State? Only so can we know what the factions are disputing about, in the streets or in the Diet. A nation's assumptions about government are of much more general and permanent importance than figures of party strength. In the United States, the Government, to both Republicans and Democrats, is almost a necessary evil and it limits individual freedom; Government employment, too, except perhaps in wartime, does not give a man the standing he gets from an equivalent job in private enterprise. This version of the State is a far cry from the Japanese version, and even from that of many European nations. What we need to know first of all is just what their version is. Their view is embodied in their folkways, in their comments on successful men, in their myth of their national history, in their speeches on national holidays; and it can be studied in these indirect manifestations. But it requires systematic study.

The basic assumptions which any nation makes about living, the solutions it has sanctioned, can be studied with as much attention and as much detail as we give to finding out what proportion of a population will vote yes and no in an election. Japan was a country whose fundamental assumptions were well worth exploring. Certainly I found that once I had seen where my Occidental assumptions did not fit into their view of life and had got some idea of the categories and symbols they used, many contradictions Westerners are accustomed to see in Japanese behavior were no longer contradictions. I began to see how it was that the Japanese themselves saw certain violent swings of behavior as integral parts of a system consistent within itself. I can try to show why. As I worked with them, they began to use strange phrases and ideas which turned out to have great implications and to be full of age-long emotion. Virtue and vice as the Occident understands them had undergone a sea-change. The system was singular. It was not Buddhism and it was not Confucianism. It was Japanese—the strength and the weakness of Japan.

2

The Japanese in the War

In Every cultural tradition there are orthodoxies of war and certain of these are shared in all Western nations, no matter what the specific differences. There are certain clarion calls to all-out war effort, certain forms of reassurance in case of local defeats, certain regularities in the proportion of fatalities to surrenders, and certain rules of behavior for prisoners of war which are predictable in wars between Western nations just because they have a great shared cultural tradition which covers even warfare.

All the ways in which the Japanese departed from Western conventions of war were data on their view of life and on their convictions of the whole duty of man. For the purposes of a systematic study of Japanese culture and behavior it did not matter whether or not their deviations from our orthodoxies were crucial in a military sense; any of them might be important because they raised questions about the character of the Japanese to which we needed answers.

The very premises which Japan used to justify her war were the opposite of America's. She defined the international situation differently. America laid the war to the aggressions of the Axis. Japan, Italy, and Germany had unrighteously offended against international peace by their acts of conquest. Whether the Axis had seized power in Manchukuo or in Ethiopia or in Poland, it proved that they had embarked on an evil course of oppressing weak peoples. They had sinned against an international code of 'live and let live' or at least of 'open doors' for free enterprise. Japan saw the cause of the war in another light. There was anarchy in the world as long as every nation had absolute sovereignty; it was necessary for her to fight to establish a hierarchy—under Japan, of course, since she alone represented a nation truly hierarchal from top to bottom and hence understood the necessity of taking 'one's proper place.' Japan, having attained unification and peace in her homeland, having put down banditry and built up roads and electric power and steel industries, having, according to her official figures, educated 99.5 per cent of her rising generation in her public schools, should, according to Japanese premises of hierarchy, raise her backward younger brother China. Being of the same race as Greater East Asia, she should eliminate the United States, and after her Britain and Russia, from that part of the world and 'take her proper place.' All nations were to be one world, fixed in an international hierarchy. In the next chapter we shall examine what this high value placed on hierarchy meant in Japanese culture. It was an appropriate fantasy for Japan to create. Unfortunately for her the countries she occupied did not see it in the same light. Nevertheless not even defeat has drawn from her moral repudiation of her Greater East Asia ideals, and even her prisoners of war who were least jingoistic rarely went so far as to arraign the purposes of Japan on the continent and in the Southwest Pacific. For a long, long time Japan will necessarily keep some of her inbred attitudes and one of the most important of these is her faith and confidence in hierarchy. It is alien to equality-loving Americans but it is nevertheless necessary for us to understand what Japan meant by hierarchy and what advantages she has learned to connect with it.

Japan likewise put her hopes of victory on a different basis from that prevalent in the United States. She would win, she cried, a victory of spirit over matter. America was big, her armaments were superior, but what did that matter? All this, they said, had been foreseen and discounted. 'If we had been afraid of mathematical figures,' the Japanese read in their great newspaper, the *Mainichi Shimbun*, 'the war would not have started. The enemy's great resources were not created by this war.'

Even when she was winning, her civilian statesmen, her High Command, and her soldiers repeated that this was no contest between armaments; it was a pitting of our faith in things against their faith in spirit. When we were winning they repeated over and over that in such a contest material power must necessarily fail. This dogma became, no doubt, a convenient alibi about the time of the defeats at Saipan and Iwo Jima, but it was not manufactured as an alibi for defeats. It was a clarion call during all the months of Japanese victories, and it had been an accepted slogan long before Pearl Harbor. In the nineteen-thirties General Araki, fanatical militarist and one-time Minister of War, wrote in a pamphlet addressed 'To the whole Japanese

Race' that 'the true mission' of Japan was 'to spread and glorify the Imperial way to the end of the Four Seas. Inadequacy of strength is not our worry. Why should we worry about that which is material?'

Of course, like any other nation preparing for war, they did worry. All through the nineteen-thirties the proportion of their national income which was devoted to armament grew astronomically. By the time of their attack on Pearl Harbor very nearly half the entire national income was going to military and naval purposes, and of the total expenditures of the government only 17 per cent were available for financing anything having to do with civilian administration. The difference between Japan and Western nations was not that Japan was careless about material armament. But ships and guns were just the outward show of the undying Japanese Spirit. They were symbols much as the sword of the samurai had been the symbol of his virtue.

Japan was as completely consistent in playing up nonmaterial resources as the United States was in its commitment to bigness. Japan had to campaign for all-out production just as the United States did, but her campaigns were based on her own premises. The spirit, she said, was all and was everlasting; material things were necessary, of course, but they were subordinate and fell by the way. 'There are limits to material resources,' the Japanese radio would cry: 'it stands to reason that material things cannot last a thousand years.' And this reliance on spirit was taken literally in the routine of war; their war catechisms used the slogan—and it was a traditional one, not made to order for this war

—'To match our training against their numbers and our flesh against their steel.' Their war manuals began with the bold-type line, 'Read this and the war is won.' Their pilots who flew their midget planes in a suicidal crash into our warships were an endless text for the superiority of the spiritual over the material. They named them the Kamikaze Corps, for the *kamikaze* was the divine wind which had saved Japan from Genghis Khan's invasion in the thirteenth century by scattering and overturning his transports.

Even in civilian situations Japanese authorities took literally the dominance of spirit over material circumstances. Were people fatigued by twelve-hour work in the factories and all-night bombings? 'The heavier our bodies, the higher our will, our spirit, rises above them.' 'The wearier we are, the more splendid the training.' Were people cold in the bomb shelters in winter? On the radio the Dai Nippon Physical Culture Society prescribed body-warming calisthenics which would not only be a substitute for heating facilities and bedding, but, better still, would substitute for food no longer available to keep up people's normal strength. 'Of course some may say that with the present food shortages we cannot think of doing calisthenics. No! The more shortage of food there is, the more we must raise our physical strength by other means.' That is, we must increase our physical strength by expending still more of it. The American's view of bodily energy which always reckons how much strength he has to use by whether he had eight or five hours of sleep last night, whether he has eaten his regular meals, whether he has been cold, is here confronted with a calculus that does not rely on storing up energy. That would be materialistic.

Japanese broadcasts went even farther during the war. In battle, spirit surmounted even the physical fact of death. One broadcast described a hero-pilot and the miracle of his conquest of death:

> After the air battles were over, the Japanese planes returned to their base in small formations of three or four. A Captain was in one of the first planes to return. After alighting from his plane, he stood on the ground and gazed into the sky through binoculars. As his men returned, he counted. He looked rather pale, but he was quite steady. After the last plane returned he made out a report and proceeded to Headquarters. At Headquarters he made his report to the Commanding Officer. As soon as he had finished his report, however, he suddenly dropped to the ground. The officers on the spot rushed to give assistance but alas! he was dead. On examining his body it was found that it was already cold, and he had a bullet wound in his chest, which had proved fatal. It is impossible for the body of a newly-dead person to be cold. Nevertheless the body of the dead captain was as cold as ice. The Captain must have been dead long before, and it was his spirit that made the report. Such a miraculous fact must have been achieved by the strict sense of responsibility that the dead Captain possessed.

To Americans, of course, this is an outrageous yarn but educated Japanese did not laugh at this broadcast. They felt sure it would not be taken as a tall tale by listeners in Japan. First they pointed out that the broadcaster had truthfully said that the captain's feat was 'a miraculous fact.'

But why not? The soul could be trained; obviously the captain was a past-master of self-discipline. If all Japan knew that 'a composed spirit could last a thousand years,' could it not last a few hours in the body of an air-force captain who had made 'responsibility' the central law of his whole life? The Japanese believed that technical disciplines could be used to enable a man to make his spirit supreme. The captain had learned and profited.

As Americans we can completely discount these Japanese excesses as the alibis of a poor nation or the childishness of a deluded one. If we did, however, we would be, by that much, the less able to deal with them in war or in peace. Their tenets have been bred into the Japanese by certain taboos and refusals, by certain methods of training and discipline, and these tenets are not mere isolated oddities. Only if Americans have recognized them can we realize what they are saying when, in defeat, they acknowledge that spirit was not enough and that defending positions 'with bamboo spears' was a fantasy. It is still more important that we be able to appreciate their acknowledgment that *their* spirit was insufficient and that it was matched in battle and in the factory by the spirit of the American people. As they said after their defeat: during the war they had 'engaged in subjectivity.'

Japanese ways of saying all kinds of things during the war, not only about the necessity of hierarchy and the supremacy of spirit, were revealing to a student of comparative cultures. They talked constantly about security and morale being only a matter of being forewarned. No matter what the catastrophe, whether it was civilian bombing or defeat at Saipan or their failure to defend the Philippines, the Japanese line to their people was that this was foreknown and that there was therefore nothing to worry about. The radio went to great lengths, obviously counting on the reassurance it gave to the Japanese people to be told that they were living still in a thoroughly known world. 'The American occupation of Kiska brings Japan within the radius of American bombers. But we were well aware of this contingency and have made the necessary preparations.' 'The enemy doubtless will make an offensive against us by combined land, sea and air operations, but this has been taken account of by us in our plans.' Prisoners of war, even those who hoped for Japan's early defeat in a hopeless war, were sure that bombing would not weaken Japanese on the home front 'because they were forewarned.' When Americans began bombing Japanese cities, the vice-president of the Aviation Manufacturer's Association broadcast: 'Enemy planes finally have come over our very heads. However, we who are engaged in the aircraft production industry and who had always expected this to happen had made complete preparations to cope with this. Therefore, there is nothing to worry about.' Only granted all was foreknown, all was fully planned, could the Japanese go on to make the claim so necessary to them that everything had been actively willed by themselves alone; nobody had put anything over on them. 'We should not think that we have been passively attacked but that we have actively pulled the enemy toward us.' 'Enemy, come if you wish. Instead of saying, "Finally what was to come has come," we will say rather, "That which we were waiting for has come. We are glad it has come." ' The Navy Minister quoted in the Diet the teachings of the great warrior of the eighteen-seventies, Takamori Saigo, 'There are two kinds of opportunities: one which we chance upon, the other which we create. In time of great difficulty, one must not fail to create his opportunity.' And General Yamashito, when American troops marched into Manila, 'remarked with a broad smile,' the radio said, 'that now the enemy is in our bosom. . . .' 'The rapid fall of Manila, shortly after the enemy landings in Lingayen Bay, was only possible as a result of General Yamashito's tactics and in accordance with his plans. General Yamashito's operations are now making continuous progress.' In other words, nothing succeeds like defeat.

Americans went as far in the opposite direction as the Japanese in theirs. Americans threw themselves into the war effort *because* this fight had been forced upon us. We had been attacked, therefore let the enemy beware. No spokesman, planning how he could reassure the rank and file of Americans, said of Pearl Harbor or of Bataan, 'These were fully taken account of by us in our plans.' Our officials said instead, 'The enemy asked for it. We will show them what we can do.' Americans gear all their living to a constantly challenging world—and are prepared to accept the challenge. Japanese reassurances are based rather on a way of life that is planned and charted beforehand and where the greatest threat comes from the unforeseen.

Another constant theme in Japanese conduct of the war was also revealing about Japanese life. They continually spoke of how 'the eyes of the world were upon them.' Therefore they must show to the full the spirit of Japan. Americans landed on Guadalcanal, and Japanese orders to troops were that now they were under direct observation 'by the world' and should show what they were made of. Japanese seamen were warned that in case they were torpedoed and the order given to abandon ship, they should man the lifeboats with the utmost decorum or 'the world will laugh at you. The Americans will take movies of you and show them in New York.' It mattered what account they gave of themselves to the world. And their concern with this point also was a concern deeply imbedded in Japanese culture.

The most famous question about Japanese attitudes concerned His Imperial Majesty, the Emperor. What was the hold of the Emperor on his subjects? Some American authorities pointed out that through all Japan's seven feudal centuries the Emperor was a shadowy figurehead. Every man's immediate loyalty was due to his lord, the *daimyo*, and, beyond that, to the military Generalissimo, the Shogun. Fealty to the Emperor was hardly an issue. He was kept secluded in an isolated court whose ceremonies and activities were rigorously circumscribed by the Shogun's regulations. It was treason even for a great feudal lord to pay his respects to the Emperor, and for the people of Japan he hardly existed. Japan could only be understood by its history, these American analysts insisted; how could an Emperor who had been brought out from obscurity within the memory of still living people be the real rallying point of a conservative nation like Japan? The Japanese publicists who again and again reiterated the undying hold of the Emperor upon his subjects were over-protesting, they said, and their insistence only proved the weakness of their case. There was no reason, therefore, that American policy during the war should draw on kid gloves in dealing with the Emperor. There was every reason rather why we should direct our strongest attacks against this evil Fuehrer concept that Japan had recently concocted. It was the very heart of its modern nationalistic Shinto religion and if we undermined and challenged the sanctity of the Emperor, the whole structure of enemy Japan would fall in ruins.

Many capable Americans who knew Japan and who saw the reports from the front lines and from Japanese sources were of the opposite persuasion. Those who had lived in Japan well knew that nothing stung the Japanese people to bitterness and whipped up their morale like any depreciatory word against the Emperor or any outright attack on him. They did not believe that in attacking the Emperor we would in the eyes of the Japanese be attacking militarism. They had seen that reverence for the Emperor had been equally strong in those years after the First World War when 'de-mok-ra-sie' was the great watchword and militarism was so discredited that army men prudently changed to mufti before they went out on the streets of Tokyo. The reverence of the Japanese for their Imperial chief could not be compared, these old Japanese residents insisted, with Heil-Hitler veneration which was a barometer of the fortunes of the Nazi party and bound up with all the evils of a fascist program.

Certainly the testimony of Japanese prisoners of war bore them out. Unlike Western soldiers, these prisoners had not been instructed about what to say and what to keep silent about when captured and their responses on all subjects were strikingly unregimented. This failure to indoctrinate was of course due to Japan's no-surrender policy. It was not remedied until the last months of the war, and even then only in certain armies or local units. The prisoners' testimony was worth paying attention to for they represented a cross-section of opinion in the Japanese Army. They were not troops whose low morale had caused them to surrender—and who might therefore be atypical. All but a few were wounded and unconscious soldiers unable to resist when captured.

Japanese prisoners of war who were out-and-out bitter-enders imputed their extreme militarism to the Emperor and were 'carrying out his will,' 'setting his mind at rest,' 'dying at the Emperor's command.' 'The Emperor led the people into war and it was my duty to obey.' But those who rejected this present war and future Japanese plans of conquest just as regularly ascribed their peaceful persuasions to the Emperor. He was all things to all men. The war-weary spoke of him as 'his peace-loving Majesty'; they insisted that he 'had always been liberal and against the war.' 'He had been deceived by Tojo.' 'During the Manchurian Incident he showed that he was against the military.' 'The war was started without the Emperor's knowledge or permission. The Emperor does not like war and would not have permitted his people to be dragged into it. The Emperor does not know how badly treated his soldiers are.' These were not statements like those of German prisoners of war who, however much they complained that Hitler had been betrayed by his generals or his high command, nevertheless ascribed war and the preparations for war to Hitler as supreme inciter. The Japanese prisoner of war was quite explicit that the reverence given the Imperial Household was separable from militarism and aggressive war policies.

The Emperor was to them, however, inseparable from Japan. 'A Japan without the Emperor is not Japan.' 'Japan without the Emperor cannot be imagined.' 'The Japanese Emperor is the symbol of the Japanese people, the center of their religious lives. He is a super-religious object.' Nor would he be blamed for the defeat if Japan lost the war. 'The people did not consider the Emperor responsible for the war.' 'In the event of defeat the Cabinet and the military leaders would take the blame, not the Emperor.' 'Even if Japan lost the war ten out of ten Japanese would still revere the Emperor.'

All this unanimity in reckoning the Emperor above criticism appeared phoney to Americans who are accustomed to exempt no human man from skeptical scrutiny and criticism. But there was no question that it was the voice of Japan even in defeat. Those most experienced in interrogating the prisoners gave it as their verdict that it was unnecessary to enter on each interview sheet: 'Refuses to speak against the Emperor'; all prisoners refused, even those who co-operated with the Allies and broadcast for us to the Japanese troops. Out of all the collected interviews of prisoners of war, only three were even mildly anti-Emperor and only one went so far as to say: 'It would be a mistake to leave the Emperor on the throne.' A second said the Emperor was 'a feeble-minded person, nothing more than a puppet.' And the third got no farther than supposing that the Emperor might abdicate in favor of his son and that if the monarchy were abolished young Japanese women would hope to get a freedom they envied in the women of America.

Japanese commanders, therefore, were playing on an all but unanimous Japanese veneration when they distributed cigarettes to the troops 'from the Emperor,' or led them on his birthday in bowing three times to the east and shouting 'Banzai'; when they chanted with all their troops morning and evening, 'even though the unit was subjected to day and night bombardment,' the 'sacred words' the Emperor himself had given to the armed forces in the Rescript for Soldiers and Sailors while 'the sound of chanting echoed through the forest.' The militarists used the appeal of loyalty to the Emperor in every possible way. They called on their men to 'fulfill the wishes of His Imperial Majesty,' to 'dispel all the anxieties of your Emperor,' to 'demonstrate your respect for His Imperial benevolence,' to 'die for the Emperor.' But this obedience to his will could cut both ways. As many prisoners said, the Japanese 'will fight unhesitatingly, even with nothing more than bamboo poles, if the Emperor so decrees. They would stop just as quickly if he so decreed'; 'Japan would throw down arms tomorrow if the Emperor should issue such an order'; 'Even the Kwantung Army in Manchuria'—most militant and jingoistic—'would lay down their arms'; 'only his words can make the Japanese people accept a defeat and be reconciled to live for reconstruction.'

This unconditional and unrestricted loyalty to the Emperor was conspicuously at odds with criticisms of all other persons and groups. Whether in Japanese newspapers and magazines or in war prisoners' testimony, there was criticism of the government and of military leaders. Prisoners of war were free with their denunciation of their local commanders, especially those who had not shared the dangers and hardships of their soldiers. They were especially critical of those who had evacuated by plane and left their troops behind to fight it out. Usually they praised some officers and bitterly criticized others; there was no sign that they lacked the will to discriminate the good from the bad in things Japanese. Even in the home islands newspapers and magazines criticized 'the government.' They called for more leadership and greater co-ordination of effort and noted that they were not getting from the government what was necessary. They even criticized the restrictions on freedom of speech. A report on a panel of editors, former members of the Diet, and directors of Japan's totalitarian party, the Imperial Rule Assistance Association, printed in a Tokyo paper in July, 1944, is a good example. One speaker said: 'I think there are various ways to arouse the Japanese people but the most important one is freedom of speech. In these few years, the people have not been able to say frankly what they think. They have been afraid that they might be blamed if they spoke certain matters. They hesitated, and tried to patch up the surface, so the public mind has really become timid. We can never develop the total power of the people in this way.' Another speaker expanded the same theme: 'I have held symposiums almost every night with the people of the electoral districts and asked them about many things, but they were all afraid to speak. Freedom of speech has been denied. This is certainly not a proper way to stimulate their will to fight. The people are so badly restricted by the so-called Special Penal Law of War Time and the National Security Law that they have become as timid as the people in the feudalistic period. Therefore the fighting power which could have been developed remains undeveloped now.'

Even during the war, therefore, the Japanese criticized the government, the High Command, and their immediate superiors. They did not unquestioningly acknowledge the virtues of the whole hierarchy. But the Emperor was exempt. How could this be when his primacy was so recent? What quirk of Japanese character made it possible that he should so attain a sacrosanct position? Were Japanese prisoners of war right in claiming that just as the people would fight to the death 'with bamboo spears' as long as he so ordered, they would peaceably accept defeat and occupation if that was his command? Was this nonsense meant to mislead us? Or was it, possibly, the truth?

All these crucial questions about Japanese behavior in the war, from their anti-materialistic bias to their attitudes toward the Emperor concerned the homeland Japan as well as the fighting fronts. There were other attitudes which had to do more specifically with the Japanese Army. One of these concerned the expendability of their fighting forces. The Japanese radio put well the contrast with the American attitudes when it described with shocked incredulity the Navy's decoration of Admiral George S. McCain, commander of a task force off Formosa.

> The official reason for the decoration was not that Commander John S. McCain was able to put the Japanese to flight, though we don't see why not since that is what the

> Nimitz communiqué claimed. . . . Well, the reason given for Admiral McCain's decoration was that he was able successfully to rescue two damaged American warships and escort them safely to their home base. What makes this bit of information important is not that it is a fiction but that it is the truth. . . . So we are not questioning the veracity of Admiral McCain's rescuing two ships, but the point we want you to see is the curious fact that the rescuing of damaged ships merits decoration in the United States.

Americans thrill to all rescue, all aid to those pressed to the wall. A valiant deed is all the more a hero's act if it saves the 'damaged.' Japanese valor repudiates such salvaging. Even the safety devices installed in our B-29's and fighter planes raised their cry of 'Cowardice.' The press and the radio returned to the theme over and over again. There was virtue only in accepting life and death risks; precautions were unworthy. This attitude found expression also in the case of the wounded and of malarial patients. Such soldiers were damaged goods and the medical services provided were utterly inadequate even for reasonable effectiveness of the fighting force. As time went on, supply difficulties of all kinds aggravated this lack of medical care, but that was not the whole story. Japanese scorn of materialism played a part in it; her soldiers were taught that death itself was a victory of the spirit and our kind of care of the sick was an interference with heroism—like safety devices in bombing planes. Nor are the Japanese used to such reliance on physicians and surgeons in civilian life as Americans are. Preoccupation with mercy toward the damaged rather than with other welfare measures is especially high in the United

States, and is often commented on even by visitors from some European countries in peacetime. It is certainly alien to the Japanese. At all events, during the war the Japanese army had no trained rescue teams to remove the wounded under fire and to give first aid; it had no medical system of front line, behind-the-lines and distant recuperative hospitals. Its attention to medical supplies was lamentable. In certain emergencies the hospitalized were simply killed. Especially in New Guinea and the Philippines, the Japanese often had to retreat from a position where there was a hospital. There was no routine of evacuating the sick and wounded while there was still opportunity; only when the 'planned withdrawal' of the battalion was actually taking place or the enemy was occupying was anything done. Then, the medical officer in charge often shot the inmates of the hospital before he left or they killed themselves with hand grenades.

If this attitude of the Japanese toward damaged goods was fundamental in their treatment of their own countrymen, it was equally important in their treatment of American prisoners of war. According to our standards the Japanese were guilty of atrocities to their own men as well as to their prisoners. The former chief medical officer of the Philippines, Colonel Harold W. Glattly, said after his three years' internment as a prisoner of war on Formosa that 'the American prisoners got better medical treatment than the Japanese soldiers. Allied medical officers in the prison camps were able to take care of their men while the Japanese didn't have any doctors. For a while the only medical personnel they had for their own men was a corporal and later on a sergeant.' He saw a Japanese medical officer only once or twice a year.*

The furthest extreme to which this Japanese theory of expendability could be pushed was their no-surrender policy. Any Occidental army which has done its best and finds itself facing hopeless odds surrenders to the enemy. They still regard themselves as honorable soldiers and by international agreement their names are sent back to their countries so that their families may know that they are alive. They are not disgraced either as soldiers or as citizens or in their own families. But the Japanese defined the situation differently. Honor was bound up with fighting to the death. In a hopeless situation a Japanese soldier should kill himself with his last hand grenade or charge weaponless against the enemy in a mass suicide attack. But he should not surrender. Even if he were taken prisoner when he was wounded and unconscious, he 'could not hold up his head in Japan' again; he was disgraced; he was 'dead' to his former life.

There were Army orders to this effect, of course, but there was apparently no need of special official indoctrination at the front. The Army lived up to the code to such an extent that in the North Burma campaign the proportion of the captured to the dead was 142 to 17,166. That was a ratio of 1:120. And of the 142 in the prison camps, all except a small minority were wounded or unconscious when taken; only a very few had 'surrendered' singly or in groups of two or three. In the armies of Occidental nations it is almost a truism that troops cannot stand the death of one-

* Reported in the *Washington Post*, October 15, 1945.

fourth to one-third of their strength without giving up; surrenders run about 4:1. When for the first time in Hollandia, however, any appreciable number of Japanese troops surrendered, the proportion was 1:5 and that was a tremendous advance over the 1:120 of North Burma.

To the Japanese therefore Americans who had become prisoners of war were disgraced by the mere fact of surrender. They were 'damaged goods' even when wounds or malaria or dysentery had not also put them outside the category of 'complete men.' Many Americans have described how dangerous a thing American laughter was in the prison camps and how it stung their warders. In Japanese eyes they had suffered ignominy and it was bitter to them that the Americans did not know it. Many of the orders which American prisoners had to obey, too, were those which had also been required of their Japanese keepers by their own Japanese officers; the forced marches and the close-packed transshipments were commonplaces to them. Americans tell, too, of how rigorously sentries required that the prisoners should cover up evasions of rules; the great crime was to evade openly. In camps where the prisoners worked off-bounds on roads or installations during the day the rule that no food be brought back with them from the countryside was sometimes a dead letter—if the fruit and vegetables were covered up. If they could be seen, it was a flagrant offense which meant that the Americans had flouted the sentry's authority. Open challenging of authority was terribly punished even if it were mere 'answering back.' Japanese rules are very strict against a man's answering back even in civilian life and their own army practices penalized it heavily. It is no exoneration of the atrocities and wanton cruelties that did occur in the prison camps to distinguish between these and those acts which were the consequences of cultural habituations.

Especially in the earlier stages of the conflict the shame of capture was reinforced by a very real belief among the Japanese that the enemy tortured and killed any prisoners. One rumor of tanks that had been driven across the bodies of those captured on Guadalcanal spread through almost all areas. Some Japanese who tried to give themselves up, too, were regarded with so much suspicion by our troops that they were killed as a precaution, and this suspicion was often justified. A Japanese for whom there was nothing left but death was often proud that he could take an enemy with him when he died; he might do it even after he was captured. Having determined, as one of them put it, 'to be burned on the altar of victory, it would be a disgrace to die with no heroic deed achieved.' Such possibilities put our Army on its guard and diminished the number of surrenders.

The shame of surrender was burned deeply into the consciousness of the Japanese. They accepted as a matter of course a behavior which was alien to our conventions of warfare. And ours was just as alien to them. They spoke with shocked disparagement of American prisoners of war who *asked* to have their names reported to their government so that their families would know they were alive. The rank and file, at least, were quite unprepared for the surrender of American troops at Bataan for they had assumed that they would fight it out the Japanese way. And they could not accept the fact that Americans had no shame in being prisoners of war.

The most melodramatic difference in behavior between Western soldiers and the Japanese was undoubtedly the co-operation the latter gave to the Allied forces as prisoners of war. They knew no rules of life which applied in this new situation; they were dishonored and their life as Japanese was ended. Only in the last months of the war did more than a handful imagine any return to their homeland, no matter how the war ended. Some men asked to be killed, 'but if your customs do not permit this, I will be a model prisoner.' They were better than model prisoners. Old Army hands and long-time extreme nationalists located ammunition dumps, carefully explained the disposition of Japanese forces, wrote our propaganda and flew with our bombing pilots to guide them to military targets. It was as if they had turned over a new page; what was written on the new page was the opposite of what was written on the old, but they spoke the lines with the same faithfulness.

This is of course not a description of all prisoners of war. Some few were irreconcilable. And in any case certain favorable conditions had to be set up before such behavior was possible. American Army commanders were very understandably hesitant to accept Japanese assistance at face value and there were camps where no attempt was made to use any services they might have given. In camps where this was done, however, the original suspicion had to be withdrawn and more and more dependence was placed on the good faith of the Japanese prisoners.

Americans had not expected this right-about-face from

prisoners of war. It was not according to our code. But the Japanese behaved as if, having put everything they had into one line of conduct and failed at it, they naturally took up a different line. Was it a way of acting which we could count on in post-war days or was it behavior peculiar to soldiers who had been individually captured? Like the other peculiarities of Japanese behavior which obtruded themselves upon us during the war, it raised questions about the whole way of life to which they were conditioned, the way their institutions functioned and the habits of thought and action they had learned.

3

Taking One's Proper Station

ANY ATTEMPT to understand the Japanese must begin with their version of what it means to 'take one's proper station.' Their reliance upon order and hierarchy and our faith in freedom and equality are poles apart and it is hard for us to give hierarchy its just due as a possible social mechanism. Japan's confidence in hierarchy is basic in her whole notion of man's relation to his fellow man and of man's relation to the State and it is only by describing some of their national institutions like the family, the State, religious and economic life that it is possible for us to understand their view of life.

The Japanese have seen the whole problem of international relations in terms of their version of hierarchy just as they have seen their internal problems in the same light. For the last decade they have pictured themselves as attaining the apex of that pyramid, and now that this position belongs instead to the Western Nations, their view of hierarchy just as certainly underlies their acceptance of the present dispensation. Their international documents have constantly stated the weight they attach to it. The preamble to the Tripartite Pact with Germany and Italy which Japan signed in 1940 reads: 'The Governments of Japan, Germany and Italy consider it as the condition precedent to any lasting peace that all nations of the world be given each its proper station . . .' and the Imperial Rescript given on the signing of the Pact said the same thing again:

> To enhance our great righteousness in all the earth and to make of the world one household is the great injunction bequeathed by our Imperial Ancestors and we lay this to heart day and night. In the stupendous crisis now confronting the world it appears that war and confusion will be endlessly aggravated and mankind suffer incalculable disasters. We fervently hope that disturbances will cease and peace be restored as soon as possible. . . . We are therefore deeply gratified that this pact has been concluded between the Three Powers.
>
> The task of enabling each nation to find its proper place and all individuals to live in peace and security is of the greatest magnitude. It is unparalleled in history. This goal is still far distant. . . .

On the very day of the attack on Pearl Harbor, too, the Japanese envoys handed to Secretary of State Cordell Hull a most explicit statement on this point:

> It is the immutable policy of the Japanese Government . . . to enable each nation to find its proper place in the world. . . . The Japanese Government cannot tolerate the perpetuation of the present situation since it runs directly counter to Japan's fundamental policy to enable each nation to enjoy its proper station in the world.

This Japanese memorandum was in response to Secretary Hull's a few days previous which had invoked American principles just as basic and honored in the United States as hierarchy is in Japan. Secretary Hull enumerated four:

inviolability of sovereignty and of territorial integrity; non-intervention in other nations' internal affairs; reliance on international co-operation and conciliation; and the principle of equality. These are all major points in the American faith in equal and inviolable rights and are the principles on which we believe daily life should be based no less than international relations. Equality is the highest, most moral American basis for hopes for a better world. It means to us freedom from tyranny, from interference, and from unwanted impositions. It means equality before the law and the right to better one's condition in life. It is the basis for the rights of man as they are organized in the world we know. We uphold the virtue of equality even when we violate it and we fight hierarchy with a righteous indignation.

It has been so ever since America was a nation at all. Jefferson wrote it into the Declaration of Independence, and the Bill of Rights incorporated in the Constitution is based on it. These formal phrases of the public documents of a new nation were important just because they reflected a way of life that was taking shape in the daily living of men and women on this continent, a way of life that was strange to Europeans. One of the great documents of international reporting is the volume a young Frenchman, Alexis de Tocqueville, wrote on this subject of equality after he had visited the United States in the early eighteen-thirties. He was an intelligent and sympathetic observer who was able to see much good in this alien world of America. For it was alien. The young de Tocqueville had been bred in the aristocratic society of France which within the memory of still active and influential men had first been jolted and shocked by the French Revolution and then by the new and drastic laws of Napoleon. He was generous in his appreciation of a strange new order of life in America but he saw it through the eyes of a French aristocrat and his book was a report to the Old World on things to come. The United States, he believed, was an advance post of developments which would take place, though with differences, in Europe also.

He reported therefore at length on this new world. Here people really considered themselves the equals of others. Their social intercourse was on a new and easy footing. They fell into conversation as man to man. Americans did not care about the little attentions of a hierarchal etiquette; they did not demand them as their due nor offer them to others. They liked to say they owed nothing to any man. There was no family here in the old aristocratic or Roman sense, and the social hierarchy which had dominated the Old World was gone. These Americans trusted equality as they trusted nothing else; even liberty, he said, they often in practice let fly out of the window while they looked the other way. But they lived equality.

It is invigorating for Americans to see their forebears through the eyes of this stranger, writing about our way of life more than a century ago. There have been many changes in our country but the main outlines have not altered. We recognize, as we read, that America in 1830 was already America as we know it. There have been, and there still are, those in this country who, like Alexander Hamilton in Jefferson's day, are in favor of a more aristocratic ordering of society. But even the Hamiltons recognize that our way of life in this country is not aristocratic.

When we stated to Japan therefore just before Pearl Harbor the high moral bases on which the United States based her policy in the Pacific we were voicing our most trusted principles. Every step in the direction in which we pointed would according to our convictions improve a still imperfect world. The Japanese, too, when they put their trust in 'proper station' were turning to the rule of life which had been ingrained in them by their own social experience. Inequality has been for centuries the rule of their organized life at just those points where it is most predictable and most accepted. Behavior that recognizes hierarchy is as natural to them as breathing. It is not, however, a simple Occidental authoritarianism. Both those who exercise control and those who are under others' control act in conformity to a tradition which is unlike our own, and now that the Japanese have accepted the high hierarchal place of American authority in their country it is even more necessary for us to get the clearest possible idea of their conventions. Only so can we picture to ourselves the way in which they are likely to act in their present situation.

Japan for all its recent Westernization is still an aristocratic society. Every greeting, every contact must indicate the kind and degree of social distance between men. Every time a man says to another 'Eat' or 'Sit down' he uses different words if he is addressing someone familiarly or is speaking to an inferior or to a superior. There is a different 'you' that must be used in each case and the verbs have different stems. The Japanese have, in other words, what is called a 'respect language,' as many other peoples do in the Pacific, and they accompany it with proper bows and kneelings. All such behavior is governed by meticulous rules and conventions; it is not merely necessary to know to whom one bows but it is necessary to know how much one bows. A bow that is right and proper to one host would be resented as an insult by another who stood in a slightly different relationship to the bower. And bows range all the way from kneeling with forehead lowered to the hands placed flat upon the floor, to the mere inclination of head and shoulders. One must learn, and learn early, how to suit the obeisance to each particular case.

It is not merely class differences which must be constantly recognized by appropriate behavior, though these are important. Sex and age, family ties and previous dealings between two persons all enter into the necessary calculations. Even between the same two persons different degrees of respect will be called for on different occasions: a civilian may be on familiar terms with another and not bow to him at all, but when he wears a military uniform his friend in civilian clothes bows to him. Observance of hierarchy is an art which requires the balancing of innumerable factors, some of which in any particular case may cancel each other out and some of which may be additive.

There are of course persons between whom there is relatively little ceremony. In the United States these people are one's own family circle. We shed even the slight formalities of our etiquette when we come home to the bosom of our family. In Japan it is precisely in the family where respect rules are learned and meticulously observed. While the mother still carries the baby strapped to her back she will push his head down with her hand, and his first lessons as a toddler are to observe respect behavior to his father or older brother. The wife bows to her husband, the child bows to his father, younger brothers bow to elder brothers, the sister bows to all her brothers of whatever age. It is no empty gesture. It means that the one who bows acknowledges the right of the other to have his way in things he might well prefer to manage himself, and the one who receives the bow acknowledges in his turn certain responsibilities incumbent upon his station. Hierarchy based on sex and generation and primogeniture are part and parcel of family life.

Filial piety is, of course, a high ethical law which Japan shares with China, and Chinese formulations of it were early adopted in Japan along with Chinese Buddhism, Confucian ethics and secular Chinese culture in the sixth and seventh centuries A.D. The character of filial piety, however, was inevitably modified to suit the different structure of the family in Japan. In China, even today, one owes loyalty to one's vast extended clan. It may number tens of thousands of people over whom it has jurisdiction and from whom it receives support. Conditions differ in different parts of that vast country but in large parts of China all people in any village are members of the same clan. Among all of China's 450,000,000 inhabitants there are only 470 surnames and all people with the same surname count themselves in some degree clan-brothers. Over a whole area all people may be exclusively of one clan and, in addition, families living in far-away cities are their clan fellows. In populous areas like Kwangtung all the clan members unite in keeping up great clan-halls and on stated days they venerate as many as a thousand ancestral tablets of dead clan members stemming from a common forebear. Each clan owns property, lands and temples and has clan funds which are used to pay for the education of any promising clan son. It keeps track of dispersed members and publishes elaborate genealogies which are brought up to date every decade or so to show the names of those who have a right to share in its privileges. It has ancestral laws which might even forbid them to surrender family criminals to the State if the clan was not in agreement with the authorities. In Imperial times these great communities of semi-autonomous clans were governed in the name of the larger State as casually as possible by easy-going mandarinates headed by rotating State appointees who were foreigners in the area.

All this was different in Japan. Until the middle of the nineteenth century only noble families and warrior (*samurai*) families were allowed to use surnames. Surnames were fundamental in the Chinese clan system and without these, or some equivalent, clan organization cannot develop. One of these equivalents in some tribes is keeping a genealogy. But in Japan only the upper classes kept genealogies and even in these they kept the record, as Daughters of the American Revolution do in the United States, backward in time from the present living person, not downward in time to include every contemporary who stemmed from an original ancestor. It is a very different matter. Besides, Japan was a feudal country. Loyalty was due, not to a great group of relatives, but to a feudal lord. He was resident overlord, and the contrast with the temporary bureaucratic mandarins of China, who were always strangers in their districts, could not have been greater. What was important in Japan was that one was of the fief of Satsuma or the fief of Hizen. A man's ties were to his fief.

Another way of institutionalizing clans is through the worship of remote ancestors or of clan gods at shrines or holy places. This would have been possible for the Japanese 'common people' even without surnames and genealogies. But in Japan there is no cult of veneration of remote ancestors and at the shrines where 'common people' worship all villagers join together without having to prove their common ancestry. They are called the 'children' of their shrine-god, but they are 'children' because they live in his territory. Such village worshipers are of course related to each other as villagers in any part of the world are after generations of fixed residence but they are not a tight clan group descended from a common ancestor.

The reverence due to ancestors is paid at a quite different shrine in the family living room where only six or seven recent dead are honored. Among all classes in Japan obeisance is done daily before this shrine and food set out for parents and grandparents and close relatives remembered in the flesh, who are represented in the shrine by little miniature gravestones. Even in the cemetery the markers on the graves of great-grandparents are no longer relettered and the identity even of the third ancestral generation sinks rapidly into oblivion. Family ties in Japan are whittled down almost to Occidental proportions and the French family is perhaps the nearest equivalent.

'Filial piety' in Japan, therefore, is a matter within a limited face-to-face family. It means taking one's proper station according to generation, sex, and age within a group which includes hardly more than one's father and father's father, their brothers and their descendants. Even in important houses, where larger groups may be included, the family splits up into separate lines and younger sons establish branch families. Within this narrow face-to-face group the rules that regulate 'proper station' are meticulous. There is strict subservience to elders until they elect to go into formal retirement (*inkyo*). Even today a father of grown sons, if his own father has not retired, puts through no transaction without having it approved by the old grandfather. Parents make and break their children's marriages even when the children are thirty and forty years old. The father as male head of the household is served first at meals, goes first to the family bath, and receives with a nod the deep bows of his family. There is a popular riddle in Japan which might be translated into our conundrum form: 'Why is a son who wants to offer advice to his parents like a Buddhist priest who wants to have hair on the top of his head?' (Buddhist priests had a tonsure.) The answer is, 'However much he wants to do it, he can't.'

Proper station means not only differences of generation but differences of age. When the Japanese want to express utter confusion, they say that something is 'neither elder brother nor younger brother.' It is like our saying that something is neither fish nor fowl, for to the Japanese a man should keep his character as elder brother as drastically as a fish should stay in water. The eldest son is the heir. Travelers speak of 'that air of responsibility which the eldest son so early acquires in Japan.' The eldest son shares to a high degree in the prerogatives of the father. In the old days his younger brother would have been inevitably dependent upon him in time; nowadays, especially in towns and villages, it is he who will stay at home in the old rut while his younger brothers will perhaps press forward and get more education and a better income. But old habits of hierarchy are strong.

Even in political commentary today the traditional prerogatives of elder brothers are vividly stated in discussions of Greater East Asia policy. In the spring of 1942 a Lieutenant Colonel, speaking for the War Office, said on the subject of the Co-prosperity Sphere: 'Japan is their elder brother and they are Japan's younger brothers. This fact must be brought home to the inhabitants of the occupied territories. Too much consideration shown for the inhabitants might engender in their minds the tendency to presume on Japan's kindness with pernicious effects on Japanese rule.' The elder brother, in other words, decides what is good for his younger brother and should not show 'too much consideration' in enforcing it.

Whatever one's age, one's position in the hierarchy depends on whether one is male or female. The Japanese woman walks behind her husband and has a lower status. Even women who on occasions when they wear American clothes walk alongside and precede him through a door, again fall to the rear when they have donned their kimonos. The Japanese daughter of the family must get along as best she can while the presents, the attentions, and the money for education go to her brothers. Even when higher schools were established for young women the prescribed courses were heavily loaded with instruction in etiquette and bodily movement. Serious intellectual training was not on a par with boys', and one principal of such a school, advocating for his upper middle class students some instruction in European languages, based his recommendation on the desirability of their being able to put their husband's books back in the bookcase right side up after they had dusted them.

Nevertheless, the Japanese women have great freedom as compared to most other Asiatic countries and this is not just a phase of Westernization. There never was female footbinding as in the Chinese upper classes, and Indian women today exclaim over Japanese women going in and out of shops, up and down the streets and never secreting themselves. Japanese wives do the family shopping and carry the family purse. If money fails, it is they who must select something from the household and carry it to the pawnshop. A woman runs her servants, has great say in her children's marriages, and when she is a mother-in-law commonly runs her household realm with as firm a hand as if she had never been, for half her life, a nodding violet.

The prerogatives of generation, sex, and age in Japan are great. But those who exercise these privileges act as trustees rather than as arbitrary autocrats. The father or the elder brother is responsible for the household, whether its members are living, dead, or yet unborn. He must make weighty decisions and see that they are carried out. He does not, however, have unconditional authority. He is expected to act responsibly for the honor of the house. He recalls to his son and younger brother the legacy of the family, both in material and in spiritual things, and he challenges them to be worthy. Even if he is a peasant he invokes *noblesse oblige* to the family forebears, and if he belongs to more exalted classes the weight of responsibility to the house becomes heavier and heavier. The claims of the family come before the claims of the individual.

In any affair of importance the head of a family of any standing calls a family council at which the matter is debated. For a conference on a betrothal, for instance, members of the family may come from distant parts of Japan. The process of coming to a decision involves all the imponderables of personality. A younger brother or a wife may sway the verdict. The master of the house saddles himself with great difficulties if he acts without regard for group opinion. Decisions, of course, may be desperately unwelcome to the individual whose fate is being settled. His elders, however, who have themselves submitted in their lifetimes to decisions of family councils, are impregnable in demanding of their juniors what they have bowed to in their day. The sanction behind their demand is very different from that which, both in law and in custom, gives the Prussian father arbitrary rights over his wife and children. What is demanded is not for this reason less exacting in Japan, but the effects are different. The Japanese do not learn in their home life to value arbitrary authority, and the habit of submitting to it easily is not fostered. Submission to the will of the family is demanded in the name of a supreme value in which, however onerous its requirements, all of them have a stake. It is demanded in the name of a common loyalty.

Every Japanese learns the habit of hierarchy first in the bosom of his family and what he learns there he applies in wider fields of economic life and of government. He learns that a person gives all deference to those who outrank him in assigned 'proper place,' no matter whether or not they are the really dominant persons in the group. Even a husband who is dominated by his wife, or an elder brother who is dominated by a younger brother, receives no less formal deference. Formal boundaries between prerogatives are not broken down just because some other person is operating behind the scenes. The façade is not changed to suit the facts of dominance. It remains inviolable. There is even a certain tactical advantage in operating without the trappings of formal status; one is in that case less vulnerable. The Japanese learn, too, in their family experience that the greatest weight that can be given to a decision comes from the family conviction that it maintains the family honor. The decision is not a decree enforced by an iron fist at the whim of a tyrant who happens to be head of the family. He is more nearly a trustee of a material and spiritual estate which is important to them all and which demands of them all that they subordinate their personal wills to its requirements. The Japanese repudiate the use of the mailed fist, but they do not for that reason subordinate themselves any the less to the demands of the family, nor do they for that reason give to those with assigned status any less extreme deference. Hierarchy in the family is maintained even though the family elders have little opportunity to be strong-armed autocrats.

Such a bald statement of hierarchy in the Japanese family does not, when Americans read it with their different standards of interpersonal behavior, do justice to the acceptance of strong and sanctioned emotional ties in Japanese families. There is very considerable solidarity in the household and how they achieve it is one of the subjects of this book. Meanwhile it is important in trying to understand their demand for hierarchy in the wider fields of government and economic life to recognize how thoroughly the habit is learned in the bosom of the family.

The hierarchal arrangements of Japanese life have been as drastic in relations between the classes as they have been in the family. In all her national history Japan has been a strong class and caste society, and a nation which has a centuries-long habit of caste arrangements has certain strengths and certain weaknesses which are of the utmost importance. In Japan caste has been the rule of life through all her recorded history and even back in the seventh century A.D. she was already adapting the ways of life she borrowed from casteless China to suit her own hierarchal culture. In that era of the seventh and eighth centuries, the Japanese Emperor and his court set themselves the task of enriching Japan with the customs of the high civilization that had greeted the amazed eyes of their envoys in the great kingdom of China. They went about it with incomparable energy. Before that time Japan had not even had a written language; in the seventh century she took the ideographs of China and used them to write her own totally different language. She had had a religion which named forty thousand gods who presided over mountains and villages and gave people good fortune—a folk religion which with all its subsequent changes has survived as modern Shinto. In the seventh century, Japan adopted Buddhism wholesale from China as a religion 'excellent for protecting the State.'* She had had no great permanent architecture, either public or private; the Emperors built a new capital city, Nara, on the model of a Chinese capital, and great ornate Buddhist temples and vast Buddhist monasteries were erected in Japan after the Chinese pattern. The Emperors introduced titles and ranks and laws their envoys reported to them from China. It is difficult to find anywhere in the history of the world any other such successfully planned importation of civilization by a sovereign nation.

Japan, however, from the very first, failed to reproduce China's casteless social organization. The official titles Japan adopted were in China given to administrators who had passed the State examinations, but in Japan they were given to hereditary nobles and feudal lords. They became part of the caste arrangements of Japan. Japan was laid out in a great number of semi-sovereign fiefs whose lords were constantly jealous of each other's powers, and the social arrangements that mattered were those that had to do with the prerogatives of lords and vassals and retainers. No matter how assiduously Japan imported civilization from China she could not adopt ways of life which put in the place of her hierarchy anything like China's administrative bureaucracy or her system of extended clans which united people from the most different walks of life into one great clan. Nor did Japan adopt the Chinese idea of a secular Emperor. The

* Quoted from a contemporary chronicle of the Nara period by Sir George Sansom, *Japan: A Short Cultural History*, p. 131.

Japanese name for the Imperial House is 'Those who dwell above the clouds' and only persons of this family can be Emperor. Japan has never had a change of dynasty, as China so often had. The Emperor was inviolable and his person was sacred. The Japanese Emperors and their courts who introduced Chinese culture in Japan no doubt could not even imagine what the Chinese arrangements were in these matters and did not guess what changes they were making.

In spite of all Japan's cultural importations from China, therefore, this new civilization only paved the way for centuries of conflict as to which of these hereditary lords and vassals was in control of the country. Before the eighth century had ended the noble Fujiwara family had seized dominance and had thrust the Emperor into the background. When, as time went on, the Fujiwaras' dominance was disputed by feudal lords and the whole country plunged into civil war, one of these, the famous Yoritomo Minamoto, vanquished all rivals and became actual ruler of the country under an old military title, the Shogun, which in full means literally 'Barbarian-subduing Generalissimo.' This title, as was usual in Japan, Yoritomo made hereditary in the Minamoto family for as long as his descendants could hold the other feudal lords in check. The Emperor became an impotent figure. His chief importance was that the Shogun still depended upon him for his ritual investiture. He had no civil power. The actual power was held by a military camp, as it was called, which tried to hold its dominance by armed force over unruly fiefs. Each feudal lord, the *daimyo*, had his armed retainers, the *samurai*, whose swords were at his disposal, and they were always ready in periods of disorder to dispute the 'proper place' of a rival fief or of the ruling Shogun.

In the sixteenth century civil war had become endemic. After decades of disorder the great Ieyasu won out over all rivals and in 1603 became the first Shogun of the House of Tokugawa. The Shogunate remained in Ieyasu's line for two centuries and a half and was ended only in 1868 when the 'dual rule' of Emperor and Shogun was abolished at the beginning of the modern period. In many ways this long Tokugawa Era is one of the most remarkable in history. It maintained an armed peace in Japan up to the very last generation before it ended and it put into effect a centralized administration that admirably served the Tokugawas' purposes.

Ieyasu was faced with a most difficult problem and he did not choose an easy solution. The lords of some of the strongest fiefs had been against him in the civil war and had bowed to him only after a final disastrous defeat. These were the so-called Outside Lords. These lords he left in control of their fiefs and of their samurai, and indeed of all the feudal lords of Japan they continued to have the greatest autonomy in their domains. Nevertheless, he excluded them from the honor of being his vassals and from all important functions. These important positions were reserved for the Inside Lords, Ieyasu's supporters in the civil war. To maintain this difficult regime the Tokugawas relied upon a strategy of keeping the feudal lords, the daimyos, from accumulating power and of preventing any possible combination among them which might threaten the Shogun's control. Not only did the Tokugawas not abolish the feudal scheme; for the purpose of maintaining peace in Japan and dominance of the House of Tokugawa, they attempted to strengthen it and make it more rigid.

Japanese feudal society was elaborately stratified and each man's status was fixed by inheritance. The Tokugawas solidified this system and regulated the details of each caste's daily behavior. Every family head had to post on his doorway his class position and the required facts about his hereditary status. The clothes he could wear, the foods he could buy, and the kind of house he could legally live in were regulated according to this inherited rank. Below the Imperial Family and the court nobles, there were four Japanese castes ranked in hierarchal order: the warriors (samurai), the farmers, the artisans, and the merchants. Below these, again, were the outcasts. The most numerous and famous of these outcasts were the Eta, workers in tabooed trades. They were scavengers, buriers of the executed, skinners of dead animals and tanners of hides. They were Japan's untouchables, or, more exactly, their uncountables, for even the mileage of roads through their villages went uncounted as if the land and the inhabitants of the area did not exist at all. They were desperately poor, and, though guaranteed the exercise of their trades, they were outside the formal structure.

The merchants ranked just above the outcasts. However strange this seems to Americans, it was highly realistic in a feudal society. A merchant class is always disruptive of feudalism. As business men become respected and prosperous, feudalism decays. When the Tokugawas, by the most drastic laws any nation has ever enforced, decreed the isolation of Japan in the seventeenth century, they cut the ground from under the feet of the merchants. Japan had had an overseas trade all up and down the coast of China and Korea and a class of traders had been inevitably developing. The Tokugawas stopped all this by making it an offense worthy of capital punishment to build or operate any boat larger than a certain size. The small boats allowed could not cross to the continent or carry loads of trade goods. Domestic trade was severely restricted, too, by customs barriers which were set up on the borders of each fief with strict rules against letting goods in or out. Other laws were directed toward emphasizing the merchants' low social position. Sumptuary laws regulated the clothes they could wear, the umbrellas they could carry, the amount they could spend for a wedding or a funeral. They could not live in a samurai district. They had no legal protection against the swords of the samurai, the privileged warriors. The Tokugawa policy of keeping the merchants in inferior stations failed of course in a money economy, and Japan at that period was run on a money economy. But it was attempted.

The two classes which are appropriate to a stable feudalism, the warriors and the farmers, the Tokugawa regime froze into rigid forms. During the civil wars that were finally ended by Ieyasu, the great war-lord, Hideyoshi, had already completed, by his famous 'sword hunt,' the separation of these two classes. He had disarmed the peasants and given to the samurai the sole right to wear swords. The warriors could no longer be farmers nor artisans nor merchants. Not even the lowest of them could any longer legally be a producer; he was a member of a parasitic class which drew its annual rice stipend from taxes levied upon the peasants. The daimyo handled this rice and distributed to each samurai retainer his allotted income. There was no question about where the samurai had to look for support; he was wholly dependent upon his lord. In earlier eras of Japanese history strong ties between the feudal chief and his warriors had been forged in almost ceaseless war between the fiefs; in the Tokugawa era of peace the ties became economic. For the warrior-retainer, unlike his European counterpart, was not a sub-seigneur owning his own land and serfs nor was he a soldier of fortune. He was a pensioner on a set stipend which had been fixed for his family line at the beginning of the Tokugawa Era. It was not large. Japanese scholars have estimated that the average stipend of all samurai was about what farmers were earning and that was certainly bare subsistence.* Nothing could be more to the family's disadvantage than division of this stipend among heirs and in consequence the samurai limited their families. Nothing could be more galling to them than prestige dependent on wealth and display, so they laid great stress in their code on the superior virtues of frugality.

A great gulf separated the samurai from the other three classes: the farmers, the artisans and the merchants. These last three were 'common people.' The samurai were not. The swords the samurai wore as their prerogative and sign of caste were not mere decorations. They had the right to use them on the common people. They had traditionally

* Quoted by Herbert Norman, *Japan's Emergence as a Modern State*, p. 17, n. 12.

done so before Tokugawa times and the laws of Ieyasu merely sanctioned old customs when they decreed: 'Common people who behave unbecomingly to the samurai or who do not show respect to their superiors may be cut down on the spot.' It was no part of Ieyasu's design that mutual dependence should be built up between common people and the samurai retainers. His policy was based on strict hierarchal regulations. Both classes headed up to the daimyo and reckoned directly with him; they were on different stairways, as it were. Up and down each stairway there was law and regulation and control and reciprocity. Between the people on two stairways there was merely distance. The separateness of the two classes was necessarily bridged by circumstances over and over again but it was not a part of the system.

During the Tokugawa Era samurai retainers were not mere sword-swingers. They became increasingly the stewards of their overlords' estates and specialists in peaceful arts like the classical drama and the tea ceremony. All protocol lay in their sphere and the daimyo's intrigues were carried out by their skilled manipulations. Two hundred years of peace is a long time and mere individual sword-swinging had its limits. Just as the merchants, in spite of the caste regulations, developed a way of life that gave high place to urbane and artistic and pleasurable pursuits, so the samurai, in spite of their ready swords, developed arts of peace.

The farmers, in spite of their legal defenselessness against the samurai, the heavy levies of rice made upon them and all the restrictions imposed upon them, had certain securities guaranteed them. They were guaranteed the possession of their farms and to have land gives a man prestige in Japan. Under the Tokugawa regime, land could not be permanently alienated and this law was a guarantee for the individual cultivator, not, as in European feudalism, for the feudal lord. The farmer had a permanent right to something which he valued supremely and he appears to have worked his land with the same diligence and unstinting care with which his descendants cultivate their rice fields today. Nevertheless, he was the Atlas who supported the whole parasitic upper class of about two million persons, including the government of the Shogun, the establishments of the daimyo and the stipends of the samurai retainers. He was taxed in kind, that is, he paid to the daimyo a percentage of his crops. Whereas in Siam, another wet-rice country, the traditional tax is 10 per cent, in Tokugawa Japan it was 40 per cent. But in reality it was higher than this. In some fiefs it was 80 per cent and always there was corvée or work requisitions, which bore down on the strength and time of the farmer. Like the samurai, the farmers also limited their families and the population of the whole of Japan stood at almost the same figure during all the Tokugawa centuries. For an Asiatic country during a long period of peace these static population figures tell a great deal about the regime. It was Spartan in its restrictions, both on the tax-supported retainers and on the producing class, but between each dependent and his superior, it was relatively dependable. A man knew his obligations, his prerogatives and his station and if these were infringed upon the poorest might protest.

The farmers, even in the direst poverty, carried their protests not only to the feudal lord but to the Shogunate authorities. There were at least a thousand of these revolts during the two and a half Tokugawa centuries. They were not occasioned by the traditional heavy rule of '40 per cent to the prince and 60 per cent to the cultivators'; they were all protests against additional levies. When conditions were no longer bearable, the farmers might march in great numbers against their overlords but the procedure of petition and judgment was orderly. The farmers drew up formal petitions for redress which they submitted to the daimyo's chamberlain. When this petition was intercepted or the daimyo took no notice of their complaints they sent their representatives to the capital to present their written complaints to the Shogunate. In famous cases they could insure its delivery only by inserting it into some high official's palanquin as he rode through the streets of the capital. But, no matter what risks the farmers took in delivering the petition, it was then investigated by the Shogunate authorities and about half of the judgments were in favor of the peasants.*

Japan's requirements of law and order were not satisfied, however, with the Shogunate's judgment on the farmers' claims. Their complaints might be just and it might be advisable for the State to honor them, but the peasant leaders had transgressed the strict law of hierarchy. Regardless of any decision in their favor, they had broken the essential law of their allegiance and this could not be overlooked. They were therefore condemned to death. The righteousness of their cause had nothing to do with the matter. Even

* Borton, Hugh, *Peasant Uprisings in Japan of the Tokugawa Period*, Transactions of the Asiatic Society of Japan, 2nd Series, 16 (1938).

the peasants accepted this inevitability. The condemned men were their heroes and the people came in numbers to the execution where the leaders were boiled in oil or beheaded or crucified, but at the execution the crowds did not riot. This was law and order. They might afterward build the dead men shrines and honor them as martyrs, but they accepted the execution as part and parcel of the hierarchal laws by which they lived.

The Tokugawa Shoguns, in short, attempted to solidify the caste structure within each fief and to make each class dependent on the feudal lord. The daimyo stood at the apex of the hierarchy in each fief and he was allowed to exercise his prerogatives over his dependents. The Shogun's great administrative problem was to control the daimyo. In every way he prevented them from forming alliances or from carrying out schemes of aggression. Passport and customs officials were maintained at the frontiers of the fiefs to keep strict watch for 'outgoing women and incoming guns' lest any daimyo try to send his women away and smuggle arms in. No daimyo could contract a marriage without the Shogun's permission lest it might lead to a dangerous political alliance. Trade between the fiefs was hindered even to the extent of allowing bridges to become impassable. The Shogun's spies too kept him well informed on the daimyo's expenditures and if the feudal coffers were filling up, the Shogun required him to undertake expensive public works to bring him in line again. Most famous regulation of all was that the daimyo live half of each year in the capital and, even when he returned to his fief for his residence there, he had to leave his wife behind him in Yedo (Tokyo) as a hos-lage in the hands of the Shoguns. In all these ways the administration made certain that it maintain the upper hand and enforce its dominant position in the hierarchy.

The Shogun was not, of course, the final keystone in this arch for he held sway as the appointee of the Emperor. The Emperor with his court of hereditary nobles (*kuge*) was isolated in Kyoto and was without actual power. The Emperor's financial resources were less than those of even lesser daimyos and the very ceremonies of the court were strictly circumscribed by Shogunate regulations. Not even the most powerful Tokugawa Shoguns, however, took any steps to do away with this dual rule of Emperor and actual ruler. It was no new thing in Japan. Since the twelfth century a Generalissimo (Shogun) had ruled the country in the name of a throne shorn of actual authority. In some centuries division of function had gone so far that the real power which the shadowy Emperor delegated to a hereditary secular chief was exercised in turn by a hereditary advisor of that chief. There has always been delegation upon delegation of original authority. Even in the last and desperate days of the Tokugawa regime, Commodore Perry did not suspect the existence of an Emperor in the background and our first envoy, Townsend Harris, who negotiated the first commercial treaty with Japan in 1858, had to discover for himself that there was an Emperor.

The truth is that Japan's conception of her Emperor is one that is found over and over among the islands of the Pacific. He is the Sacred Chief who may or may not take part in administration. In some Pacific islands he did and in some he delegated his authority. But always his person was sacred. Among New Zealand tribes the Sacred Chief was so sacrosanct that he might not feed himself and even the spoon with which he was fed must not be allowed to touch his sacred teeth. He had to be carried when he went abroad, for any land upon which he set his sacred foot became automatically so holy that it must pass into the Sacred Chief's possession. His head was particularly sacrosanct and no man could touch it. His words reached the tribal gods. In some Pacific islands, like Samoa and Tonga, the Sacred Chief did not descend into the arena of life. A Secular Chief performed all the duties of State. James Wilson, who visited the island of Tonga in the Eastern Pacific at the end of the eighteenth century, wrote that its government 'resembles most the government of Japan where the sacred majesty is a sort of state prisoner to the captain-general.'* The Tongan Sacred Chiefs were isolated from public affairs, but they performed ritual duties. They had to receive the first fruits of the gardens and conduct a ceremony before any man could eat of them. When the Sacred Chief died, his death was announced by the phrase, 'The heavens are void.' He was buried with ceremony in a great royal tomb. But he took no part in administration.

The Emperor, even when he was politically impotent and 'a sort of State prisoner to the Captain-general,' filled, according to Japanese definitions, a 'proper station' in the hierarchy. The Emperor's active participation in mundane affairs was to them no measure of his status. His court at

* Wilson, James, *A missionary voyage to the Southern Pacific Ocean performed in the years 1796, 1797 and 1798 in the ship Duff.* London, 1799, p. 384. Quoted by Edward Winslow Gifford, Tongan Society. Bernice P. Bishop Museum, Bulletin 61. Hawaii, 1929.

Kyoto was a value they preserved all through the long centuries of the rule of the Barbarian-subduing Generalissimos. His functions were superfluous only from a Western point of view. The Japanese, who at every point were accustomed to rigorous definition of hierarchal rôle, looked at the matter differently.

The extreme explicitness of the Japanese hierarchal system in feudal times, from outcast to Emperor, has left its strong impress on modern Japan. After all, the feudal regime was legally ended only about seventy-five years ago, and strong national habits do not pass away within one man's lifetime. Japanese statesmen of the modern period, too, laid their careful plans, as we shall see in the next chapter, to preserve a great deal of the system in spite of radical alterations in their country's objectives. The Japanese, more than any other sovereign nation, have been conditioned to a world where the smallest details of conduct are mapped and status is assigned. During two centuries when law and order were maintained in such a world with an iron hand, the Japanese learned to identify this meticulously plotted hierarchy with safety and security. So long as they stayed within known boundaries, and so long as they fulfilled known obligations, they could trust their world. Banditry was controlled. Civil war between the daimyo was prevented. If subjects could prove that others had overstepped their rights, they could appeal as the farmers did when they were exploited. It was personally dangerous but it was approved. The best of the Tokugawa Shoguns even had a Complaint Box into which any citizen could drop his protest, and the Shogun alone had a key to his box. There were genuine guarantees in Japan that aggressions would be rectified if they were acts that were not allowed on the existing map of conduct. One trusted the map and was safe only when one followed it. One showed one's courage, one's integrity in conforming to it, not in modifying it or in revolting against it. Within its stated limits, it was a known and, in their eyes, a dependable world. Its rules were not abstract ethical principles of a decalogue but tiny specifications of what was due in this situation and what was due in that situation; what was due if one were a samurai and what was due if one were a common man; what was proper to elder brother and what was proper to younger brother.

The Japanese did not become a mild and submissive people under this system, as some nations have under a stronghanded hierarchal regime. It is important to recognize that certain guarantees were given to each class. Even the outcasts were guaranteed a monopoly of their special trades and their self-governing bodies were recognized by the authorities. Restrictions upon each class were great but there were order and security too.

The caste restrictions also had a certain flexibility they do not have, for instance, in India. Japanese customs provided several explicit techniques for manipulating the system without doing violence to the accepted ways. A man could change his caste status in several ways. When money lenders and merchants became wealthy, as they inevitably did under Japan's money economy, the rich used various traditional devices to infiltrate the upper classes. They became 'land owners' by the use of liens and rents. It is true that the peasants' land was inalienable but farm rents were excessively high in Japan and it was profitable to leave the peasants on their land. Money lenders settled on the land and collected their rents, and such 'ownership' of land gave prestige as well as profit in Japan. Their children married samurai. They became gentry.

Another traditional manipulation of the caste system was through the custom of adoption. It provided a way of 'buying' samurai status. As merchants became richer in spite of all Tokugawa restrictions, they arranged for their sons' adoption into samurai families. In Japan one seldom adopts a son; one adopts a husband for one's daughter. He is known as an 'adopted husband.' He becomes the heir of his father-in-law. He pays a high price, for his name is stricken from his own family register and entered on his wife's. He takes her name and goes to live with his mother-in-law. But if the price is high, the advantages are also great. For the prosperous merchant's descendants become samurai and the impoverished samurai's family gets an alliance with wealth. No violence is done to the caste system which remains just what it always was. But the system has been manipulated to provide upper-class status for the wealthy.

Japan therefore did not require castes to marry only among themselves. There were approved arrangements which allowed intermarriage among them. The resulting infiltration of prosperous traders into the lower samurai class played a large part in furthering one of the greatest contrasts between Western Europe and Japan. When feudalism broke down in Europe it was due to the pressure of a growing and increasingly powerful middle class and this class dominated the modern industrial period. In Japan no such strong middle class arose. The merchants and money lenders 'bought' upper-class status by sanctioned methods. Merchants and lower samurai became allies. It is a curious and surprising thing to point out that at the time when feudalism was in its death throes in both civilizations, Japan sanctioned class mobility to a greater degree than continental Europe did, but no evidence for such a statement could be more convincing than the lack of any sign of a class war between aristocracy and bourgeoisie.

It is easy to point out that the common cause made by these two classes was mutually advantageous in Japan, but it would have been mutually advantageous in France too. It was advantageous in Western Europe in those individual instances where it occurred. But class rigidity was strong in Europe and the conflict of classes led in France to the expropriation of the aristocracy. In Japan they drew closer together. The alliance that overthrew the effete Shogunate was an alliance between the merchant-financiers and the samurai retainers. The modern era in Japan preserved the aristocratic system. It could hardly have happened without Japan's sanctioned techniques for class mobility.

If the Japanese loved and trusted their meticulously explicit map of behavior, they had a certain justification. It guaranteed security so long as one followed the rules; it allowed protests against unauthorized aggressions and it could be manipulated to one's own advantage. It required the fulfillment of reciprocal obligations. When the Tokugawa regime crumbled in the first half of the nineteenth century, no group in the nation was in favor of tearing up the map. There was no French Revolution. There was not even an 1848. Yet the times were desperate. From the common people to the Shogunate, every class had fallen into debt to the money lenders and merchants. The mere numbers of the non-productive classes and the scale of customary official expenditures had proved insupportable. The daimyo as the grip of poverty tightened upon them were unable to pay the fixed stipends to their samurai retainers and the whole network of feudal ties became a mockery. They tried to keep afloat by increasing the already heavy taxes upon the peasants. These were collected years in advance and the farmers were reduced to extreme want. The Shogunate too was bankrupt and could do little to keep the status quo. Japan was in dire domestic extremity by 1853 when Admiral Perry appeared with his men of war. His forced entry was followed in 1858 by a trade treaty with the United States which Japan was in no position to refuse.

The cry that went up from Japan, however, was *Isshin*—to dig back into the past, to restore. It was the opposite of revolutionary. It was not even progressive. Joined with the cry 'Restore the Emperor' was the equally popular cry 'Expel the Barbarians.' The nation supported the program of going back to a golden age of isolation and the few leaders who saw how impossible such a course would be were assassinated for their pains. There seemed not the slightest likelihood that this non-revolutionary country of Japan would alter its course to conform to any Occidental patterns, still less that in fifty years it would compete with Western nations on their own grounds. Nevertheless, that is what happened. Japan used her own strengths, which were not at all the Occidental strengths, to achieve a goal which no powerful high-placed group and no popular opinion in Japan demanded. No Westerner in the eighteen-sixties would have believed if he had seen the future in a crystal ball. There seemed to be no cloud the size of a man's hand on the horizon to indicate the tumult of activity which swept Japan during the next decades. Nevertheless, the impossible happened. Japan's backward and hierarchy-ridden population swung to a new course and held it.

4

The Meiji Reform

THE BATTLECRY that ushered in the modern era in Japan was *Sonno joi,* 'Restore the Emperor and expel the Barbarian.' It was a slogan that sought to keep Japan uncontaminated by the outside world and to restore a golden age of the tenth century before there had been a 'dual rule' of Emperor and Shogun. The Emperor's court at Kyoto was reactionary in the extreme. The victory of the Emperor's party meant to his supporters the humiliation and expulsion of foreigners. It meant reinstatement of traditional ways of life in Japan. It meant that 'reformers' would have no voice in affairs. The great Outside Lords, the daimyo of Japan's strongest fiefs who spearheaded the overthrow of the Shogunate, thought of the Restoration as a way in which they, instead of the Tokugawa, could rule Japan. They wanted a mere change of personnel. The farmers wanted to keep more of the rice they raised but they hated 'reforms.' The samurai wanted to keep their pensions and be allowed to use their swords for greater glory. The merchants, who financed the Restoration forces, wanted to expand mercantilism but they never arraigned the feudal system.

When the anti-Tokugawa forces triumphed and 'dual

rule' was ended in 1868 by the Restoration of the Emperor, the victors were committed, by Western standards, to a fiercely conservative isolationist policy. From the first the regime followed the opposite course. It had been in power hardly a year when it abolished the daimyo's right of taxation in all fiefs. It called in the land-registers and appropriated to itself the peasants' tax of '40 per cent to the daimyo.' This expropriation was not without compensation. The government allotted to each daimyo the equivalent of half his normal income. At the same time also the government freed the daimyo of the support of his samurai retainers and of the expenses of public works. The samurai retainers, like the daimyo, received pensions from the government. Within the next five years all legal inequality among the classes was summarily abolished, insignia and distinctive dress of caste and class were outlawed—even queues had to be cut,—the outcasts were emancipated, the laws against alienation of land withdrawn, the barriers that had separated fief from fief were removed and Buddhism was disestablished. By 1876 the daimyo and samurai pensions were commuted to lump sum payments which were to become due in five to fifteen years. These payments were either large or small according to the fixed income these individuals had drawn in Tokugawa days and the money made it possible for them to start enterprises in the new non-feudal economy. 'It was the final stage in the sealing of that peculiar union of merchants and financial princes with the feudal or landed princes which was already evident in the Tokugawa period.'*

These remarkable reforms of the infant Meiji regime

* Norman, p. 96.

were not popular. There was far more general enthusiasm for an invasion of Korea from 1871 to 1873 than for any of these measures. The Meiji government not only persisted in its drastic course of reform, it killed the project of the invasion. Its program was so strongly opposed to the wishes of a great majority of those who had fought to establish it that by 1877 Saigo, their greatest leader, had organized a full-scale rebellion against the government. His army represented all the pro-feudal longings of Imperial supporters which had from the first year of the Restoration been betrayed by the Meiji regime. The government called up a non-samurai voluntary army and defeated Saigo's samurai. But the rebellion was an indication of the extent of the dissatisfaction the regime aroused in Japan.

The farmers' dissatisfaction was equally marked. There were at least 190 agrarian revolts between 1868 and 1878, the first Meiji decade. In 1877 the new government made its first tardy moves to lessen the great tax burden upon the peasants, and they had reason to feel that the regime had failed them. The farmers objected in addition to the establishment of schools, to conscription, to land surveys, to having to cut their queues, to legal equality of the outcasts, to the drastic restrictions on official Buddhism, to calendar reforms and to many other measures which changed their settled ways of life.

Who, then, was this 'government' which undertook such drastic and unpopular reforms? It was that 'peculiar union' in Japan of the lower samurai and the merchant class which special Japanese institutions had fostered even in feudal times. They were the samurai retainers who had learned statecraft as chamberlains and stewards for the daimyos, who had run the feudal monopolies in mines, textiles, pasteboards and the like. They were merchants who had bought samurai status and spread knowledge of productive techniques in that class. This samurai-merchant alliance rapidly put to the fore able and self-confident administrators who drew up the Meiji policies and planned their execution. The real problem, however, is not from what class they came but how it happened that they were so able and so realistic. Japan, just emerging from medievalism in the last half of the nineteenth century and as weak then as Siam is today, produced leaders able to conceive and to carry out one of the most statesmanlike and successful jobs ever attempted in any nation. The strength, and the weakness too, of these leaders was rooted in traditional Japanese character and it is the chief object of this book to discuss what that character was and is. Here we can only recognize how the Meiji statesmen went about their undertaking.

They did not take their task to be an ideological revolution at all. They treated it as a job. Their goal as they conceived it was to make Japan into a country which must be reckoned with. They were not iconoclasts. They did not revile and beggar the feudal class. They tempted them with pensions large enough to lure them into eventual support of the regime. They finally ameliorated the peasants' condition; their ten-year tardiness appears to have been due rather to the pitiful condition of the early Meiji treasury than to a class rejection of peasants' claims upon the regime.

The energetic and resourceful statesmen who ran the Meiji government rejected, however, all ideas of ending hierarchy in Japan. The Restoration had simplified the hierarchal order by placing the Emperor at its apex and eliminating the Shogun. The post-Restoration statesmen, by abolishing the fiefs, eliminated the conflict between loyalty to one's own seigneur and to the State. These changes did not unseat hierarchal habits. They gave them a new locus. 'Their Excellencies,' the new leaders of Japan, even strengthened centralized rule in order to impose their own workmanlike programs upon the people. They alternated demands from above with gifts from above and in this way they managed to survive. But they did not imagine that they had to cater to a public opinion which might not want to reform the calendar or to establish public schools or to outlaw discrimination against the outcasts.

One of these gifts from above was the Constitution of Japan, which was given by the Emperor to his people in 1889. It gave the people a place in the State and established the Diet. It was drawn up with great care by Their Excellencies after critical study of the varied constitutions of the Western World. The writers of it however, took 'every possible precaution to guard against popular interference and the invasion of public opinion.'* The very bureau which drafted it was a part of the Imperial Household Department and was therefore sacrosanct.

Meiji statesmen were quite conscious about their objective. During the eighteen-eighties Prince Ito, framer of the Constitution, sent the Marquis Kido to consult Herbert

* Quoted from a Japanese authority who bases his remarks on statements by Baron Kaneko who was one of the drafters. See Norman, *ibid.*, p. 88.

Spencer in England on the problems lying ahead of Japan and after lengthy conversations Spencer wrote Ito his judgments. On the subject of hierarchy Spencer wrote that Japan had in her traditional arrangements an incomparable basis for national well-being which should be maintained and fostered. Traditional obligations to superiors, he said, and beyond all to the Emperor, were Japan's great opportunity. Japan could move forward solidly under its 'superiors' and defend itself against the difficulties inevitable in more individualistic nations. The great Meiji statesmen were well satisfied with this confirmation of their own convictions. They meant to retain in the modern world the advantages of observing 'proper station.' They did not intend to undermine the habit of hierarchy.

In every field of activity, whether political or religious or economic, the Meiji statesmen allocated the duties of 'proper station' between the State and the people. Their whole scheme was so alien to arrangements in the United States or England that we usually fail to recognize its basic points. There was, of course, strong rule from above which did not have to follow the lead of public opinion. This government was administered by a top hierarchy and this could never include elected persons. At this level the people could have no voice. In 1940 the top government hierarchy consisted of those who had 'access' to the Emperor, those who constituted his immediate advisors, and those whose high appointments bore the privy seal. These last included Cabinet Ministers, prefectural governors, judges, chiefs of national bureaus and other like responsible officers. No elected official had any such status in the hierarchy and it would have been out of the question for elected members of the Diet, for instance, to have any voice in selecting or approving a Cabinet Minister or head of the Bureau of Finance or of Transportation. The elected Lower House of the Diet was a voice of the people which had the not inconsiderable privilege of interrogating and criticizing the Higher Officials, but it had no real voice in appointments or in decisions or in budgetary matters and it did not initiate legislation. The Lower House was even checked by a non-elected Upper House, half of them nobility and another quarter Imperial appointees. Since its power to approve legislation was about equal to that of the Lower House, a further hierarchal check was provided.

Japan therefore ensured that those who held high government posts remain 'Their Excellencies,' but this does not mean that there was not self-government in its 'proper place.' In all Asiatic nations, under whatever regime, authority from above always reaches down and meets in some middle ground local self-government rising from below. The differences between different countries all concern matters of how far up democratic accountability reaches, how many or few its responsibilities are and whether local leadership remains responsive to the whole community or is preempted by local magnates to the disadvantage of the people. Tokugawa Japan had, like China, tiny units of five to ten families, called in recent times the *tonari gumi,* which were the smallest responsible units of the population. The head of this group of neighboring families assumed leadership in their own affairs, was responsible for their good behavior, had to turn in reports of any doubtful acts and surrender any wanted individual to the government. Meiji statesmen at first abolished these, but they were later restored and called the *tonari gumi*. In the towns and cities the government has sometimes actively fostered them, but they seldom function today in villages. The hamlet (*buraku*) units are more important. The buraku were not abolished nor were they incorporated as units in the government. They were an area in which the State did not function. These hamlets of fifteen or so houses continue even today to function in an organized fashion through their annually rotating headmen, who 'look after hamlet property, supervise hamlet aid given to families in the event of a death or a fire, decide the proper days for co-operative work in agriculture, housebuilding or road repair, and announce by ringing the fire bell or beating two blocks together in a certain rhythm the local holidays and rest days.'* These headmen are not responsible, as in some Asiatic nations, also for collecting the State taxes in their community and they do not therefore have to carry this onus. Their position is quite unambivalent; they function in the area of democratic responsibility.

Modern civil government in Japan officially recognizes local administration of cities, towns and villages. Elected 'elders' choose a responsible headman who serves as the representative of the community in all dealings with the State, which is represented by the prefectural and national governments. In the villages the headman is an old resident, a member of a land-owning farm family. He serves at a financial loss but the prestige is considerable. He and the

* Embree, John F., *The Japanese Nation*, p. 88.

elders are responsible for village finances, public health, maintenance of the schools and especially for property records and individual dossiers. The village office is a busy place; it has charge of the spending of the State's appropriation for primary school education for all children and of the raising and spending of its own much larger local share of school expenses, management and rent of village-owned property, land improvement and afforestation, and records of all property transactions, which become legal only when they are properly entered at this office. It must also keep an up-to-date record of residence, marital status, birth of children, adoption, any encounter with the law and other facts on each individual who still maintains official residence in the community, besides a family record which shows similar data about one's family. Any such information is forwarded from any part of Japan to one's official home office and is entered on one's dossier. Whenever one applies for a position or is tried before a judge or in any way is asked for identification, one writes one's home community office or visits it and obtains a copy to submit to the interested person. One does not face lightly the possibility of having a bad entry inscribed on one's own or one's family's dossier.

The city, town, and village therefore has considerable responsibility. It is a community responsibility. Even in the nineteen-twenties, when Japan had national political parties, which in any country means an alternation of tenure between 'ins' and 'outs,' local administration generally remained untouched by this development and was directed by elders acting for the whole community. In three respects, however, local administrations do not have autonomy; all judges are nationally appointed, all police and school teachers are employees of the State. Since most civil cases in Japan are still settled by arbitration or through go-betweens, the courts of law figure very little in local administration. Police are more important. Police have to be on hand at public meetings but these duties are intermittent and most of their time is devoted to keeping the personal and property records. The State may transfer policemen frequently from one post to another so that they may remain outsiders without local ties. School teachers also are transferred. The State regulates every detail of the schools, and, as in France, every school in the country is studying on the same day the same lesson from the same textbook. Every school goes through the same calisthenics to the same radio broadcast at the same hour of the morning. The community does not have local autonomy over schools or police or courts of justice.

The Japanese government at all points thus greatly differs from the American, where elected persons carry the highest executive and legislative responsibility and local control is exercised through local direction of police and police-courts. It does not, however, differ formally from the governmental set-up of such thoroughly Occidental nations as Holland and Belgium. In Holland, for instance, as in Japan, the Queen's Ministry drafts all proposed laws; the Diet has in practice not initiated legislation. The Dutch Crown legally appoints even mayors of towns and cities and thus its formal right reaches further down into local areas of concern than it did in Japan before 1940; this is true even though in practice the Dutch Crown usually approves a local nomination. The direct responsibility to the Crown of the police and of the courts is also Dutch. Though, in Holland, schools may be set up at will by any sectarian group, the Japanese school system is duplicated in France. Local responsibility for canals, polders and local improvements, also, is a duty of the community as a whole in Holland, not of a mayor and officials politically elected.

The true difference between the Japanese form of government and such cases in Western Europe lies not in form but in functioning. The Japanese rely on old habits of deference set up in their past experience and formalized in their ethical system and in their etiquette. The State can depend upon it that, when their Excellencies function in their 'proper place,' their prerogatives will be respected, not because the policy is approved but because it is wrong in Japan to override boundaries between prerogatives. At the topmost level of policy 'popular opinion' is out of place. The government asks only 'popular support.' When the State stakes out its own official field in the area of local concern, also, its jurisdiction is accepted with deference. The State, in all its domestic functions, is not a necessary evil as it is so generally felt to be in the United States. The State comes nearer, in Japanese eyes, to being the supreme good.

The State, moreover, is meticulous in recognizing 'proper place' for the will of the people. In areas of legitimate popular jurisdiction it is not too much to say that the Japanese State has had to woo the people even for their own good. The State agricultural extension agent can act with about as little authoritarianism in improving old methods of agriculture as his counterpart can in Idaho. The State official advocating State-guaranteed farmers' credit associations or farmers' co-operatives for buying and selling must hold long-drawn-out round-tables with the local notables and then abide by their decision. Local affairs require local management. The Japanese way of life allocates proper authority and defines its proper sphere. It gives much greater deference—and therefore freedom of action—to 'superiors' than Western cultures do, but they too must keep their station. Japan's motto is: Everything in its place.

In the field of religion the Meiji statesmen made much more bizarre formal arrangements than in government. They were however carrying out the same Japanese motto. The State took as its realm a worship that specifically upholds the symbols of national unity and superiority, and in all the rest it left freedom of worship to the individual. This area of national jurisdiction was State Shinto. Since it was concerned with proper respect to national symbols, as saluting the flag is in the United States, State Shinto was, they said, 'no religion.' Japan therefore could require it of all citizens without violating the Occidental dogma of religious freedom any more than the United States violates it in requiring a salute to the Stars and Stripes. It was a mere sign of allegiance. Because it was 'not religion,' Japan could teach it in the schools without risk of Occidental criticism. State Shinto in the schools becomes the history of Japan from the age of the gods and the veneration of the Emperor, 'ruler from ages eternal.' It was State-supported, State-regulated. All other areas of religion, even denominational or cult Shinto, to say nothing of Buddhist and Christian sects, were left to individual initiative much as in the United States. The two areas were even administratively and financially separated; State Shinto was in the charge of its own bureau in the Home Office and its priests and ceremonies and shrines were supported by the State. Cult Shinto and Buddhist and Christian sects were the concern of a Bureau of Religion in the Department of Education and were supported by voluntary contributions of members.

Because of Japan's official position on the subject one cannot speak of State Shinto as a vast Established Church, but one can at least call it a vast Establishment. There were over 110,000 shrines ranging all the way from the great Ise Shrine, temple of the Sun Goddess, to small local shrines which the officiating priest cleans up for the occasion of a special ceremony. The national hierarchy of priests paralleled the political and the lines of authority ran from the lowest priest through the district and prefectural priests to their priestly Excellencies at the top. They performed ceremonies for the people rather than conducting worship by the people, and there was in State Shinto nothing paralleling our familiar church-going. Priests of State Shinto—since it was no religion—were forbidden by law to teach any dogma and there could be no church services as Westerners understand them. Instead, on the frequent days of rites official representatives of the community came and stood before the priest while he purified them by waving before them a wand with hemp and paper streamers. He opened the door of the inner shrine and called down the gods, with a high-pitched cry, to come to partake of a ceremonial meal. The priest prayed and each participant in order of rank presented with deep obeisance that omnipresent object in old and new Japan: a twig of their sacred tree with pendant strips of white paper. The priest then sent back the gods with another cry and closed the doors of the inner shrine. On the festival days of State Shinto the Emperor in his turn observed rites for the people and government offices were closed. But these holidays were not great popular fête-days like the ceremonies in honor of local shrines or even Buddhist holidays. Both of these are in the 'free' area outside of State Shinto.

In this area the Japanese people carry on the great sects and fête-days which are close to their hearts. Buddhism remains the religion of the great mass of the people and the various sects with their different teachings and founding prophets are vigorous and omnipresent. Even Shinto has its great cults which stand outside of State Shinto. Some were strongholds of pure nationalism even before the government in the nineteen-thirties took up the same position, some are faith-healing sects often compared to Christian Science, some hold by Confucian tenets, some have specialized in trance states and pilgrimages to sacred mountain shrines. Most of the popular fête-days, too, have been left outside of State Shinto. The people on such days throng to the shrines. Each person purifies himself by rinsing out his mouth and he summons the god to descend by pulling a bell rope or clapping his hands. He bows in veneration, sends back the god by another pull of the bell cord or clapping of hands, and goes off for the main business of the day which is buying knickknacks and tidbits from the vendors who have set up their stalls, watching wrestling matches or exorcism or *kagura* dances, which are liberally enlivened by clowns, and generally enjoying the great throng. An Englishman who had lived in Japan quoted William Blake's verse which he always remembered on Japanese fête-days:

> If at the church they would give us some ale,
> And a pleasant fire our souls to regale,
> We'd sing and we'd pray all the livelong day,
> Nor ever once wish from the church to stray.

Except for those few who have professionally dedicated themselves to religious austerities, religion is not austere in Japan. The Japanese are also addicted to religious pilgrimages and these too are greatly enjoyed holidays.

Meiji statesmen, therefore, carefully marked out the area of State functioning in government and of State Shinto in the field of religion. They left other areas to the people but they ensured to themselves as top officials of the new hierarchy dominance in matters which in their eyes directly concerned the State. In setting up the Armed Forces they had a similar problem. They rejected, as in other fields, the old caste system but in the Army they went farther than in civilian life. They outlawed in the Armed Services even the respect language of Japan, though in actual practice old usage of course persists. The Army also promoted to officer's rank on the basis of merit, not of family, to a degree which could hardly be put into effect in other fields. Its reputation among Japanese in this respect is high and apparently deservedly so. It was certainly the best means available by which to enlist popular support for the new Army. Companies and platoons, too, were formed from neighbors of the same region and peacetime military service was spent at posts close to one's home. This meant not only that local ties were conserved but that every man who went through Army training spent two years during which the relationship between officers and men, between second-year men and first-year men, superseded that between samurai and farmers or between rich and poor. The Army functioned in many ways as a democratic leveler and it was in many ways a true people's army. Whereas the Army in most other nations is depended upon as the strong arm to defend the status quo, in Japan the Army's sympathy with the small peasant has lined it up in repeated protests against the great financiers and industrialists.

Japanese statesmen may not have approved of all the consequences of building up a people's army but it was not at this level where they saw fit to ensure Army supremacy in the hierarchy. That objective they made sure of by arrangements in the very highest spheres. They did not write these arrangements into the Constitution but continued as customary procedure the already recognized independence of the High Command from the civil government. The Ministers of the Army and the Navy, in contrast for instance to the head of the Foreign Office and domestic bureaus, had direct access to the Emperor himself and could therefore use his name in forcing through their measures. They did not need to inform or consult their civilian colleagues of the Cabinet. In addition the Armed Services held a whip hand over any Cabinet. They could prevent the formation of a Cabinet they distrusted by the simple expedient of refusing to release generals and admirals to hold military portfolios in the Cabinet. Without such high officers of the active service to fill the positions of Army and Navy Ministers there could be no cabinet; no civilians or retired officers could hold these posts. Similarly, if the Armed Services were displeased at any act of the Ministry, they could cause its dissolution by recalling their Cabinet representatives. On this highest policy level the top military hierarchy made sure that it need brook no interference. If it needed any further guarantees it had one in the Constitution: 'If the Diet fails to approve the budget submitted, the budget of the previous year is automatically available to the Government for the current year.' The exploit of the Army in occupying Manchuria when the Foreign Office had promised that the Army would not take this step was only one of the instances when the Army hierarchy successfully supported its commanders in the field in the absence of agreed Cabinet policy. As in other fields, so with the Army: where hierarchal privileges are concerned the Japanese tend to accept all the consequences, not because of agreement about the policy but because they do not countenance overriding boundaries between prerogatives.

In the field of industrial development Japan pursued a course which is unparalleled in any Western nation. Again their Excellencies arranged the game and set the rules. They not only planned, they built and financed on government money the industries they decided they needed. A State bureaucracy organized and ran them. Foreign technicians were imported and Japanese were sent to learn abroad. Then when, as they said, these industries were 'well organized and business was prosperous,' the government disposed of them to private firms. They were sold gradually at 'ridiculously low prices'* to a chosen financial oligarchy, the famous Zaibatsu, chiefly the Mitsui and Mitsubishi families. Her statesmen judged that industrial development was too important to Japan to be entrusted to laws of supply and demand or to free enterprise. But this policy was in no way due to socialistic dogma; it was precisely the Zaibatsu who reaped the advantages. What Japan accomplished was that with the minimum of fumbling and wastage the industries she deemed necessary were established.

Japan was by these means able to revise 'the normal order of the starting point and succeeding stages of capitalist production.'† Instead of beginning with the production of consumer goods and light industry, she first undertook key heavy industries. Arsenals, shipyards, iron works, construction of railroads had priority and were rapidly brought to a high stage of technical efficiency. Not all of these were released to private hands and vast military industries remained under government bureaucracy and were financed by special government accounts.

In this whole field of the industries to which the government gave priority, the small trader or the non-bureaucratic manager had no 'proper place.' Only the State and the great trusted and politically favored financial houses operated in this area. But as in other fields of Japanese life there was a free area in industry too. These were the 'left-over' industries which operated with minimum capitalization and maximum utilization of cheap labor. These light indus-

* Norman, *op. cit.*, p. 131. This discussion is based on the illuminating analysis given by Norman.

† *Ibid.*, p. 125.

tries could exist without modern technology and they do. They function through what we used to call in the United States home sweat-shops. A small-time manufacturer buys the raw material, lets it out to a family or a small shop with four or five workers, takes it back again, repeats by letting it out again for another step in processing and at last sells the product to the merchant or exporter. In the nineteen-thirties no less than 53 per cent of all persons industrially employed in Japan were working in this way in shops and homes having less than five workers.* Many of these workers are protected by old paternalistic customs of apprenticeship and many are mothers who in Japan's great cities sit in their own homes over their piecework with their babies strapped on their backs.

This duality of Japanese industry is quite as important in Japanese ways of life as duality in the field of government or religion. It is as if, when Japanese statesmen decided that they needed an aristocracy of finance to match their hierarchies in other fields, they built up for them the strategic industries, selected the politically favored merchant houses and affiliated them in their 'proper stations' with the other hierarchies. It was no part of their plan for government to cut loose from these great financial houses and the Zaibatsu profited by a kind of continued paternalism which gave them not only profit but high place. It was inevitable, granted old Japanese attitudes toward profit and money, that a financial aristocracy should fall under attack from the people, but the government did what it could to build

* Professor Uyeda, quoted by Miriam S. Farley, *Pigmy Factories.* Far Eastern Survey, VI (1937), p. 2.

it up according to accepted ideas of hierarchy. It did not entirely succeed, for the Zaibatsu has been under attack from the so-called Young Officers' groups of the Army and from rural areas. But it still remains true that the greatest bitterness of Japanese public opinion is turned not against the Zaibatsu but against the *narikin*. Narikin is often translated 'nouveau riche' but that does not do justice to the Japanese feeling. In the United States nouveaux riches are strictly 'newcomers'; they are laughable because they are gauche and have not had time to acquire the proper polish. This liability, however, is balanced by the heartwarming asset that they have come up from the log cabin, they have risen from driving a mule to controlling oil millions. But in Japan a narikin is a term taken from Japanese chess and means a pawn promoted to queen. It is a pawn rampaging about the board as a 'big shot.' It has no hierarchal right to do any such thing. The narikin is believed to have obtained his wealth by defrauding or exploiting others and the bitterness directed toward him is as far as possible from the attitude in the United States toward the 'home boy who makes good.' Japan provided a place in her hierarchy for great wealth and kept an alliance with it; when wealth is achieved in the field outside, Japanese public opinion is bitter against it.

The Japanese, therefore, order their world with constant reference to hierarchy. In the family and in personal relations, age, generation, sex, and class dictate proper behavior. In government, religion, the Army, and industry, areas are carefully separated into hierarchies where neither the higher nor the lower may without penalty overstep their prerogatives. As long as 'proper station' is maintained the Japanese carry on without protest. They feel safe. They are of course often not 'safe' in the sense that their best good is protected but they are 'safe' because they have accepted hierarchy as legitimate. It is as characteristic of their judgment on life as trust in equality and free enterprise is of the American way of life.

Japan's nemesis came when she tried to export her formula for 'safety.' In her own country hierarchy fitted popular imagination because it had moulded it. Ambitions could only be such as could take shape in that kind of a world. But it was a fatal commodity for export. Other nations resented Japan's grandiloquent claims as an impertinence and worse. Japan's officers and troops, however, in each occupied country continued to be shocked that the inhabitants did not welcome them. Was Japan not offering them a place, however lowly, in a hierarchy and was not hierarchy desirable even for those on the lower steps of it? Their War Services continued to get out series of war films which figured China's 'love' for Japan under the image of desperate and disordered Chinese girls who found happiness by falling in love with a Japanese soldier or a Japanese engineer. It was a far cry from the Nazi version of conquest yet it was no more successful in the long run. They could not exact from other nations what they had exacted of themselves. It was their mistake that they thought they could. They did not recognize that the system of Japanese morality which had fitted them to 'accept their proper station' was something they could not count on elsewhere. Other nations did not have it. It is a genuine product of Japan. Her writers take this system of ethics so much for granted that they do not describe it and a description of it is necessary before one can understand the Japanese.

5

Debtor to the Ages and the World

In the English Language we used to talk about being 'heirs of the ages.' Two wars and a vast economic crisis have diminished somewhat the self-confidence it used to bespeak but this shift has certainly not increased our sense of indebtedness to the past. Oriental nations turn the coin to the other side: they are debtors to the ages. Much of what Westerners name ancestor worship is not truly worship and not wholly directed toward ancestors: it is a ritual avowal of man's great indebtedness to all that has gone before. Moreover, he is indebted not only to the past; every day-by-day contact with other people increases his indebtedness in the present. From this debt his daily decisions and actions must spring. It is the fundamental starting point. Because Westerners pay such extremely slight attention to their debt to the world and what it has given them in care, education, well-being or even in the mere fact of their ever having been born at all, the Japanese feel that our motivations are inadequate. Virtuous men do not say, as they do in America, that they owe nothing to any man. They do not discount the past. Righteousness in Japan depends upon recognition of one's place in the great network of mutual indebtedness that embraces both one's forebears and one's contemporaries.

It is simple to put in words this contrast between East and West but it is difficult to appreciate what a difference it makes in living. Until we understand it in Japan we shall not be able to plumb either the extreme sacrifice of self with which we became familiar during the war or the quick resentments which Japanese are capable of in situations where we think resentments are not called for. To be a debtor can make a man extremely quick to take offense and the Japanese prove it. It also puts upon him great responsibilities.

Both the Chinese and the Japanese have many words meaning 'obligations.' The words are not synonyms and their specific meanings have no literal translation into English because the ideas they express are alien to us. The word for 'obligations' which covers a person's indebtedness from greatest to least is *on*. In Japanese usage it is translated into English by a whole series of words from 'obligations' and 'loyalty' to 'kindness' and 'love,' but these words distort its meaning. If it really meant love or even obligation the Japanese would certainly be able to speak of *on* to their children, but that is an impossible usage of the word. Nor does it mean loyalty, which is expressed by other Japanese words, which are in no way synonymous with *on*. *On* is in all its uses a load, an indebtedness, a burden, which one carries as best one may. A man receives *on* from a superior and the act of accepting an *on* from any man not definitely one's superior or at least one's equal gives one an uncomfortable sense of inferiority. When they say, 'I wear an *on* to him' they are saying, 'I carry a load of obligations to him,' and they call this creditor, this benefactor, their '*on* man.'

'Remembering one's *on*' may be a pure outpouring of reciprocal devotion. A little story in a Japanese second-grade school reader entitled 'Don't forget the *on*' uses the word in this sense. It is a story for little children in their ethics classes.

> Hachi is a cute dog. As soon as he was born he was taken away by a stranger and was loved like a child of the house. For that reason, even his weak body became healthy and when his master went to his work every morning, he would accompany him (master) to the street car station and in the evening around the time when he (master) came home, he went again up to the station to meet him.
>
> In due time, the master passed away. Hachi, whether he knew of this or not, kept looking for his master every day. Going to the usual station he would look to see if his master was in the crowd of people who came out whenever the street car arrived.
>
> In this way days and months passed by. One year passed, two years passed, three years passed, even when ten years had passed, the aged Hachi's figure can be seen every day in front of the station, still looking for his master.

The moral of this little tale is loyalty which is only another name for love. A son who cares deeply for his mother can speak of not forgetting the *on* he has received from his mother and mean that he has for her Hachi's single-minded devotion to his master. The term, however, refers specifically not to his love, but to all that his mother did for him as a baby, her sacrifices when he was a boy, all that she has done to further his interests as a man, all that he owes her from the mere fact that she exists. It implies a return upon this indebtedness and therefore it means love. But the primary meaning is the debt, whereas we think of love as something freely given unfettered by obligation.

On is always used in this sense of limitless devotion when it is used of one's first and greatest indebtedness, one's 'Imperial *on*.' This is one's debt to the Emperor, which one should receive with unfathomable gratitude. It would be impossible, they feel, to be glad of one's country, of one's life, of one's great and small concerns without thinking also of receiving these benefits. In all Japanese history this ultimate person among living men to whom one was indebted was the highest superior within one's horizon. It has been at different periods the local seigneur, the feudal lord, and the Shogun. Today it is the Emperor. Which superior it was is not nearly so significant as the centuries-long primacy in Japanese habit of 'remembering the *on*.' Modern Japan has used every means to center this sentiment upon the Emperor. Every partiality they have for their own way of living increases each man's Imperial *on*; every cigarette distributed to the Army on the front lines in the Emperor's name during the war underscored the *on* each soldier wore for him; every sip of *sake* doled out to them before going into battle was a further Imperial *on*. Every kamikaze pilot of a suicide plane was, they said, repaying his Imperial *on*; all the troops who, they claimed, died to a man defending some island of the Pacific were said to be discharging their limitless *on* to the Emperor.

A man wears an *on* also to lesser people than the Emperor. There is of course the *on* one has received from one's parents. This is the basis of the famous Oriental filial piety which places parents in such a strategic position of authority over their children. It is phrased in terms of the debt their children owe them and strive to repay. It is therefore the children who must work hard at obedience rather than as in Germany—another nation where parents have authority over their children—where the parents must work hard to exact and enforce this obedience. The Japanese are very realistic in their version of Oriental filial piety and they have a saying about *on* one receives from parents which can be freely translated 'Only after a person is himself a parent does he know how indebted he is to his own parents.' That is, the parental *on* is the actual daily care and trouble to which fathers and mothers are put. The Japanese limitation of ancestor veneration to recent and remembered forebears brings this emphasis on actual dependency in childhood very much to the fore in their thinking, and of course it is a very obvious truism in any culture that every man and woman was once a helpless infant who would not have survived without parental care; for years until he was an adult he was provided with a home and food and clothing. Japanese feel strongly that Americans minimize all this, and that, as one writer says, 'In the United States remembering *on* to parents is hardly more than being good to your father and mother.' No person can leave *on* to his children, of course, but devoted care of one's children is a return on one's indebtedness to one's parents when one was oneself helpless. One makes part payment on *on* to one's own parents by giving equally good or better rearing to one's children. The obligations one has to one's children are merely subsumed under '*on* to one's parents.'

One has particular *on* too to one's teacher and to one's master (*nushi*). They have both helped bring one along the way and one wears an *on* to them which may at some future time make it necessary to accede to some request of theirs when they are in trouble or to give preference, perhaps to a young relative of theirs, after they are dead. One should go to great lengths to pay the obligation and time does not lessen the debt. It increases rather than decreases with the years. It accumulates a kind of interest. An *on* to anyone is a serious matter. As their common saying has it: 'One never returns one ten-thousandth of an *on*.' It is a heavy burden and 'the power of the *on*' is regarded as always rightly overriding one's mere personal preferences.

The smooth working of this ethics of indebtedness depends upon each man's being able to consider himself a great debtor without feeling too much resentment in discharging the obligations he is under. We have already seen how thoroughly hierarchal arrangements have been organized in Japan. The attendant habits diligently pursued make it possible for the Japanese to honor their moral indebtedness to a degree that would not cross the mind of an Occidental. This is easier to do if the superiors are regarded as well-wishers. There is interesting evidence from their language that superiors were indeed credited with being 'loving' to their dependents. *Ai* means 'love' in Japan and it was this word *ai* which seemed to the missionaries of the last century the only Japanese word it was possible to use in their translations of the Christian concept of 'love.' They used it in translating the Bible to mean God's love for man and man's love for God. But *ai* means specifically the love of a superior for his dependents. A Westerner might perhaps feel that it meant 'paternalism,' but in its Japanese usage it means more than that. It was a word that meant affection. In contemporary Japan *ai* is still used in this strict sense of love from above to below, but, perhaps partly due to the Christian usage, and certainly as a consequence of official efforts to break down caste distinctions, it may today be used also of love between equals.

In spite of all cultural alleviations, however, it is nevertheless a fortunate circumstance in Japan when *on* is 'worn' with no offense. People do not like to shoulder casually the debt of gratitude which *on* implies. They are always talking of 'making a person wear an *on*' and often the nearest translation is 'imposing upon another'—though in the United States 'imposing' means demanding something of another, and in Japan the phrase means giving him something or doing him a kindness. Casual favors from relative strangers are the ones most resented, for with neighbors and in old-established hierarchal relationships a man knows and has accepted the complications of *on*. But with mere acquaintances and near-equals men chafe. They would prefer to avoid getting entangled in all the consequences of *on*. The passivity of a street crowd in Japan when an accident occurs is not just lack of initiative. It is a recognition that any non-official interference would make the recipient wear an *on*. One of the best-known laws of pre-Meiji days was: 'Should a quarrel or dispute occur, one shall not unnecessarily meddle with it,' and a person who helps another person in such situations in Japan without clear authorization is suspected of taking an unjustifiable advantage. The fact that the recipient will be greatly indebted to him acts, not to make any man anxious to avail himself of this advantage to himself but to make him very chary of helping. Especially in unformalized situations the Japanese are extremely wary of getting entangled in *on*. Even the offer of a cigarette from a person with whom a man has previously had no ties makes him uncomfortable and the polite way for him to express thanks is to say: 'Oh, this poisonous feeling (*kino doku*).' 'It's easier to bear,' a Japanese said to me, 'if you come right out and acknowledge how bad it makes you feel. You had never thought of doing anything for him and so you are shamed by receiving the *on*.' '*Kino doku*' therefore is translated sometimes as 'Thank you,' i.e., for the cigarettes, sometimes as 'I'm sorry,' i.e., for the indebtedness, sometimes as 'I feel like a heel,' i.e., because you beat me to this act of generosity. It means all of these and none.

The Japanese have many ways of saying 'Thank you' which express this same uneasiness in receiving *on*. The least ambivalent, the phrase that has been adopted in modern city department stores, means 'Oh, this difficult thing' (*arigato*). The Japanese usually say that this 'difficult thing' is the great and rare benefit the customer is bestowing on the store in buying. It is a compliment. It is used also when one receives a present and in countless circumstances. Other just as common words for 'thank you' refer like *kino doku* to the difficulty of receiving. Shopkeepers who run their own shops most commonly say literally: 'Oh, this doesn't end,' (*sumimasen*), i.e., 'I have received *on* from you and under modern economic arrangements I can never repay you; I am sorry to be placed in such a position.' In English *sumimasen* is translated 'Thank you,' 'I'm grateful,' or 'I'm sorry,' 'I apologize.' You use the word, for instance, in preference to all other thank-you's if anyone chases the hat you lost on a windy street. When he returns it to you politeness requires that you acknowledge your own internal discomfort in receiving. 'He is offering me an *on* and I never saw him before. I never had a chance to offer him the first *on*. I feel guilty about it but I feel better if I apologize to him. *Sumimasen* is probably the commonest word for thank-you in Japan. I tell him that I recognize that I have received *on* from him and it doesn't end with the act of taking back my hat. But what can I do about it? We are strangers.'

The same attitude about indebtedness is expressed even more strongly from the Japanese standpoint by another word for thank-you, *katajikenai*, which is written with the character 'insult,' 'loss of face.' It means both 'I am insulted' and 'I am grateful.' The all-Japanese dictionary says that by this term you say that by the extraordinary benefit you have received you are shamed and insulted because you are not worthy of the benefaction. In this phrase you explicitly acknowledge your shame in receiving *on*, and shame, *haji*, is, as we shall see, a thing bitterly felt in Japan. *Katajikenai*, 'I am insulted,' is still used by conservative shopkeepers in thanking their customers, and customers use it when they ask to have their purchases charged. It is the word found constantly in pre-Meiji romances. A beautiful girl of low class who serves in the court and is chosen by the lord as his mistress, says to him *Katajikenai*; that is, 'I am shamed in unworthily accepting this *on*; I am awed by your graciousness.' Or the samurai in a feudal brawl who is let go scot-free by the authorities says *Katajikenai*, 'I have lost face that I accept this *on*; it is not proper for me to place myself in such a humble position; I am sorry; I humbly thank you.'

These phrases tell, better than any generalizations, the 'power of the *on*.' One wears it constantly with ambivalence. In accepted structuralized relations the great indebtedness it implies often stimulates a man only to put forward in repayment all that is in him. But it is hard to be a debtor and resentments come easily. How easily is described vividly in the famous novel *Botchan* by one of Japan's best-known novelists, Soseki Natsume. Botchan, the hero, is a Tokyo boy who is teaching school for the first time in a small town in the provinces. He finds very soon that he despises most of his fellow teachers, certainly he does not get along with them. But there is one young teacher he warms to and while they are out together this new-found friend whom he calls Porcupine treats him to a glass of ice water. He pays one sen and a half for it, something like one-fifth of a cent.

Not long afterward another teacher reports to Botchan that Porcupine has spoken slightingly of him. Botchan believes the trouble-maker's report and is instantly concerned about the *on* he had received from Porcupine.

> 'To wear an *on* from such a fellow even if it is for so trifling a thing as ice water, affects my honor. One sen or half a sen, I shall not die in peace if I wear this *on*. . . The fact that I receive somebody's *on* without protesting is an act of good-will, taking him at his par value as a decent fellow.

> Instead of insisting on paying for my own ice water, I took the *on* and expressed gratitude. That is an acknowledgement which no amount of money can purchase. I have neither title nor official position but I am an independent fellow, and to have an independent fellow accept the favor of *on* is far more than if he gave a million yen in return. I let Porcupine blow one sen and a half, and gave him my thanks which is more costly than a million yen.'

The next day he throws a sen and a half on Porcupine's desk, for only after having ceased to wear the *on* for the glass of ice water can he begin to settle the current issue between them: the insulting remark he has been told of. That may involve blows, but the *on* has to be wiped out first because the *on* is no longer between friends.

Such acute sensitivity about trifles, such painful vulnerability occurs in American records of adolescent gangs and in case-histories of neurotics. But this is Japanese virtue. Not many Japanese would carry the matter to this extreme, they think, but of course many people are lax. Japanese commentators writing about Botchan describe him as 'hot-tempered, pure as crystal, a champion of the right.' The author too identifies himself with Botchan and the character is indeed always recognized by critics as a portrait of himself. The story is a tale of high virtue because the person who receives *on* can lift himself out of the debtor's position only by regarding his gratitude as worth 'a million yen' and acting accordingly. He can take it only from 'a decent fellow.' In Botchan's anger he contrasts his *on* to Porcupine with an *on* he had received long since from his old nurse. She was blindly partial to him and felt that none of the rest of his family appreciated him. She used to bring him secretly little gifts of candy and colored pencils and once she gave him three yen. 'Her constant attention to me chilled me to the marrow.' But though he was 'insulted' at the offer of the three yen he had accepted it as a loan and he had never repaid it in all the years between. But that, he says to himself, contrasting the way he feels about his *on* to Porcupine, was because '*I regard her as part of myself.*' This is the clue to Japanese reactions to *on*. They can be borne, with whatever mixed feelings, so long as the '*on* man' is actually oneself; he is fixed in 'my' hierarchal scheme, or he is doing something I can imagine myself doing, like returning my hat on a windy day, or he is a person who admires me. Once these identifications break down, the *on* is a festering sore. However trivial the debt incurred it is virtue to resent it.

Every Japanese knows that if one makes the *on* too heavy under any circumstances whatsoever one will get into trouble. A good illustration is from the 'Consulting Department' of a recent magazine. The Department is a kind of 'Advice to the Lovelorn' and is a feature of the *Tokyo Psychoanalytic Journal*. The advice offered is hardly Freudian but it is thoroughly Japanese. An elderly man wrote asking for counsel:

> I am the father of three boys and one girl. My wife died sixteen years ago. Because I was sorry for my children, I did not remarry, and my children considered this fact as my virtue. Now my children are all married. Eight years ago when my son married, I retired to a house a few blocks away. It is embarrassing to state, but for three years I have played with a girl in the dark [a prostitute under contract in a public house]. She told me her circumstances and I felt

sorry for her. I bought her freedom for a small sum, took her to my home, taught her etiquette, and kept her as a maid. Her sense of responsibility is strong and she is admirably economical. However, my sons and daughter-in-law and my daughter and son-in-law look down on me for this and treat me as a stranger. I do not blame them; it is my fault.

The parents of the girl did not seem to understand the situation and since she is of marriageable age they wrote wanting her returned. I have met the parents and explained the circumstances. They are very poor but are not golddiggers. They have promised to consider her as dead and to consent that she continue in her situation. She herself wants to remain by my side till my death. But our ages are as father and daughter and therefore I sometimes consider sending her home. My children consider that she is after my property.

I have a chronic illness and I think I have only one or two years to live. I would appreciate your showing me what course to take. Let me say in conclusion that though the girl was once only a 'girl in the dark,' that was because of circumstances. Her character is good and her parents are not golddiggers.

The Japanese doctor regards this as a clear case of the old man's having put too heavy an *on* upon his children. He says:

You have described an event of daily occurrence. . . .

Let me preface my remarks by saying that I gather from your letter that you are asking from me the answer *you* want, and that this makes me have some antagonism to you. I of course appreciate your long unmarriedness, but you have used this to make your children wear the *on* and also to justify yourself in your present line of action. I don't like this. I'm not saying that you are sly, but your personality is very weak. It would have been better to have explained to your children that you had to live with a woman,—if you couldn't help having one,—and not to have let them wear the *on* (for your remaining unmarried). The children naturally are against you because you have laid such emphasis on this *on*. After all human beings don't lose their sexual desires and you can't help having desire. But one tries to overcome the desire. Your children expected you to because they expected you to live up to the ideal they had formed of you. On the contrary, they were betrayed and I can see how they feel, though it is egoistic on their part. They are married and sexually satisfied and they're selfish to deny this to their father. You're thinking this way and your children the other way (as above). The two ways of thinking don't meet.

You say that the girl and her parents are good people. That is what you want to think. One knows that people's good and evil depend on the circumstances, the situation, and because they are not at the moment seeking an advantage one can't say they're 'good people.' I think the girl's parents are dumb to let her serve as concubine of a man about to die. If they're going to consider their daughter's being a concubine, they ought to seek some profit or advantage from it. It's only your fantasy to see it otherwise.

I don't wonder the children are worried about the girl's parents seeking some property; I really think they are. The girl is young and may not have this in mind, but her parents should have.

There are two courses open to you:

1) As 'a complete man' (one so well rounded that nothing is impossible to him) cut off the girl and settle with her. But I don't think you could do that; your human feelings wouldn't permit.
2) 'Come back to being a common man' (give up your pretensions) and break up the children's illusion about you as an ideal man.

> About the property, make a will immediately and state what the girl's and the children's shares are.
>
> In conclusion, remember that you are old, you are getting childish, as I can see by your handwriting. Your thinking is emotional rather than rational. You want this girl as a mother substitute, though you phrase this as wanting to save her from the gutter. I don't think any infant can live if its mother leaves—therefore, I advise you to take the second course.

This letter says several things about *on*. A person once having elected to make even his children wear an extra heavy *on* can change his course of action only at his own risk. He should know that he will suffer for it. In addition, no matter what the cost to him of the *on* his children received, he may not lay it up for himself as merit to be drawn upon; it is wrong to use it 'to justify yourself in your present line of action.' His children are 'naturally' resentful; because their father started something he couldn't maintain, they were 'betrayed.' It is foolish for a father to imagine that just because he has devoted himself entirely to them while they needed his care, the now-grown children are going to be extra solicitous for him. Instead they are conscious only of the *on* they have incurred and 'naturally they are against you.'

Americans do not judge such a situation in this light. We think that a father who dedicated himself to his motherless children should in later years merit some warm spot in their hearts, not that they are 'naturally against him.' In order to appreciate it as the Japanese see it, we can, however, regard it as a financial transaction for in that sphere we have comparable attitudes. It would be perfectly possible for us to say to a father who has lent money to his children in a formal transaction which they have to live up to with interest, 'they are naturally against you.' In these terms too we can understand why a person who has accepted a cigarette speaks of his 'shame' instead of saying a straightforward 'Thank you.' We can understand the resentment with which they speak of a person's making another wear an *on*. We can at least get a clue to Botchan's grandiose magnification of the debt of a glass of ice water. But Americans are not accustomed to applying these financial criteria to a casual treat at the soda counter or to the years' long devotion of a father to his motherless children or to the devotion of a faithful dog like Hachi. Japan does. Love, kindness, generosity, which we value just in proportion as they are given without strings attached, necessarily must have their strings in Japan. And every such act received makes one a debtor. As their common saying has it: 'It requires (an impossible degree of) inborn generosity to receive *on*.'

6

Repaying One-Ten-Thousandth

ON IS A DEBT and must be repaid, but in Japan all repayments are regarded as falling into another category entirely. The Japanese find our morals, which confuse these two categories in our ethics and in our neutral words like obligation and duty, as strange as we would find financial dealings in some tribe whose language did not separate 'debtor' from 'creditor' in money transactions. To them the primary and ever-present indebtedness called *on* is worlds apart from the active, bowstring-taut repayment which is named in a whole series of other concepts. A man's indebtedness (*on*) is not virtue; his repayment is. Virtue begins when he dedicates himself actively to the job of gratitude.

It will help Americans to understand this matter of virtue in Japan if we keep in mind the parallel with financial transactions and think of it as having behind it the sanctions against defaulting which property transactions have in America. Here we hold a man to his bond. We do not count extenuating circumstances when a man takes what is not his. We do not allow it to be a matter of impulse whether or not a man pays a debt to a bank. And the debtor is just as responsible for the accrued interest as he is for the original money he borrowed. Patriotism and love of our families we regard as quite different from all this. Love, with us, is a matter of the heart and is best when freely given. Patriotism, in the sense of putting our country's interests above everything else, is regarded as rather quixotic or certainly as not compatible with fallible human nature until the United States is attacked by the armed forces of an enemy. Lacking the basic Japanese postulate of great indebtedness automatically incurred by every man and woman born, we think that a man should pity and help his needy parents, should not beat his wife, and should provide for his children. But these things are not quantitatively reckoned like a debt of money and they are not rewarded as success in business is. In Japan they are regarded quite as financial solvency is in America and the sanctions behind them are as strong as they are in the United States behind being able to pay one's bills and the interest on one's mortgage. They are not matters that must be attended to only at crises such as a proclamation of war or the serious illness of a parent; they are one's constant shadow like a small New York farmer's worry about his mortgage or a Wall Street financier's as he watches the market climb when he has sold short.

The Japanese divide into distinct categories, each with its different rules, those repayments on *on* which are limitless both in amount and in duration and those which are quantitatively equivalent and come due on special occasions. The limitless repayments on indebtedness are called *gimu* and they say of it: 'One never repays one ten-thousandth of (this) *on*.' One's gimu groups together two differ-

SCHEMATIC TABLE OF JAPANESE OBLIGATIONS AND THEIR RECIPROCALS

I. *On:* obligations passively incurred. One 'receives an *on*'; one 'wears an *on*,' i.e., *on* are obligations from the point of view of the passive recipient.

ko on. *On* received from the Emperor.
oya on. *On* received from parents.
nushi no on. *On* received from one's lord.
shi no on. *On* received from one's teacher.
on received in all contacts in the course of one's life.

NOTE: All these persons from whom one receives *on* become one's *on jin*, '*on* man.'

II. Reciprocals of *on*. One 'pays' these debts, one 'returns these obligations' to the *on* man, i.e., these are obligations regarded from the point of view of active repayment.

A. *Gimu*. The fullest repayment of these obligations is still no more than partial and there is no time limit.

chu. Duty to the Emperor, the law, Japan.
ko. Duty to parents and ancestors (by implication, to descendants).
nimmu. Duty to one's work.

B. *Giri*. These debts are regarded as having to be repaid with mathematical equivalence to the favor received and there are time limits.

1. *Giri*-to-the-world.

Duties to liege lord.
Duties to affinal family.
Duties to non-related persons due to *on* received, e.g., on a gift of money, on a favor, on work contributed (as a 'work party').
Duties to persons not sufficiently closely related (aunts, uncles, nephews, nieces) due to *on* received not from them but from common ancestors.

2. *Giri*-to-one's-name. This is a Japanese version of *die Ehre*.

One's duty to 'clear' one's reputation of insult or imputation of failure, i.e., the duty of feuding or vendetta. (N.B. This evening of scores is not reckoned as aggression.)
One's duty to admit no (professional) failure or ignorance.
One's duty to fulfill the Japanese proprieties, e.g., observing all respect behavior, not living above one's station in life, curbing all displays of emotion on inappropriate occasions, etc.

ent types of obligations: repayment of one's *on* to parents, which is *ko*, and repayment of one's *on* to the Emperor, which is *chu*. Both these obligations of gimu are compulsory and are man's universal lot; indeed Japan's elementary schooling is called 'gimu education' because no other word so adequately renders the meaning of 'required.' The accidents of life may modify the details of one's gimu, but gimu is automatically incumbent upon all men and is above all fortuitous circumstances.

Both forms of gimu are unconditional. In thus making these virtues absolute Japan has departed from the Chinese concepts of duty to the State and of filial piety. The Chinese ethical system has been repeatedly adopted in Japan ever since the seventh century and chu and ko are Chinese words. But the Chinese did not make these virtues unconditional. China postulates an overriding virtue which is a condition of loyalty and piety. It is usually translated 'benevolence' (*jen*) but it means almost everything Occidentals mean by good interpersonal relations. A parent must have *jen*. If a ruler does not have it it is righteous for his people to rebel against him. It is a condition upon which one's gift of loyalty is predicated. The Emperor's tenure and that of his officials depended on their doing jen. Chinese ethics applies this touchstone in all human relations.

This Chinese ethical postulate was never accepted in Japan. The great Japanese student, Kanichi Asakawa, speaking of this contrast in medieval times, says: 'In Japan these ideas were obviously incompatible with her imperial sovereignty and were therefore never accepted in entirety even as theories.'* In fact jen became in Japan an outlaw virtue and was entirely demoted from the high estate it had in Chinese ethics. In Japan it is pronounced *jin* (it is written with the same character the Chinese use) and 'doing jin' or its variant 'doing jingi' is very far indeed from being a virtue required even in the highest quarters. It has been so thoroughly banished from their ethical system that it means something done outside the law. It may indeed be a praiseworthy act like putting one's name on a subscription list for public charity or granting mercy to a criminal. But it is emphatically a work of supererogation. It means that the act was not required of you.

'Doing jingi' is used in another sense of 'outside the law,' too; it is used of virtue among gangsters. The honor among thieves of the raiding and slashing swashbucklers of the Tokugawa period—they were one-sword men as contrasted with the two-sworded swashbuckling samurai—was 'doing jingi'; when one of these outlaws asked shelter of another who was a stranger, that stranger, as an insurance against future vengeance from the petitioner's gang, would grant it and thereby 'do jingi.' In modern usage 'doing jingi' has fallen even lower. It occurs frequently in discussions of punishable acts: 'Common laborers,' their newspapers say, 'still do jingi and they must be punished. Police should see to it that jingi is stopped in the holes and corners where it flourishes in Japan.' They mean of course the 'honor among thieves' which flourishes in racketeering and gangsterdom. Especially the small labor contractor in modern Japan is said to 'do jingi' when, like the Italian labor padrone at Amer-

* *Documents of Iriki*, 1929, p. 380, n. 19.

ican ports at the turn of the century, he enters into outside-the-law relationships with unskilled laborers and gets rich off farming them out at a profit. The degradation of the Chinese concept of *jen* could hardly go farther.* The Japanese, having entirely reinterpreted and demoted the crucial virtue of the Chinese system and put nothing else in its place that might make gimu conditional, filial piety became in Japan a duty one had to fulfill even if it meant condoning a parent's vice and injustice. It could be abrogated only if it came into conflict with one's obligation to the Emperor, but certainly not when one's parent was unworthy or when he was destroying one's happiness.

In one of their modern movies a mother comes upon some money her married son, a village schoolmaster, has collected from the villagers to redeem a young schoolgirl about to be sold by her parents to a house of prostitution because they are starving in a rural famine. The schoolmaster's mother steals the money from her son although she is not poor; she runs a respectable restaurant of her own. Her son knows that she has taken it but he has to shoulder the blame himself. His wife discovers the truth, leaves a suicide note taking all responsibility for the loss of the money, and drowns herself and their baby. Publicity follows but the mother's part in the tragedy is not even called in question. The son has fulfilled the law of filial piety and goes off alone to Hokkaido to build his character so that he can strengthen himself for like tests in coming years. He is a

* When the Japanese use the phrase 'knowing jin,' they are somewhat closer to Chinese usage. Buddhists exhort people to 'know jin' and this means to be merciful and benevolent. But, as the all-Japanese dictionary says, 'knowing jin refers to ideal man rather than to acts.'

virtuous hero. My Japanese companion vigorously protested my obvious American verdict that the person responsible for the whole tragedy was the thieving mother. Filial piety, he said, was often in conflict with other virtues. If the hero had been wise enough, he might have found a way to reconcile them without loss of self-respect. But it would have been no possible occasion for self-respect if he blamed his mother even to himself.

Both novels and real life are full of the heavy duties of filial piety after a young man is married. Except in 'modan' (modern) circles it is taken for granted in respectable families that the parents select their son's wife, usually through the good offices of go-betweens. The family, not the son, is chiefly concerned about the matter of a good selection, not only because of the money transactions involved but because the wife will be entered in the family genealogy and will perpetuate the family line through her sons. It is the custom for the go-betweens to arrange a seemingly casual meeting between the two young principals in the presence of their parents but they do not converse. Sometimes the parents choose to make for their son a marriage of convenience in which case the girl's father will profit financially and the boy's parents by alliance with a good family. Sometimes they choose to select the girl for her personally acceptable qualities. The good son's repayment of parental *on* does not allow him to question his parents' decision. After he is married his repayment continues. Especially if the son is the family heir he will live with his parents and it is proverbial that the mother-in-law does not like her daughter-in-law. She finds all manner of fault with her, and she may send her away and break up the marriage even when the young husband is happy with his wife and asks nothing better than to live with her. Japanese novels and personal histories are just as apt to stress the suffering of the husband as of the wife. The husband of course is doing *ko* in submitting to the break-up of his marriage.

One 'modan' Japanese now in America took into her own rooms in Tokyo a pregnant young wife whose mother-in-law had forced her to leave her grieving young husband. She was sick and brokenhearted but she did not blame her husband. Gradually she became interested in the baby she was soon to bear. But when the child was born, the mother came accompanied by her silent and submissive son to claim the baby. It belonged of course to the husband's family and the mother-in-law took it away. She disposed of it immediately to a foster home.

All this is on occasion included in filial piety, and is proper repayment of indebtedness to parents. In the United States all such stories are taken as instances of outside interference with an individual's rightful happiness. Japan cannot consider this interference as 'outside' because of her postulate of indebtedness. Such stories in Japan, like our stories of honest men who pay off their creditors by incredible personal hardships, are tales of the truly virtuous, of persons who have earned their right to respect themselves, who have proved themselves strong enough to accept proper personal frustrations. Such frustrations, however virtuous, may naturally leave a residue of resentment and it is well worth noting that the Asiatic proverb about the Hateful Things, which in Burma, for instance, lists 'fire, water, thieves, governors and malicious men,' in Japan itemizes 'earthquake, thunder and the Old Man (head of the house; the father).'

Filial piety does not, as in China, encompass the line of ancestors for centuries back nor the vast proliferating living clan descended from them. Japan's veneration is of recent ancestors. A gravestone must be relettered annually to keep its identity and when living persons no longer remember an ancestor his grave is neglected. Nor are tablets for them kept in the family shrine. The Japanese do not value piety except to those remembered in the flesh and they concentrate on the here and now. Many writers have commented on their lack of interest in disembodied speculation or in forming images of objects not present, and their version of filial piety serves as another instance of this when it is contrasted with China's. The greatest practical importance of their version, however, is in the way it limits the obligations of ko among living persons.

For filial piety, both in China and Japan, is far more than deference and obedience to one's own parents and forebears. All that care of the child which Westerners phrase as being contingent on maternal instinct and on paternal responsibility, they phrase as contingent on piety to one's ancestors. Japan is very explicit about it: one repays one's debts to one's forebears by passing on to one's children the care one oneself received. There is no word to express 'obligation of the father to his children' and all such duties are covered by ko to the parents and their parents. Filial piety enjoins all the numerous responsibilities which rest upon the head of a family to provide for his children, educate his sons and younger brothers, see to the management of the estate, give shelter to relatives who need it and a thousand similar everyday duties. The drastic limitation of the institutionalized family in Japan sharply limits the number of persons toward whom any man has this gimu. If a son dies it is an obligation of filial piety to bear the burden of supporting his widow and her children. So also is the occasional providing of shelter to a widowed daughter and her family. But it is not a gimu to take in a widowed niece; if one does so, one is fulfilling a quite different obligation. It is gimu to rear and educate your own children. But if one educates a nephew, it is customary to adopt him legally as one's own son; it is not a gimu if he retains the status of nephew.

Filial piety does not require that assistance even to one's immediate needy relatives in the descending generations be given with deference and loving-kindness. Young widows in the family are called 'cold-rice relatives,' meaning that they eat rice when it is cold, are at the beck and call of every member of the inner family, and must accept with deep obedience any decisions about their affairs. They are poor relations, along with their children, and when in particular cases they fare better than this it is not because the head of the family owes them this better treatment as a gimu. Nor is it a gimu incumbent upon brothers to carry out their mutual obligations with warmth; men are often praised for having fully lived up to obligations to a younger brother when it is freely admitted that the two hate each other like poison.

Greatest antagonism is between mother-in-law and daughter-in-law. The daughter-in-law comes into the household as a stranger. It is her duty to learn how her mother-in-law likes to have things done and then to learn to do them. In many cases the mother-in-law quite explicitly takes the position that the young wife is not nearly good enough for her son and in other cases it can be inferred that she has considerable jealousy. But, as the Japanese saying goes, 'The hated daughter-in-law keeps on bearing beloved grandsons' and ko is therefore always present. The young daughter-in-law is on the surface endlessly submissive but generation after generation these mild and charming creatures grow up into mothers-in-law as exacting and as critical as their own mothers-in-law were before them. They cannot express their aggressions as young wives but they do not therefore become genuinely mild human beings. In later life they turn, as it were, an accumulated weight of resentment against their own daughters-in-law. Japanese girls today openly talk about the great advantage of marrying a son who is not an heir so that they will not have to live with a dominating mother-in-law.

To 'work for ko' is not necessarily to achieve loving-kindness in the family. In some cultures this is the crux of the moral law in the extended family. But not in Japan. As one Japanese writer says, 'Just because he esteems the family highly, the Japanese has anything but a high estimation of the individual members or of the family tie between them.'* That is not always true, of course, but it gives the picture. The emphasis is upon obligations and repaying the debt and the elders take great responsibility upon themselves, but one of these responsibilities is to see to it that those below them make the requisite sacrifices. If they re-

* Nohara, K., *The True Face of Japan*. London, 1936, p. 45.

sent these, it makes little difference. They must obey their elders' decisions or they have failed in gimu.

The marked resentments between members of the family which are so typical of filial piety in Japan are absent in the other great obligation which like filial piety is a gimu: fealty to the Emperor. Japanese statesmen planned well in secluding their Emperor as a Sacred Chief and in removing him from the hurlyburly of life; only so in Japan could he serve to unify all people in unambivalent service to the State. It was not enough to make him a father to his people, for the father in the household, despite all the obligations rendered him, was a figure of whom one might have 'anything but a high estimation.' The Emperor had to be a Sacred Father removed from all secular considerations. A man's fealty to him, chu, the supreme virtue, must become an ecstatic contemplation of a fantasied Good Father untainted by contacts with the world. Early Meiji statesmen wrote after they had visited the nations of the Occident that in all these countries history was made by the conflict between ruler and people and that this was unworthy of the Spirit of Japan. They returned and wrote into the Constitution that the Ruler was to 'be sacred and inviolable' and not reckoned responsible for any acts of his Ministers. He was to serve as supreme symbol of Japanese unity, not as responsible head of a State. Since the Emperor had not served as an executive ruler for some seven centuries it was simple to perpetuate his back-stage rôle. Meiji statesmen needed only to attach to him, in the minds of all Japanese, that unconditional highest virtue, chu. In feudal Japan chu had been obligation to the Secular Chief, the Shogun, and its long history warned Meiji statesmen what it was necessary to do in the new dispensation to accomplish their objective, the spiritual unification of Japan. In those centuries the Shogun had been Generalissimo and chief administrator and in spite of the chu that was due him plots against his supremacy and against his life were frequent. Fealty to him often came into conflict with obligations to one's own feudal overlord, and the higher loyalty frequently was less compelling than the lower. Fealty to one's own overlord was, after all, based on face to face ties and fealty to the Shogun might well seem cold in comparison. Retainers too fought in troubled times to unseat the Shogun and to establish their own feudal lord in his place. The prophets and leaders of the Meiji Restoration had for a century fought against the Tokugawa Shogunate with the slogan that chu was due to the Emperor secluded in the shadowy background, a figure whose lineaments every person could draw for himself according to his own desires. The Meiji Restoration was the victory for this party and it was precisely this shifting of chu from Shogun to symbolic Emperor which justified the use of the term 'restoration' for the year 1868. The Emperor remained secluded. He invested Their Excellencies with authority but he did not himself run the government or the army or personally dictate policies. The same sort of advisors, though they were better chosen, went on running the government. The real upheaval was in the spiritual realm, for chu became every man's repayment to the Sacred Chief—high priest and symbol of the unity and perpetuity of Japan.

The ease with which chu was transferred to the Emperor was aided of course by the traditional folklore that the Imperial House was descended from the Sun Goddess. But this folkloristic claim to divinity was not so crucial as Westerners thought it was. Certainly Japanese intellectuals who entirely rejected these claims did not therefore question chu to the Emperor, and even the mass of the populace who accepted divine birth did not mean by that what Westerners would mean. *Kami*, the word rendered as 'god,' means literally 'head,' i.e., pinnacle of the hierarchy. The Japanese do not fix a great gulf between human and divine as Occidentals do, and any Japanese becomes kami after death. Chu in the feudal eras had been due to heads of the hierarchy who had no divine qualifications. Far more important in transferring chu to the Emperor was the unbroken dynasty of a single imperial house during the whole history of Japan. It is idle for Westerners to complain that this continuity was a hoax because the rules of succession did not conform to those of the royal families of England or of Germany. The rules were Japan's rules and according to her rules the succession had been unbroken 'from ages eternal.' Japan was no China with thirty-six different dynasties in recorded history. She was a country which, in all the changes she had embraced, had never torn her social fabric in shreds; the pattern had been permanent. It was this argument, and not divine ancestry, which the anti-Tokugawa forces exploited during the hundred years before the Restoration. They said that chu, which was due him who stood at the apex of the hierarchy, was due the Emperor alone. They built him up as high priest of the nation and that rôle does not necessarily mean divinity. It was more crucial than descent from a goddess.

Every effort has been made in modern Japan to personalize chu and to direct it specifically to the figure of the Emperor himself. The first Emperor after the Restoration was an individual of consequence and dignity and during his long reign he easily became a personal symbol to his subjects. His infrequent public appearances were staged with all the appurtenances of worship. No murmur rose from the assembled multitudes as they bowed before him. They did not raise their eyes to gaze upon him. Windows were shuttered everywhere above the first story for no man might look down from a height upon the Emperor. His contacts with his high counselors were similarly hierarchal. It was not said that he summoned his administrators; a few specially privileged Excellencies 'had access' to him. Rescripts were not issued on controversial political issues; they were on ethics or thrift or they were designed as landmarks to indicate an issue closed and hence to reassure his people. When he was on his deathbed all Japan became a temple where devotees devoted themselves to intercession in his behalf.

The Emperor was in all these ways made into a symbol which was placed beyond all reach of domestic controversy. Just as loyalty to the Stars and Stripes is above and beyond all party politics so the Emperor was 'inviolable.' We surround our handling of the flag with a degree of ritual which we regard as completely inappropriate for any human being. The Japanese, however, capitalized to the hilt on the humanness of their supreme symbol. They could love and he could respond. They were moved to ecstasy that he 'turned his thoughts to them.' They dedicated their lives to 'ease his heart.' In a culture based as fully as Japan's has been on personal ties, the Emperor was a symbol of loyalty far surpassing a flag. Teachers in training were flunked if they phrased man's highest duty as love of country; it had to be phrased as repayment to the Emperor in person.

Chu provides a double system of subject-Emperor relationship. The subject faces upward directly to the Emperor without intermediaries; he personally 'eases his heart' by his actions. The subject receiving the commands of the Emperor, however, hears these orders relayed through all the intermediaries that stand between them. 'He speaks for the Emperor' is a phrase that invokes chu and is probably a more powerful sanction than any other modern State can invoke. Lory describes an incident of peacetime Army maneuvers when an officer took a regiment out with orders not to drink from their canteens without his permission. Japanese Army training placed great emphasis on ability to march fifty and sixty miles without intermission under difficult conditions. On this day twenty men fell by the way from thirst and exhaustion. Five died. When their canteens were examined they were found to be untouched. 'The officer had given the command. He spoke for the Emperor.'*

In civil administration chu sanctions everything from death to taxes. The tax collector, the policeman, the local conscription officials are instrumentalities through which a subject renders chu. The Japanese point of view is that obeying the law is repayment upon their highest indebtedness, their ko-on. The contrast with folkways in the United States could hardly be more marked. To Americans any

* Lory, Hillis, *Japan's Military Masters*, 1943, p. 40.

new laws, from street stop-lights to income taxes, are resented all over the country as interferences with individual liberty in one's own affairs. Federal regulations are doubly suspect for they interfere also with the freedom of the individual state to make its own laws. It is felt that they are put over on the people by Washington bureaucrats and many citizens regard the loudest outcry against these laws as less than what is rightly due to their self-respect. The Japanese judge therefore that we are a lawless people. We judge that they are a submissive people with no ideas of democracy. It would be truer to say that the citizens' self-respect, in the two countries, is tied up with different attitudes; in our country it depends on his management of his own affairs and in Japan it depends on repaying what he owes to accredited benefactors. Both arrangements have their own difficulties: ours is that it is difficult to get regulations accepted even when they are to the advantage of the whole country, and theirs is that, in any language, it is difficult to be in debt to such a degree that one's whole life is shadowed by it. Every Japanese has probably at some point invented ways of living within the law and yet circumventing what is asked of him. They also admire certain forms of violence and direct action and private revenge which Americans do not. But these qualifications, and any others that can be urged, still do not bring in question the hold that chu has upon the Japanese.

When Japan capitulated on August 14, 1945, the world had an almost unbelievable demonstration of its working. Many Westerners with experience and knowledge of Japan had held that it would be impossible for her to surrender;

it would be naïve, they insisted, to imagine that her armies scattered over Asia and the Pacific Islands would peacefully yield up their arms. Many of Japan's armed forces had suffered no local defeat and they were convinced of the righteousness of their cause. The home islands, too, were full of bitter-enders and an occupying army, its advance guard being necessarily small, would run the risk of massacre when it moved beyond range of naval guns. During the war the Japanese had stopped at nothing and they are a warlike people. Such American analysts reckoned without chu. The Emperor spoke and the war ceased. Before his voice went upon the radio bitter opponents had thrown a cordon around the palace and tried to prevent the proclamation. But, once read, it was accepted. No field commander in Manchuria or Java, no Tojo in Japan, put himself in opposition. Our troops landed at the airfields and were greeted with courtesy. Foreign correspondents, as one of them wrote, might land in the morning fingering their small arms but by noon they had put these aside and by evening they were shopping for trinkets. The Japanese were now 'easing the Emperor's heart' by following the ways of peace; a week earlier it had been by dedicating themselves to repulse the barbarian even with bamboo spears.

There was no mystery about it except to those Westerners who could not grant how various are the emotions that sway men's conduct. Some had proclaimed that there was no alternative to practical extermination. Some had proclaimed that Japan could save itself only if the liberals seized power and overthrew the government. Either of these analyses made sense in terms of a Western nation fighting an all-out and popularly supported war. They were wrong, however, because they attributed to Japan courses of action which are essentially Occidental. Some Western prophets still thought after months of peaceful occupation that all was lost because no Western-type revolution had occurred or because 'the Japanese did not know they were defeated.' This is good Occidental social philosophy based on Occidental standards of what is right and proper. But Japan is not the Occident. She did not use that last strength of Occidental nations: revolution. Nor did she use sullen sabotage against the enemy's occupying army. She used her own strength: the ability to demand of herself as chu the enormous price of unconditional surrender before her fighting power was broken. In her own eyes this enormous payment nevertheless bought something she supremely valued: the right to say that it was the Emperor who had given the order even if that order was capitulation. Even in defeat the highest law was still chu.

7

The Repayment 'Hardest to Bear'

'GIRI,' runs the Japanese saying, is 'hardest to bear.' A person must repay giri as he must repay gimu, but it is a series of obligations of a different color. There is no possible English equivalent and of all the strange categories of moral obligations which anthropologists find in the culture of the world, it is one of the most curious. It is specifically Japanese. Both chu and ko Japan shares with China and in spite of the changes she has made in these concepts they have certain family likeness to moral imperatives familiar in other Eastern nations. But giri she owes to no Chinese Confucianism and to no Oriental Buddhism. It is a Japanese category and it is not possible to understand their courses of action without taking it into account. No Japanese can talk about motivations or good repute or the dilemmas which confront men and women in his home country without constantly speaking of giri.

To an Occidental, giri includes a most heterogeneous list of obligations (see chart on p. 116) ranging from gratitude for an old kindness to the duty of revenge. It is no wonder that the Japanese have not tried to expound giri to Westerners; their own all-Japanese dictionaries can hardly define it. One of these renders it—I translate:—'righteous way; the road human beings should follow; something one does unwillingly to forestall apology to the world.' This does not give a Westerner much idea of it but the word 'unwillingly' points up a contrast with gimu. Gimu, no matter how many difficult demands it makes upon a person, is at least a group of duties he owes within the immediate circle of his intimate family and to the Ruler who stands as a symbol for his country, his way of life, and his patriotism. It is due to persons because of strong ties drawn tight at his very birth. However unwilling specific acts of compliance may be, gimu is never defined as 'unwilling.' But 'repaying giri' is full of malaise. The difficulties of being a debtor are at their maximum in 'the circle of giri.'

Giri has two quite distinct divisions. What I shall call 'giri to the world'—literally 'repaying giri'—is one's obligation to repay *on* to one's fellows, and what I shall call 'giri to one's name' is the duty of keeping one's name and reputation unspotted by any imputation, somewhat after the fashion of German 'honor.' Giri to the world can roughly be described as the fulfillment of contractual relations—as contrasted with gimu which is felt as the fulfillment of intimate obligations to which one is born. Thus giri includes all the duties one owes to one's in-law's family; gimu, those to one's own immediate family. The term for father-in-law is father-in-giri; mother-in-law is mother-in-giri, and brother- and sister-in-law are brother-in-giri and sister-in-giri. This terminology is used either for spouse's sibling or for sibling's spouse. Marriage in Japan is of course a contract between families and carrying out these contractual obligations throughout life to the opposite family is 'working for giri.' It is heaviest toward the generation which arranged the contract—the parents—and heaviest of all on the young wife toward her mother-in-law because, as the Japanese say, the bride has gone to live in a house where she was not born. The husband's obligations to his parents-in-law are different, but they too are dreaded, for he may have to lend them money if they are in distress and must meet other contractual responsibilities. As one Japanese said, 'If a grown son does things for his own mother, it is because he loves her and therefore it couldn't be giri. You don't work for giri when you act from the heart.' A person fulfills his duties to his in-laws punctiliously, however, because at all costs he must avoid the dreaded condemnation: 'a man who does not know giri.'

The way they feel about this duty to the in-law family is vividly clear in the case of the 'adopted husband,' the man who is married after the fashion of a woman. When a family has daughters and no sons the parents choose a husband for one of their daughters in order to carry on the family name. His name is erased from the register of his own family and he takes his father-in-law's name. He enters his wife's home, is subject 'in giri' to his father- and mother-in-law, and when he dies is buried in their burying ground. In all these acts he follows the exact pattern of the woman in the usual marriage. The reasons for adopting a husband for one's daughter may not be simply the absence of a son of one's own; often it is a deal out of which both sides hope to gain. These are called 'political marriages.' The girl's family may be poor but of good family and the boy may bring ready cash and in return move up in the class hierarchy. Or the girl's family may be wealthy and able to educate the husband who in return for this benefit signs away his own family. Or the girl's father may in this way associate with himself a prospective partner in his firm. In any case, an adopted husband's giri is especially heavy—as is proper because the act of changing a man's name to another family register is drastic in Japan. In feudal Japan he had to prove himself in his new household by taking his adopted father's side in battle, even if it meant killing his own father. In modern Japan the 'political marriages' involving adopted husbands invoke this strong sanction of giri to tie the young man to his father-in-law's business or family fortunes with the heaviest bonds the Japanese can provide. Especially in Meiji times this was sometimes advantageous to both parties. But resentment at being an adopted husband is usually violent and a common Japanese saying is 'If you have three *go* of rice (about a pint), never be an adopted husband.' The Japanese say this resentment is 'because of the giri.' They do not say, as Americans probably would if we had a like custom, 'because it keeps him from playing a man's rôle.' Giri is hard enough anyway and 'unwilling' enough, so that 'because of the giri' seems to the Japanese a sufficient statement of the burdensome relation.

Not only duties to one's in-laws are giri; duties even to uncles and aunts and nephews and nieces are in the same category. The fact that in Japan duties to even such relatively close relatives do not rank as filial piety (ko) is one of the great differences in family relations between Japan and China. In China, many such relatives, and much more distant ones, would share pooled resources, but in Japan they are giri or 'contractual' relatives. The Japanese point out that it often happens that these persons have never personally done a favor (*on*) for the person who is asked to come to their aid; in helping them he is repaying *on* to their common ancestors. This is the sanction behind caring for one's own children too—which of course is a gimu—but even though the sanction is the same, assistance to these more distant relatives rates as giri. When one has to help them, as when one helps one's in-laws, one says, 'I am tangled with giri.'

The great traditional giri relationship which most Japanese think of even before the relation with in-laws, is that of a retainer to his liege lord and to his comrades at arms. It is the loyalty a man of honor owes to his superior and to his fellows of his own class. This obligation of giri is celebrated in a vast traditional literature. It is identified as the virtue of the samurai. In old Japan, before the unification of the country effected by the Tokugawas, it was often considered a greater and dearer virtue even than chu, which was at that time the obligation to the Shogun. When in the twelfth century a Minamoto Shogun demanded of one of the daimyo the surrender of an enemy lord he was sheltering, the daimyo wrote back a letter which is still preserved. He was deeply resentful of the imputation upon his giri and he refused to offend against it even in the name of chu. 'Public affairs,' he wrote, '(are a thing) over which I have little personal control but giri between men of honor is an eternal verity' which transcended the Shogun's authority. He refused 'to commit a faithless act against his honored friends.'* This transcendent samurai virtue of old Japan suffuses great numbers of historical folktales which are known today all over Japan and are worked up into *noh* dramas, *kabuki* theater and *kagura* dances.

One of the best known of these is the tale of the huge invincible *ronin* (a lordless samurai who lives by his own wits), the hero Benkei of the twelfth century. Entirely without resources but of miraculous strength he terrorizes the monks when he takes shelter in the monasteries and cuts down every passing samurai in order to make a collection of their swords to pay for outfitting himself in feudal fashion. Finally he challenges what appears to him to be a mere youngster, a slight and foppish lord. But in him he meets his match and discovers that the youth is the scion of the Minamotos who is scheming to recover the Shogunate for his family. He is indeed that beloved Japanese hero, Yoshitsune Minamoto. To him Benkei gives his passionate giri and undertakes a hundred exploits in his cause. At last, however, they have to escape with their followers from an overwhelming enemy force. They disguise themselves as monkish pilgrims traveling over Japan to collect subscriptions for a temple and to escape detection Yoshitsune dresses as one of the troop while Benkei assumes its headship. They run into a guard the enemy has set along their path and Benkei fabricates for them a long list of temple 'subscribers' which he pretends to read from his scroll. The enemy almost lets them pass. At the last moment, however,

* Quoted by Kanichi Asakawa, *Documents of Iriki*, 1929.

their suspicions are aroused by the aristocratic grace of Yoshitsune which he cannot conceal even in his disguise as an underling. They call back the troop. Benkei immediately takes a step which completely clears Yoshitsune from suspicion: he berates him on some trivial issue and strikes him across the face. The enemy is convinced; it is beyond possibility that if this pilgrim is Yoshitsune, one of his retainers should lift his hand against him. It would be an unimaginable breach of giri. Benkei's impious act saves the lives of the little band. As soon as they are in safe territory, Benkei throws himself at Yoshitsune's feet and asks him to slay him. His lord graciously offers pardon.

These old tales of times when giri was from the heart and had no taint of resentment are modern Japan's daydream of a golden age. In those days, the tales tell them, there was no 'unwillingness' in giri. If there was conflict with chu, a man could honorably stick by giri. Giri then was a loved face-to-face relation dressed in all the feudal trimmings. To 'know giri' meant to be loyal for life to a lord who cared for his retainers in return. To 'repay giri' meant to offer even one's life to the lord to whom one owed everything.

This is, of course, a fantasy. Feudal history in Japan tells of plenty of retainers whose loyalty was bought by the daimyo on the opposite side of the battle. Still more important, as we shall see in the next chapter, any slur the lord cast upon his retainer could properly and traditionally make the retainer leave his service and even enter into negotiations with the enemy. Japan celebrates the vengeance theme with as much delight as she celebrates loyalty to the death. And they were both giri; loyalty was giri to one's lord and vengeance for an insult was giri to one's name. In Japan they are two sides to the same shield.

Nevertheless the old tales of loyalty are pleasant day-dreams to the Japanese today for now 'repaying giri' is no longer loyalty to one's legitimate chieftain but is fulfilling all sorts of obligations to all sorts of people. Today's constantly used phrases are full of resentment and of emphasis on the pressure of public opinion which compels a person to do giri against his wishes. They say, 'I am arranging this marriage merely for giri'; 'merely because of giri I was forced to give him the job'; 'I must see him merely for giri.' They constantly talk of being 'tangled with giri,' a phrase the dictionary translates as 'I am obliged to it.' They say, 'He forced me with giri,' 'he cornered me with giri,' and these, like the other usages, mean that someone has argued the speaker into an act he did not want or intend by raising some issue of payment due upon an *on*. In peasant villages, in transactions in small shops, in high circles of the Zaibatsu and in the Cabinet of Japan, people are 'forced with giri' and 'cornered with giri.' A suitor may do this by taxing his prospective father-in-law with some old relationship or transaction between the two families or a man may use this same weapon to get a peasant's land. The man who is being 'cornered' will himself feel he must comply; he says, 'If I do not hold the shoulder of my *on*-man (man from whom I received *on*), my giri is in bad repute.' All these usages carry the implication of unwillingness and of compliance for 'mere decency's sake,' as the Japanese dictionary phrases it.

The rules of giri are strictly rules of required repayment;

they are not a set of moral rules like the Ten Commandments. When a man is forced with giri, it is assumed that he may have to override his sense of justice and they often say, 'I could not do right (*gi*) because of giri.' Nor do the rules of giri have anything to do with loving your neighbor as yourself; they do not dictate that a man shall act generously out of the spontaneity of his heart. A man must do giri, they say, because, 'if he does not, people will call him "a person who does not know giri" and he will be shamed before the world.' It is what people will say that makes it so necessary to comply. Indeed, 'giri to the world' often appears in English translation as 'conformity to public opinion,' and the dictionary translates 'It can't be helped because it is giri to the world' as 'People will not accept any other course of action.'

It is in this 'circle of giri' that the parallel with American sanctions on paying money one has borrowed helps us most to understand the Japanese attitude. We do not consider that a man has to pay back the favor of a letter received or a gift given or of a timely word spoken with the stringency that is necessary in keeping up his payments of interest and his repayment of a bank loan. In these financial dealings bankruptcy is the penalty for failure—a heavy penalty. The Japanese, however, regard a man as bankrupt when he fails in repaying giri and every contact in life is likely to incur giri in some way or other. This means keeping an account of little words and acts Americans throw lightly about with no thought of incurring obligations. It means walking warily in a complicated world.

There is another parallel between Japanese ideas of giri

to the world and American ideas of repaying money. Repayment of giri is thought of as repayment of an exact equivalent. In this giri is quite unlike gimu, which can never be even approximately satisfied no matter what one does. But giri is not unlimited. To American eyes the repayments are fantastically out of proportion to the original favor but that is not the way the Japanese see it. We think their gift giving is fantastic too, when twice a year every household wraps up something in ceremonious fashion as return on a gift received six months earlier, or when the family of one's maidservant brings gifts through the years as a return on the favor of hiring her. But the Japanese taboo returning gifts with larger gifts. It is no part of one's honor to return 'pure velvet.' One of the most disparaging things one can say about a gift is that the giver has 'repaid a minnow with a sea bream (a large fish).' So too in repaying giri.

Whenever possible written records are kept of the network of exchanges, whether they are of work or of goods. In the villages some of these are kept by the headman, some by one of the work-party, some are family and personal records. For a funeral it is customary to bring 'incense money.' Relatives may also bring colored cloth for funeral banners. The neighbors come to help, the women in the kitchen and the men in digging the grave and making the coffin. In the village of Suye Mura the headman made up the book in which these things were recorded. It was a valued record in the family of the deceased for it showed the tributes of their neighbors. It is also a list which shows those names to which the family owes reciprocal tributes which will be honored when a death occurs in other families. These are long-term reciprocities. There are also short-term exchanges at any village funeral just as at any kind of feast. The helpers who make the coffin are fed and they therefore bring a measure of rice to the bereaved family as part payment on their food. This rice too is entered in the headman's record. For most feasts also the guest brings some rice-wine in part payment for the party drinks. Whether the occasion is birth or death, a rice-transplanting, a housebuilding or a social party, the exchange of giri is carefully noted for future repayment.

The Japanese have another convention about giri which parallels Western conventions about money repayment. If repayment is delayed beyond due term it increases as if it drew interest. Doctor Eckstein tells a story of this in his dealings with the Japanese manufacturer who financed his trip to Japan to gather material for his biography of Noguchi. Doctor Eckstein returned to the United States to write the book and eventually sent the manuscript to Japan. He received no acknowledgement and no letters. He was naturally troubled for fear something in the volume might have offended the Japanese, but his letters remained unanswered. Some years later the manufacturer telephoned him. He was in the United States, and shortly afterward he arrived at Doctor Eckstein's home bringing with him dozens of Japanese cherry trees. The gift was lavish. Just because it had been held in abeyance so long it was proper that it should be handsome. 'Surely,' his benefactor said to Doctor Eckstein, 'you would not have wanted me to repay you *quickly*.'

A man who is 'cornered with giri' is often forced into repayments of debts which have grown with time. A man may apply for assistance to a small merchant because he is the nephew of a teacher the merchant had as a boy. Since as a young man, the student had been unable to repay his giri to his teacher, the debt has accumulated during the passing years and the merchant has to give 'unwillingly to forestall apology to the world.'

8

Clearing One's Name

GIRI to one's name is the duty to keep one's reputation unspotted. It is a series of virtues—some of which seem to an Occidental to be opposites, but which to the Japanese have a sufficient unity because they are those duties which are not repayments on benefits received; they are 'outside the circle of *on*.' They are those acts which keep one's reputation bright without reference to a specific previous indebtedness to another person. They include therefore maintaining all the miscellaneous etiquette requirements of 'proper station,' showing stoicism in pain and defending one's reputation in profession or craft. Giri to one's name also demands acts which remove a slur or an insult; the slur darkens one's good name and should be got rid of. It may be necessary to take vengeance upon one's detractor or it may be necessary to commit suicide, and there are all sorts of possible courses of action between these two extremes. But one does not shrug off lightly anything that is compromising.

The Japanese do not have a separate term for what I call here 'giri to one's name.' They describe it simply as giri outside the circle of *on*. That is the basis of classification, and not the fact that giri to the world is an obligation to return kindnesses and that giri to one's name prominently includes revenge. The fact that Western languages separate the two into categories as opposite as gratitude and revenge does not impress the Japanese. Why should one virtue not cover a man's behavior when he reacts to another's benevolence and when he reacts to his scorn or malevolence?

In Japan it does. A good man feels as strongly about insults as he does about the benefits he has received. Either way it is virtuous to repay. He does not separate the two, as we do, and call one aggression and one non-aggression. To him aggression only begins outside 'the circle of giri'; so long as one is maintaining giri and clearing one's name of slurs, one is not guilty of aggression. One is evening scores. 'The world tips,' they say, so long as an insult or slur or defeat is not requited or eliminated. A good man must try to get the world back into balance again. It is human virtue, not an all-too-human vice. Giri to one's name, and even the way it is linguistically combined in Japan with gratitude and loyalty, has been a Western virtue in certain periods of European history. It flourished mightily in the Renaissance, especially in Italy, and it has much in common with *el valor Español* in classic Spain and with *die Ehre* in Germany. Something very like it underlay dueling in Europe a hundred years ago. Wherever this virtue of wiping out stains on one's honor has been in the ascendant, in Japan or in Western nations, the very core of it has always been that it transcended profit in any material sense. One was virtuous in proportion as one offered up to 'honor' one's possessions, one's family, and one's own life. This is a part of its very definition and is the basis of the claim that these countries always put forward that it is a 'spiritual' value. It certainly involves them in great material losses and can hardly be justified on a profit-and-loss basis. In this lies the great contrast between this version of honor and the cut-throat competition and overt hostility that crops up in life in the United States; in America it may be that no holds are barred in some political or financial deal but it is a war to get or to hold some material advantage. It is only in exceptional cases, as, for instance, in the feuds of the Kentucky Mountains, where codes of honor prevail which fall in the category of giri to one's name.

Giri to one's name and all the hostility and watchful waiting that accompany it in any culture, however, is not a virtue that is characteristic of the Asiatic mainland. It is not, as the phrase goes, Oriental. The Chinese do not have it, nor the Siamese, nor the Indians. The Chinese regard all such sensitivity to insults and aspersions as a trait of 'small' people—morally small. It is no part of their ideal of nobility, as it is in Japan. Violence which is wrong when a man starts it out of the blue does not become right in Chinese ethics when a man indulges in it to requite an insult. They think it is rather ridiculous to be so sensitive. Nor do they react to a slur by resolving by all that is good and great to prove the aspersion baseless. The Siamese have no place at all for this kind of sensitivity to insult. Like the Chinese they set store by making their detractor ridiculous but they do not imagine that their honor has been impugned. They say 'The best way to show an opponent up for a brute is to give in to him.'

The full significance of giri to one's name cannot be understood without placing in context all the non-aggressive virtues which are included in it in Japan. Vengeance is only one of the virtues it may require upon occasion. It includes also plenty of quiet and temperate behavior. The stoicism, the self-control that is required of a self-respecting Japanese is part of his giri to his name. A woman may not cry out in childbirth and a man should rise above pain and danger. When floods sweep down upon the Japanese village each self-respecting person gathers up the necessities he is to take with him and seeks higher ground. There is no outcry, no running hither and thither, no panic. When the equinoctial winds and rain come in hurricane strength there is similar self-control. Such behavior is a part of the respect a person has for himself in Japan even granted he may not live up to it. They think American self-respect does not require self-control. There is *noblesse oblige* in this self-control in Japan and in feudal times more was therefore required of the samurai than of the common people but the virtue, though less exigent, was a rule of life among all classes. If the samurai were required to go to extremes in rising above bodily pain, the common people had to go to extremes in accepting the aggressions of the armed samurai.

The tales of samurai stoicism are famous. They were forbidden to give way to hunger but that was too trivial to mention. They were enjoined when they were starving to pretend they had just eaten: they must pick their teeth with a toothpick. 'Baby birds,' the maxim went, 'cry for their food but a samurai holds a toothpick between his teeth.' In the past war this became an Army maxim for the enlisted soldier. Nor must they give way to pain. The Japanese attitude was like the boy soldier's rejoinder to Napoleon: 'Wounded? Nay, sire, I'm killed.' A samurai should give no sign of suffering till he fell dead and he must bear pain without wincing. It is told of Count Katsu who died in 1899 that when he was a boy his testicles were torn by a dog. He was of samurai family but his family had been reduced to beggary. While the doctor operated upon him, his father held a sword to his nose. 'If you utter one cry,' he told him, 'you will die in a way that at least will not be shameful.'

Giri to one's name also requires that one live according to one's station in life. If a man fails in this giri he has no right to respect himself. This meant in Tokugawa times that he accepted as part of his self-respect the detailed sumptuary laws which regulated practically everything he wore or had or used. Americans are shocked to the core by laws which define these things by inherited class position. Self-respect in America is bound up with improving one's status and fixed sumptuary laws are a denial of the very basis of our society. We are horrified by Tokugawa laws which stated that a farmer of one class could buy such and such a doll for his child and the farmer of another class could buy a different doll. In America, however, we get the same results by invoking a different sanction. We accept with no criticism the fact that the factory owner's child has a set of electric trains and that the sharecropper's child contents itself with a corncob doll. We accept differences in income and justify them. To earn a good salary is a part of our system of self-respect. If dolls are regulated by income that is no violation of our moral ideas. The person who has got rich buys better dolls for his children. In Japan getting rich is under suspicion and maintaining proper station is not. Even today the poor as well as the rich invest their self-respect in observing the conventions of hierarchy. It is a virtue alien to America, and the Frenchman, de Tocqueville, pointed this out in the eighteen-thirties in his book already quoted. Born himself in eighteenth-century France, he knew and loved the aristocratic way of life in spite of his generous comments about the egalitarian United States. America, he said, in spite of its virtues, lacked true dignity. 'True dignity consists in always taking one's proper station, neither too high nor too low. And this is as much within the reach of the peasant as of the prince.' De Tocqueville would have understood the Japanese attitude that class differences are not themselves humiliating.

'True dignity,' in this day of objective study of cultures, is recognized as something which different peoples can define differently, just as they always define for themselves what is humiliating. Americans who cry out today that Japan cannot be given self-respect until we enforce our egalitarianism are guilty of ethnocentrism. If what these Americans want is, as they say, a self-respecting Japan they will have to recognize her bases for self-respect. We can recognize, as de Tocqueville did, that this aristocratic 'true dignity' is passing from the modern world and that a different and, we believe, a finer dignity is taking its place. It will no doubt happen in Japan too. Meantime Japan will have to rebuild her self-respect today on her own basis, not on ours. And she will have to purify it in her own way.

Clearing One's Name

Giri to one's name is also living up to many sorts of commitments besides those of proper station. A borrower may pledge his giri to his name when he asks for a loan; a generation ago it was common to phrase it that 'I agree to be publicly laughed at if I fail to repay this sum.' If he failed, he was not literally made a laughingstock; there were no public pillories in Japan. But when the New Year came around, the date on which debts must be paid off, the insolvent debtor might commit suicide to 'clear his name.' New Year's Eve still has its crop of suicides who have taken this means to redeem their reputations.

All kinds of professional commitments involve giri to one's name. The Japanese requirements are often fantastic when particular circumstances bring one into the public eye and criticism might be general. There are for instance the long list of school principals who committed suicide because fires in their schools—with which they had nothing to do—threatened the picture of the Emperor which was hung in every school. Teachers too have been burned to death dashing into burning schools to rescue these pictures. By their deaths they showed how high they held their giri to their names and their chu to the Emperor. There are also famous stories of persons who were guilty of a slip of the tongue in ceremonious public readings of one of the Imperial Rescripts, either the one on Education or the one for Soldiers and Sailors, and who have cleared their names by committing suicide. Within the reign of the present Emperor, a man who had inadvertently named his son Hirohito—the given name of the Emperor was never spoken in Japan—killed himself and his child.

Giri to one's name as a professional person is very exigent in Japan but it need not be maintained by what an American understands as high professional standards. The teacher says, 'I cannot in giri to my name as a teacher admit ignorance of it,' and he means that if he does not know to what species a frog belongs nevertheless he has to pretend he does. If he teaches English on the basis of only a few years' school instruction, nevertheless he cannot admit that anyone might be able to correct him. It is specifically to this kind of defensiveness that 'giri to one's name as a teacher' refers. The business man too, in giri to his name as a business man, cannot let anyone know that his assets are seriously depleted or that the plans he made for his organization have failed. And the diplomat cannot in giri admit the failure of his policy. In all such giri usages there is extreme identification of a man with his work and any criticism of one's acts or one's competence becomes automatically a criticism of one's self.

These Japanese reactions to imputations of failure and inadequacy can be duplicated over and over again in the United States. We all know persons who are maddened by detraction. But we are seldom so defensive as the Japanese. If a teacher does not know to what species a frog belongs, he thinks it is better behavior to say so than to claim knowledge, even though he might succumb to the temptation to hide his ignorance. If a business man is dissatisfied with a policy he has promoted he thinks he can put out a new and different directive. He does not consider that his self-respect is conditional upon his maintaining that he was right all along and that if he admitted he was wrong he should either resign or retire. In Japan, however, this defensiveness goes very deep and it is the part of wisdom—as it is also universal etiquette—not to tell a person to his face in so many words that he has made a professional error.

This sensitivity is especially conspicuous in situations where one person has lost out to another. It may be only that another person has been preferred for a job or that the person concerned has failed in a competitive examination. The loser 'wears a shame' for such failures, and, though this shame is in some cases a strong incentive to greater efforts, in many others it is a dangerous depressant. He loses confidence and becomes melancholy or angry or both. His efforts are stymied. It is especially important for Americans to recognize that competition in Japan thus does not have the same degree of socially desirable effects that it does in our own scheme of life. We rely strongly on competition as a 'good thing.' Psychological tests show that competition stimulates us to our best work. Performance goes up under this stimulus; when we are given something to do all by ourselves we fall short of the record we make when there are competitors present. In Japan, however, their tests show just the opposite. It is especially marked after childhood is ended, for Japanese children are more playful about competition and not so worried about it. With young men and adults, however, performance deteriorated with competition. Subjects who had made good progress, reduced their mistakes and gained speed when they were working by themselves, began to make mistakes and were far slower when a competitor was introduced. They did best when they were measuring their improvement against their own record, not when they were measuring themselves against others. The Japanese experimenters rightly analyzed the reason for this poor record in competitive situations. Their subjects, they said, when the project became competitive, became principally interested in the danger that they might be defeated, and the work suffered. They felt the competition so keenly as an aggression that they turned their attention to their relation to the aggressor instead of concentrating on the job in hand.*

The students examined in these tests tended to be influenced most by the possible shame of failing. Like a teacher or a business man living up to his giri to his professional name they are stung by their giri to their name as students. Student teams who lost in competitive games, too, went to great lengths in abandoning themselves to this shame of failure. Crews might throw themselves down in their boats beside their oars and weep and bewail themselves. Defeated baseball teams might gather in a huddle and cry aloud. In the United States we would say they were bad losers. We have an etiquette that expects them to say that the better team won. It is proper for the defeated to shake hands with the victors. No matter how much we hate to be beaten we scorn people who make an emotional crisis out of it.

The Japanese have always been inventive in devising ways of avoiding direct competition. Their elementary schools minimize it beyond what Americans would think possible.

* For a summary see *The Japanese: Character and Morale* (mimeographed). Prepared by Ladislas Farago for the Committee for National Morale, 9 East 89th Street, New York City.

Their teachers are instructed that each child must be taught to better his own record and that he should not be given opportunities to compare himself with others. In their grade schools they do not even keep any students back to repeat a grade and all children who enter together go through their entire elementary education together. Their report cards grade children in elementary schools on marks for conduct but not on their school work: when really competitive situations are unavoidable, as in entrance examinations to the middle schools, the tension is understandably great. Every teacher has stories of the boys who when they know they have failed commit suicide.

This minimizing of direct competition goes all through Japanese life. An ethic that is based on *on* has small place for competition whereas the American categorical imperative is upon making good in competition with one's fellows. Their whole system of hierarchy with all its detailed rules of class minimizes direct competition. The family system minimizes it too for the father and son are not institutionally in competition as they are in America: it is possible for them to reject each other but not for them to compete. Japanese comment with amazement on the American family where the father and the son compete both for the use of the family car and for the attention of the mother-wife.

The ubiquitous institution of the go-between is one of the more conspicuous ways in which the Japanese prevent direct confrontation of two persons who are in competition with each other. An intermediary is required in any situation where a man might feel shame if he fell short and consequently go-betweens serve on a great number of occasions—negotiating marriage, offering one's services for hire, leaving a job and arranging countless everyday matters. This go-between reports to both parties, or in case of an important deal like a marriage each side employs its own intermediary and they negotiate the details between themselves before reporting to their side. By dealing in this way at second hand the principals need take no cognizance of claims and charges that would have to be resented in giri to their names if they were in direct communication. The go-between too gains prestige by acting in this official capacity, and gets the respect of the community by his successful manipulation. The chances of a peaceful arrangement are the greater because the go-between has an ego investment in smooth negotiations. The intermediary acts in the same way in feeling out an employer about a job for his client or in relaying to the employer the employee's decision to leave his job.

Etiquette of all kinds is organized to obviate shame-causing situations which might call in question one's giri to one's name. These situations which are thus minimized go far beyond direct competition. The host, they think, should greet his guest with certain ritual welcoming and in his good clothes. Therefore anyone who finds a farmer in his work clothes at home may have to wait a bit. The farmer gives no sign of recognition until he has put on suitable clothes and arranged the proper courtesies. It makes no difference even if the host has to change his clothes in the room where the guest is waiting. He simply is not present until he is there in the proper guise. In the rural areas, too, boys may visit girls at night after the household is asleep and the girl is in bed. Girls can either accept or reject their advances, but the boy wears a towel bound about his face so that if he is rejected he need feel no shame next day. The disguise is not to prevent the girl from recognizing him; it is purely an ostrich technique so that he will not have to admit that he was shamed in his proper person. Etiquette requires too that as little cognizance as possible be taken of any project until success is assured. It is part of the duties of go-betweens arranging a marriage to bring the prospective bride and groom together before the contract is completed. Everything is done to make this a casual meeting for if the purpose of the introduction were avowed at this stage any breaking-off of the negotiations would threaten the honor of one family or of both. Since the young couple must each be escorted by one or both of their parents, and the go-betweens must be the hosts or hostesses, it is most properly arranged when they all 'run into each other' casually at the annual chrysanthemum show or at a cherry-blossom viewing or in a well-known park or place of recreation.

In all such ways, and in many more, the Japanese avoid occasions in which failure might be shameful. Though they lay such emphasis on the duty to clear one's name of insult, in actual practice this leads them to arrange events so that insult need be felt as seldom as possible. This is in great contrast to many tribes of the Pacific Islands where clearing one's name holds much the same pre-eminent place that it does in Japan.

Among these primitive gardening peoples of New Guinea and Melanesia the mainspring of tribal or personal action is the insult which it is necessary to resent. They cannot have a tribal feast without one village's setting it in motion by saying that another village is so poor it cannot feed ten guests, it is so stingy it hides its taro and its coconuts, its leaders are so stupid they could not organize a feast if they tried. Then the challenged village clears its name by overwhelming all comers with its lavish display and hospitality. Marriage arrangements and financial transactions are set going in the same way. When they go on the warpath too the two sides have a tremendous insult exchange before they set their arrows to their bows. They handle the smallest matter as if it were an occasion that called for mortal fight. It is a great incentive to action and such tribes often have a great deal of vitality. But nobody has ever described them as courteous.

The Japanese on the contrary are paragons of politeness and this pre-eminent politeness is a measure of the lengths to which they have gone in limiting the occasions when it is necessary to clear one's name. They retain as an incomparable goad to achievement the resentment insult occasions but they limit the situations where it is called for. It should occur only in specified situations or when traditional arrangements to eliminate it break down under pressure. Unquestionably the use of this goad in Japan contributed to the dominant position she was able to attain in the Far East and to her policy of Anglo-American war in the last decade. Many Occidental discussions of Japan's sensitivity to insult and her eagerness to avenge herself, however, would be more appropriate to the insult-using tribes of New Guinea than they are to Japan, and many Westerners' forecasts of how Japan would behave after defeat in this war were wide of the mark because they did not recognize the special Japanese limitations upon giri to one's name.

The politeness of the Japanese should not lead Americans to minimize their sensitivity to slurs. Americans bandy personal remarks very lightly; it is a kind of game. It is hard for us to realize the deadly seriousness that attaches to light remarks in Japan. In his autobiography, published in America just as he wrote it in English, a Japanese artist, Yoshio Markino, has described vividly a perfectly proper Japanese reaction to what he interpreted as a sneer. When he wrote the book he had already lived most of his adult life in the United States and in Europe but he felt as strongly as if he were still living in his home town in rural Aichi. He was the youngest child of a landowner of good standing and had been most lovingly reared in a charming home. Toward the end of his childhood his mother died, and, not long after, his father became bankrupt and sold all his property to pay his debts. The family was broken up and Markino had not a sen to help him in realizing his ambitions. One of these ambitions was to learn English. He attached himself to a near-by mission school and did janitor work in order to learn the language. At eighteen he had still never been outside the round of a few provincial towns but he had made up his mind to go to America.

> I visited upon one of the missionaries to whom I had more confidence than any other. I told him my intention to go to America in hope that he might be able to give me some useful information. To my great disappointment he exclaimed, 'What, *You* are intending to go to America?'

His wife was in the same room, and they both *sneered* at me! At the moment I felt as if all the blood in my head went down to my feet! I stood on the same point for a few seconds in silence, then came back to my room without saying 'goodbye.' I said to myself, 'Everything is quite finished.'

On the next morning I ran away. Now I want to write the reason. I always believe that *insincerity* is the greatest crime in this world, and nothing could be more insincere than to sneer!

I always forgive the other's anger, because it is the human nature to get into bad temper. I generally forgive if one tells me a lie, because the human nature is very weak and very often one cannot have a steady mind to face the difficulty and tell all the truth. I also forgive if one makes any foundless rumor or gossip against me, because it is a very easy temptation when some others persuade in that way.

Even murderers I may forgive according to their condition. But about sneering, there is no excuse. Because one cannot sneer at innocent people without intentional insincerity.

Let me give you my own definition of two words. Murderer: one who assassinates some human *flesh.* Sneerer: one who assassinates others' SOUL and *heart.*

Soul and heart are far dearer than the flesh, therefore sneering is the worst crime. Indeed, that missionary and his wife tried to assassinate my *soul* and *heart,* and I had a great pain in my heart, which cried out, 'Why you?'*

The next morning he departed with his entire possessions tied in a handkerchief.

He had been 'assassinated,' as he felt, by the missionary's incredulity about a penniless provincial boy's going to the United States to become an artist. His name was besmirched

* Markino, Yoshio, *When I was a Child,* 1912, pp. 159–160. Italics in the original.

until he had cleared it by carrying out his purpose and after the missionary's 'sneer' he had no alternative but to leave the place and prove his ability to get to America. In English it reads curiously that he charges the missionary with 'insincerity'; the American's exclamation seems to us quite 'sincere' in our sense of the word. But he is using the word in its Japanese meaning and they regularly deny sincerity to anyone who belittles any person whom he does not wish to provoke to aggression. Such a sneer is wanton and proves 'insincerity.'

'Even murderers I may forgive according to their condition. But about sneering there is no excuse.' Since it is not proper to 'forgive,' one possible reaction to a slur is revenge. Markino cleared his name by getting to America but revenge ranks high in Japanese tradition as a 'good thing' under circumstances of insult or defeat. Japanese who write books for Western readers have sometimes used vivid figures of speech to describe the Japanese attitudes about revenge. Inazo Nitobe, one of the most benevolent men in Japan, writing in 1900, says: 'In revenge there is something that satisfies one's sense of justice. Our sense of revenge is as exact as our mathematical faculty and until both terms of the equation are satisfied we cannot get over the sense of something left undone.'* Yoshisaburo Okakura in a book on *The Life and Thought of Japan* uses a particularly Japanese custom as a parallel:

> Many of the so-called mental peculiarities of the Japanese owe their origin to the love of purity and its complementary hatred of defilement. But, pray, how could it be

* Nitobe, Inazo, *Bushido, The Soul of Japan*, 1900, p. 83.

> otherwise, being trained, as we actually are, to look upon slights inflicted, either on our family honour or on the national pride, as so many defilements and wounds that would not be clean and heal up again, unless by a thorough washing through vindication? You may consider the cases of vendetta so often met with in the public and private life of Japan, merely as a kind of morning tub which a people take with whom love of cleanliness has grown into a passion.*

And he continues, saying that thus the Japanese 'live clean, undefiled lives which seem as serene and beautiful as a cherry tree in full bloom.' This 'morning tub,' in other words, washes off dirt other people have thrown at you and you cannot be virtuous as long as any of it sticks to you. The Japanese have no ethic which teaches that a man cannot be insulted unless he thinks he is and that it is only 'what comes out of a man' that defiles him, not what is said or done against him.

Japanese tradition keeps constantly before the public this ideal of a 'morning bath' of vendetta. Countless incidents and hero tales, of which the most popular is the historical *Tale of the Forty-Seven Ronin*, are known to everybody. They are read in their school books and played in the theater, made up into contemporary movies, and printed in popular publications. They are a part of the living culture of Japan today.

Many of these tales are about sensitivity to casual failures. For instance, a daimyo called on three of his retainers to name the maker of a certain fine sword. They disagreed and when experts were called in it was found that

* Okakura, Yoshisaburo, *The Life and Thought of Japan.* London, 1913, p. 17.

Nagoya Sanza had been the only one who had correctly identified it as a Muramasa blade. The ones who were wrong took it as an insult and set out to kill Sanza. One of them found Sanza asleep and stabbed him with Sanza's own sword. Sanza, however, lived, and his attacker thereafter dedicated himself to his revenge. In the end he succeeded in killing him and his giri was satisfied.

Other tales are about the necessity of avenging oneself upon one's lord. Giri meant in Japanese ethics equally the retainer's loyalty to his lord to the death, and his right-about-face of extravagant enmity when he felt himself insulted. A good example is from the stories about Ieyasu, the first Tokugawa Shogun. It was reported to one of his retainers that Ieyasu had said of him, 'He is the sort of fellow who will die of a fishbone stuck in his throat.' The imputation that he would die in an undignified manner was not to be borne, and the retainer vowed that this was something he would not forget in life or death. Ieyasu was at the time unifying the country from the new capital Yedo (Tokyo) and was not yet secure from his enemies. The retainer made overtures to the hostile lords, offering to set fire to Yedo from within and lay it waste. Thus his giri would be satisfied and he would be avenged upon Ieyasu. Most Occidental discussions of Japanese loyalty are thoroughly un realistic because they do not recognize that giri is not merely loyalty; it is also a virtue that under certain circumstances enjoins treachery. As they say, 'A man who is beaten becomes a rebel.' So does a man who is insulted.

These two themes from the historical tales—revenge upon someone who has been right when you were wrong, and revenge for a slur, even from one's lord—are commonplaces in the best-known literature of Japan, and they have many variations. When one examines contemporary life-histories and novels and events, it is clear that, however much the Japanese appreciate revenge in their traditions, stories of vengeance are today certainly as rare as in Western nations, perhaps rarer. This does not mean that obsessions about one's honor have grown less but rather that the reaction to failures and slurs is more and more often defensive instead of offensive. People take the shame as seriously as ever, but it more and more often paralyzes their energies instead of starting a fight. The direct attack of vengeance was more possible in lawless pre-Meiji days. In the modern era law and order and the difficulties of managing a more interdependent economy have sent revenge underground or directed it against one's own breast. A man may take a private revenge against his enemy by playing a trick upon him which he never avows—somewhat after the fashion of the old story of the host who served his enemy with excrement which could not be detected in the delicious food and asked no more than to know he had done it. The guest never knew. But even this kind of underground aggression is rarer today than turning it against oneself. There one has two choices: to use it as a goad to drive oneself to the 'impossible,' or to let it eat out one's heart.

The vulnerability of the Japanese to failures and slurs and rejections makes it all too easy for them to harry themselves instead of others. Their novels describe over and over again the dead end of melancholy alternating with outbursts of anger in which educated Japanese have so often lost themselves in the last decades. The protagonists of these stories are bored—bored with the round of life, bored with their families, bored with the city, bored with the country. But it is not the boredom of reaching for the stars, where all effort seems trivial compared with a great goal pictured in their mind's eye. It is not a boredom born of the contrast between reality and the ideal. When the Japanese have a vision of a great mission they lose their boredom. They lose it completely and absolutely, no matter how distant the goal. Their particular kind of ennui is the sickness of an over-vulnerable people. They turn inward upon themselves their fear of rejection and they are stymied. The picture of boredom in the Japanese novel is quite a different state of mind from that with which we are familiar in the Russian novel where the contrast between the real and the ideal worlds is basic in all the tedium their heroes experience. Sir George Sansom has said that the Japanese lack this sense of a contrast between the real and the ideal. He is not speaking of how this underlies their boredom but of how they formulate their philosophy and their general attitude toward life. Certainly this contrast with basic Occidental notions goes far beyond the particular case in point here, but it has special relevance to their besetting depressions. Japan ranks with Russia as a nation given to depicting boredom in her novels and the contrast with the United States is marked. American novels do not do much with the theme. Our novelists trace the misery of their characters to a character-deficiency or to the buffets of a cruel world; they very seldom depict pure and simple ennui. Personal maladjustment must have a cause, a build-up, and rouse the reader's moral condemnation of some flaw in the hero or heroine, or of some evil in the social order. Japan also has her proletarian novels protesting desperate economic conditions in the cities and terrible happenings on commercial fishing boats, but their character novels uncover a world where people's emotions most often come to them, so one author says, like drifting chlorine gas. Neither the character nor the author thinks it necessary to analyze the circumstances or the hero's life history to account for the cloud. It goes and it comes. People are vulnerable. They have turned inward the aggression their old heroes used to visit upon their enemies and their depression appears to them to have no explicit causes. They may seize upon some incident as its source, but the incident leaves a curious impression of being hardly more than a symbol.

The most extreme aggressive action a modern Japanese takes against himself is suicide. Suicide, properly done, will, according to their tenets, clear his name and reinstate his memory. American condemnation of suicide makes self-destruction only a desperate submission to despair, but the Japanese respect for it allows it to be an honorable and purposeful act. In certain situations it is the most honorable course to take in giri to one's name. The defaulting debtor on New Year's Day, the official who kills himself to acknowledge that he assumes responsibility for some unfortunate occurrence, the lovers who seal their hopeless love in a double suicide, the patriot who protests the government's postponement of war with China are all, like the boy who fails in an examination or the soldier avoiding capture, turning upon themselves a final violence. Some Japanese authorities say that this liability to suicide is new in Japan. It is not easy to judge, and statistics show that observers in recent years have often overestimated its frequency. There were proportionately more suicides in Denmark in the last century and more in pre-Nazi Germany than there have ever been in Japan. But this much is certain: the Japanese love the theme. They play up suicide as Americans play up crime and they have the same vicarious enjoyment of it. They choose to dwell on events of self-destruction instead of on destruction of others. They make of it, in Bacon's phrase, their favorite 'flagrant case.' It meets some need that cannot be filled by dwelling on other acts.

Suicide is also more masochistic in modern Japan than it appears to have been in the historical tales of feudal times. In those stories a samurai committed suicide with his own hand at the command of the government to save himself from dishonorable execution, much as a Western enemy soldier would be shot instead of hanged, or he took this course to save himself the torture he expected if he fell into the enemy's hands. A warrior was allowed *harakiri* much as a Prussian officer in disgrace was sometimes allowed to shoot himself in private. Those in authority left a bottle of whiskey and a pistol on a table in his room after he knew that he had no hope of saving his honor otherwise. For the Japanese samurai, taking his own life under such circumstances was only a choice of means; death was certain. In modern times suicide is a choice to die. A man turns violence upon himself, often instead of assassinating someone else. The act of suicide, which in feudal times was the final statement of a man's courage and resolution, has become today a chosen self-destruction. During the last two generations, when Japanese have felt that 'the world tips,' that 'both terms of the equation' are not equivalent, that they need a 'morning tub' to wipe off defilements, they have increasingly destroyed themselves instead of others.

Even suicide as a final argument to win victory for one's own side, though it occurs both in feudal and in modern times, has changed in this same direction. A famous story of Tokugawa days tells of the old tutor, high in the Shogunate council, who bared his body and placed his sword in readiness for immediate harakiri in the presence of the whole council and the Shogunate regent. The threat of suicide carried the day and he thereby insured the succession of his candidate to the position of Shogun. He got his way and there was no suicide. In Occidental terminology, the tutor had blackmailed the opposition. In modern times, however, such protest suicide is the act of a martyr not of a negotiator. It is carried out after one has failed or to put oneself on record as opposing some already signed agreement like the Naval Parity Act. It is staged so that only the completed act itself, and not the threat of suicide, can influence public opinion.

This growing tendency to strike at oneself when giri to one's name is threatened need not involve such extreme steps as suicide. Aggressions directed inward may merely produce depression and lassitude and that typical Japanese boredom that was so prevalent in the educated class. There are good sociological reasons why this mood should have been widespread among this particular class for the intelligentsia was overcrowded and very insecurely placed in the hierarchy. Only a small proportion of them could satisfy their ambitions. In the nineteen-thirties, too, they were doubly vulnerable because the authorities feared they were thinking 'dangerous thoughts' and held them under suspicion. The Japanese intellectuals usually account for their frustration by complaints about the confusions of Westernization, but the explanation does not go far enough. The typical Japanese swing of mood is from intense dedication to intense boredom, and the psychic shipwreck which many intellectuals suffered was in the traditional Japanese manner. Many of them saved themselves from it, too, in the middle nineteen-thirties in traditional fashion: they embraced nationalistic goals and turned the attack outward again, away from their own breasts. In totalitarian aggression against outside nations they could 'find themselves' again. They saved themselves from a bad mood and felt a great new strength within them. They could not do it in personal relationships but they believed they could as a conquering nation.

Now that the outcome of the war has proved this confidence mistaken, lassitude is again a great psychic threat in Japan. They cannot easily cope with it, whatever their intentions. It goes very deep. 'No bombs any more,' one Japanese said in Tokyo; 'the relief is wonderful. But we are not fighting any more and there is no purpose. Everyone is in a daze, not caring much how he does things. I am like that, my wife is like that and the people in the hospital. All very slow about everything we do, dazed. People complain now that the government is slow cleaning up after the war and in providing relief, but I think the reason is that all the government officials felt the same way as we did.' This listlessness is the kind of danger in Japan that it was in France after liberation. In Germany in the first six or eight months after surrender it was not a problem. In Japan it is. Americans can understand this reaction well enough but it seems almost unbelievable to us that it should go along with such friendliness to the conqueror. Almost immediately it was clear that the Japanese people accepted the defeat and all its consequences with extreme good will. Americans were welcomed with bows and smiles, with handwavings and shouts of greeting. These people were not sullen nor angry. They had, in the phrase the Emperor used in announcing surrender, 'accepted the impossible.' Why then did these people not set their national house in order? Under the terms of occupation, they were given the opportunity to do it; there was no village-by-village foreign occupation and the administration of affairs was in their hands. The whole nation seemed to smile and wave greeting rather than to manage their affairs. Yet this was the same nation which had accomplished miracles of rehabilitation in the early days of Meiji, which had prepared for military conquest with such energy in the nineteen-thirties and whose soldiers had fought with such abandon, island by island, throughout the Pacific.

They are indeed the same people. They are reacting in character. The swing of mood that is natural to them is between intense effort and a lassitude that is sheer marking time. The Japanese at the present moment are chiefly conscious of defending their good name in defeat and they feel they can do this by being friendly. As a corollary, many feel they can do it most safely by being dependent. And it is an easy step to feeling that effort is suspect and that it is better to mark time. Lassitude spreads.

Yet the Japanese do not enjoy ennui. To 'rouse oneself from lassitude,' to 'rouse others from lassitude' is a constant call to the better life in Japan, and it was often on the lips of their broadcasters even in wartime. They campaign against their passivity in their own way. Their newspapers in the spring of 1946 keep talking about what a blot it is on the honor of Japan that 'with the eyes of the whole world upon us,' they have not cleaned up the shambles of bombing and have not got certain public utilities into operation. They complain about the lassitude of the homeless families who congregate to sleep at night in the railway stations where the Americans see them in their misery. The Japanese understand such appeals to their good name. They hope too that as a nation they will be able to put forward utmost efforts again in the future to work for a respected place in the United Nations Organization. That would be working for honor again, but in a new direction. If there is peace among the Great Powers in the future, Japan could take this road to self-respect.

For in Japan the constant goal is honor. It is necessary to command respect. The means one uses to that end are tools one takes up and then lays aside as circumstances dictate. When situations change, the Japanese can change their bearings and set themselves on a new course. Changing does not appear to them the moral issue that it does to Westerners. We go in for 'principles,' for convictions on ideological matters. When we lose, we are still of the same mind. Defeated Europeans everywhere banded together in underground movements. Except for a few diehards, the Japanese do not need to organize resistance movements and underground opposition to the occupying forces of the American Army. They feel no moral necessity to hold to the old line. From the first months, single Americans traveled safely on the sardine-packed trains to out-of-the-way corners of the country and were greeted with courtesy by erstwhile nationalistic officials. There have been no vendettas. When our jeeps drive through the villages the roads are lined with children shouting 'Hello' and 'Good-bye,' and the mother waves her baby's hand to the American soldier when he is too small to do it by himself.

This right-about-face of the Japanese in defeat is hard for Americans to take at face value. It is nothing we could do. It is even harder for us to understand than the change of attitude in their prisoners of war in our internment camps. For the prisoners regarded themselves as dead to Japan, and we judged that we really did not know what 'dead' men might be capable of. Very few of those Westerners who knew Japan predicted that the same change of front characteristic of the prisoners of war might be found in Japan, too, after the defeat. Most of them believed that Japan 'knew only victory or defeat,' and that defeat would be in her eyes an insult to be avenged by continued desperate violence. Some believed that the national characteristics of the Japanese forbade their acceptance of any terms of peace. Such students of Japan had not understood giri. They had singled out, from among all the alternative procedures that give one an honorable name, the one conspicuous traditional technique of vengeance and aggression. They did not allow for the Japanese habit of taking another tack. They confused Japanese ethics of aggression with European forms, according to which any person or nation who fights has first to be convinced of the eternal righteousness of its cause and draw strength from reservoirs of hatred or of moral indignation.

The Japanese derive their aggression in a different way. They need terribly to be respected in the world. They saw that military might had earned respect for great nations and they embarked on a course to equal them. They had to out-Herod Herod because their resources were slight and their technology was primitive. When they failed in their great effort, it meant to them that aggression was not the road to honor after all. Giri had always meant equally the use of aggression or the observance of respect relations, and in defeat the Japanese turned from one to the other, apparently with no sense of psychic violence to themselves. The goal is still their good name.

Japan has behaved in similar fashion on other occasions in her history and it has always been confusing to Westerners. The curtain had hardly risen after Japan's long feudal isolation when in 1862 an Englishman named Richardson was murdered in Satsuma. The fief of Satsuma was a hotbed of agitation against the white barbarians, and Satsuma samurai were known as the most arrogant and warlike of all Japan. The British sent a punitive expedition and bombarded Kagoshima, an important Satsuma port. The Japanese had made firearms all through the Tokugawa Era, but they were copied from antique Portuguese guns, and

Kagoshima was of course no match for British warships. The consequences of this bombardment, however, were surprising. Satsuma, instead of vowing eternal vengeance upon the British, sought British friendship. They had seen the greatness of their opponents and they sought to learn from them. They entered into trade relations with them and in the following year they established a college in Satsuma where, as a contemporary Japanese wrote, 'The mysteries of Occidental science and learning were taught. . . . The friendship which had sprung out of the Namamuga Affair continued to grow.'* The Namamuga Affair was Britain's punitive expedition against them and the bombardment of their port.

This was not an isolated case. The other fief which vied with Satsuma as the most warlike and virulent haters of foreigners was Choshu. Both fiefs were leaders in fomenting the restoration of the Emperor. The officially powerless court of the Emperor issued an imperial rescript naming the date of May 11, 1863, at which time the Shogun was directed to have expelled all barbarians from the soil of Japan. The Shogunate ignored the order but not Choshu. It opened fire from its forts upon Western merchant ships passing off its coast through the Strait of Shimonoseki. The Japanese guns and ammunition were too primitive to injure the ships but to teach Choshu a lesson an international Western war squadron soon demolished the forts. The same strange consequences of bombardment followed as in Satsuma, and this in spite of the fact that the Western powers demanded an indemnity of three million dollars. As Nor-

* Norman, E. H., *op. cit.*, pp. 44–45, and n. 85.

man says of the Satsuma and Choshu incidents, 'Whatever the complexity of motive behind the volte-face executed by these leading anti-foreign clans, one cannot but respect the realism and equanimity which this action attests.'*

This kind of situational realism is the bright face of Japanese giri to one's name. Like the moon, giri has its bright face and its dark face. It was its dark aspect which made Japan take events like the American Exclusion Act and the Naval Parity Treaty as such extravagant national insults and which goaded her to her disastrous war program. It is its bright aspect which made possible the good will with which she accepted the consequences of surrender in 1945. Japan is still acting in character.

Modern Japanese writers and publicists have made a selection from among the obligations of giri and presented them to Westerners as the cult of *bushido*, literally The Way of the Samurai. This has been misleading for several reasons. Bushido is a modern official term which has not the deep folk-feeling behind it that 'cornered with giri,' 'merely for giri,' 'working strongly for giri' have in Japan. Nor does it cover the complexities and the ambivalences of giri. It is a publicist's inspiration. Besides, it became a slogan of the nationalists and militarists and the concept is discredited with the discrediting of those leaders. That will by no means mean that the Japanese will no longer 'know giri.' It is more important than ever for Westerners to understand what giri means in Japan. The identification of bushido with the Samurai was also a source of misunderstanding. Giri is a virtue common to all classes. Like all other

* *Op. cit.*, p. 45.

obligations and disciplines in Japan giri is 'heavier' as one goes up the social scale but it is required at all levels of society. At least the Japanese think it is heavier for the samurai. A non-Japanese observer is just as likely to feel that giri requires most of the common people because the rewards for conforming seem to him less. To the Japanese it is sufficient reward to be respected in his world and 'a man who does not know giri' is still a 'miserable wretch.' He is scorned and ostracized by his fellows.

9

The Circle of Human Feelings

An Ethical Code like Japan's, which requires such extreme repayment of obligations and such drastic renunciations, might consistently have branded personal desire as an evil to be rooted out from the human breast. This is the classical Buddhist doctrine and it is therefore doubly surprising that the Japanese code is so hospitable to the pleasures of the five senses. In spite of the fact that Japan is one of the great Buddhist nations of the world, her ethics at this point contrast sharply with the teachings of Gautama Buddha and of the holy books of Buddhism. The Japanese do not condemn self-gratification. They are not Puritans. They consider physical pleasures good and worthy of cultivation. They are sought and valued. Nevertheless, they have to be kept in their place. They must not intrude upon the serious affairs of life.

Such a code keeps life at a particularly high tension. A Hindu finds it far easier to see these consequences of Japanese acceptance of the pleasures of the senses than an American does. Americans do not believe that pleasures have to be learned; a man may refuse to indulge in sensual pleasures, but he is resisting a known temptation. Pleasures, however, are learned much as duties are. In many cultures the pleasures themselves are not taught and it therefore becomes particularly easy for people to devote themselves to self-sacrificing duty. Even physical attraction between men and women has sometimes been minimized till it hardly threatens the smooth course of family life, which in such countries is based on quite other considerations. The Japanese make life hard for themselves by cultivating physical pleasures and then setting up a code in which these pleasures are the very things which must not be indulged as a serious way of life. They cultivate the pleasures of the flesh like fine arts, and then, when they are fully savored, they sacrifice them to duty.

One of the best loved minor pleasures of the body in Japan is the hot bath. For the poorest rice farmer and the meanest servant, just as much as for the rich aristocrat, the daily soak in superlatively heated water is a part of the routine of every late afternoon. The commonest tub is a wooden barrel with a charcoal fire under it to keep the water heated to 110 degrees Fahrenheit and over. People wash and rinse themselves all over before they get into the tub and then give themselves over to their enjoyment of the warmth and relaxation of soaking. They sit in the bath with their knees drawn up in fetal position, the water up to their chins. They value the daily bath for cleanliness' sake as Americans do, but they add to this value a fine art of passive indulgence which is hard to duplicate in the bathing habits of the rest of the world. The older one is, they say, the more it grows on one.

There are all sorts of ways of minimizing the cost and trouble of providing these baths, but baths they must have. In the cities and towns there are great public baths like swimming pools where one may go and soak and visit with one's chance neighbor in the water. In the farm villages several women will take turns preparing the bath in the yard—it is no part of Japanese modesty to avoid the public gaze while bathing—and their families will use it in turn. Always any family even in fine homes go into the family tub in strict succession: the guest, the grandfather, the father, the eldest son and so on down to the lowest servant of the family. They come out lobster-red, and the family gathers together to enjoy the most relaxed hour of the day before the evening meal.

Just as the hot bath is so keenly appreciated a pleasure, so 'hardening oneself' traditionally included the most excessive routine of cold douches. This routine is often called 'winter exercises' or 'the cold austerity' and is still done, but not in the old traditional form. That called for going out before dawn to sit under waterfalls of cold mountain streams. Even pouring freezing water over oneself on winter nights in their unheated Japanese houses is no slight austerity and Percival Lowell describes the custom as it existed in the eighteen-nineties. Men who aspired to special powers of curing or prophecy—but who did not then become priests—practiced the cold-austerity before they went to bed and rose again at two A.M. to do it again at the hour when 'the gods were bathing.' They repeated when they rose in the morning and again at midday and at nightfall.*

* Lowell, Percival, *Occult Japan,* 1895, pp. 106–121.

The before-dawn austerity was particularly popular with people who were merely in earnest about learning to play a musical instrument or to prepare for some other secular career. To harden oneself, one may expose oneself to any cold and it is regarded as particularly virtuous for children practicing calligraphy to finish their practice periods with their fingers numbed and chilblained. Modern elementary schools are unheated and a great virtue is made of this for it hardens the children for later difficulties of life. Westerners have been more impressed with the constant colds and snotty noses which the custom certainly does nothing to prevent.

Sleeping is another favored indulgence. It is one of the most accomplished arts of the Japanese. They sleep with complete relaxation, in any position, and under circumstances we regard as sheer impossibilities. This has surprised many Western students of the Japanese. Americans make insomnia almost a synonym for psychic tenseness, and according to our standards there are high tensions in the Japanese character. But they make child's play of good sleeping. They go to bed early, too, and it is hard to find another Oriental nation that does that. The villagers, all asleep shortly after nightfall, are not following our maxim of storing up energy for the morrow for they do not have that kind of calculus. One Westerner, who knew them well, wrote: 'When one goes to Japan one must cease to believe that it is a bounden duty to prepare for work tomorrow by sleep and rest tonight. One is to consider sleep apart from questions of recuperation, rest and recreation.' It should stand, just as a proposal to work should, too, 'on its own legs, having no reference to any known fact of life or death.'* Americans are used to rating sleeping as something one does to keep up one's strength and the first thought of most of us when we wake up in the morning is to calculate how many hours we slept that night. The length of our slumbers tells us how much energy and efficiency we will have that day. The Japanese sleep for other reasons. They like sleeping and when the coast is clear they gladly go to sleep.

By the same token they are ruthless in sacrificing sleep. A student preparing for examinations works night and day, uncurbed by any notion that sleep would equip him better for the test. In Army training, sleep is simply something to sacrifice to discipline. Colonel Harold Doud, attached to the Japanese Army from 1934 to 1935, tells of his conversation with a Captain Teshima. During peacetime maneuvers the troops 'twice went three days and two nights without sleep except what could be snatched during ten-minute halts and brief lulls in the situation. Sometimes the men slept while walking. Our junior lieutenant caused much amusement by marching squarely into a lumber pile on the side of the road while sound asleep.' When camp was finally struck, still no one got a chance to sleep; they were all assigned to outpost and patrol duty. ' "But why not let some of them sleep?" I asked. "Oh no!" he said. "That is not necessary. They already know how to sleep. They need training in how to stay awake." '† That puts the Japanese view in a nutshell.

* Watson, W. Petrie, *The Future of Japan*, 1907.

† *How the Jap Army Fights*, articles from the *Infantry Journal* published as Penguin Books, 1942, pp 54–55.

Eating, like warmth and sleeping, is both a relaxation freely enjoyed as pleasure, and a discipline imposed for hardening. As a ritual of leisure the Japanese indulge in endless course meals at which one teaspoonful of food is brought in at a time and the food is praised as much for its looks as for its flavor. But otherwise discipline is stressed. 'Quick eating, quick defecating, those together make one of the highest Japanese virtues,' Eckstein quotes a Japanese villager as saying.* 'Eating is not regarded as an act of any importance. . . . Eating is necessary to sustain life, *therefore* it should be as brief a business as possible. Children, especially boys, are not as in Europe, urged to eat slowly but are encouraged to eat as quickly as possible' (italics mine).† In the monasteries of the Buddhist faith where priests are under discipline, they ask in their grace before meals that they may remember that food is just a medicine; the idea is that those who are hardening themselves should ignore food as a pleasure and regard it only as a necessity.

According to Japanese ideas, involuntary deprivation of food is an especially good test of how 'hardened' one is. Like foregoing warmth and sleeping, so, too, being without food is a chance to demonstrate that one can 'take it,' and, like the samurai, 'hold a toothpick between one's teeth.' If one meets this test when one goes without food, one's strength is raised by one's victory of the spirit, not lowered by the lack of calories and vitamins. The Japanese do not recognize the one-to-one correspondence which Americans postulate between body nourishment and body strength.

* Eckstein, G., *In Peace Japan Breeds War*, 1943, p. 153.

† Nohara, K., *The True Face of Japan*. London, 1936, p. 140.

Therefore, Radio Tokyo could tell people in raid shelters during the war that calisthenics would make hungry people strong and vigorous again.

Romantic love is another 'human feeling' which the Japanese cultivate. It is thoroughly at home in Japan, no matter how much it runs counter to their forms of marriage and their obligations to the family. Their novels are full of it, and, as in French literature, the principals are already married. Double love-suicides are favorite themes in reading and conversation. The tenth-century *Tale of Genji* is as elaborate a novel of romantic love as any great novel any country in the world has ever produced, and tales of the loves of the lords and the samurai of the feudal period are of this same romantic sort. It is a chief theme of their contemporary novels. The contrast with Chinese literature is very great. The Chinese save themselves a great deal of trouble by underplaying romantic love and erotic pleasures, and their family life has consequently a remarkably even tenor.

Americans can, of course, understand the Japanese better than they can the Chinese on this score but this understanding nevertheless goes only a little way. We have many taboos on erotic pleasure which the Japanese do not have. It is an area about which they are not moralistic and we are. Sex, like any other 'human feeling,' they regard as thoroughly good in its minor place in life. There is nothing evil about 'human feelings' and therefore no need to be moralistic about sex pleasures. They still comment upon the fact that Americans and British consider pornographic some of their cherished books of pictures and see the Yoshiwara—

the district of geisha girls and prostitutes—in such a lurid light. The Japanese, even during early years of Western contact, were very sensitive about this foreign criticism and passed laws to bring their practices more nearly into conformity with Western standards. But no legal regulations have been able to bridge the cultural differences.

Educated Japanese are thoroughly aware that English and Americans see immorality and obscenity where they do not, but they are not as conscious of the chasm between our conventional attitudes and their tenet that 'human feelings' should not intrude upon serious affairs of life. It is, however, a major source of our difficulty in understanding Japanese attitudes about love and erotic pleasure. They fence off one province which belongs to the wife from another which belongs to erotic pleasure. Both provinces are equally open and aboveboard. The two are not divided from each other as in American life by the fact that one is what a man admits to the public and the other is surreptitious. They are separate because one is in the circle of a man's major obligations and the other in the circle of minor relaxation. This way of mapping out 'proper place' to each area makes the two as separate for the ideal father of a family as it does for the man about town. The Japanese set up no ideal, as we do in the United States, which pictures love and marriage as one and the same thing. We approve of love just in proportion as it is the basis of one's choice of a spouse. 'Being in love' is our most approved reason for marriage. After marriage a husband's physical attraction to another woman is humiliating to his wife because he bestows elsewhere something that rightly belongs to her. The Japanese judge differently. In the choice of a spouse the young man should bow to his parent's choice and marry blind. He must observe great formality in his relations with his wife. Even in the give and take of family life their children do not see an erotically affectionate gesture pass between them. 'The real aim of marriage is regarded in this country,' as a contemporary Japanese says in one of their magazines, 'as the procreation of children and thereby to assure the continuity of the family life. Any purpose other than this must simply serve to pervert the true meaning of it.'

But this does not mean that a man remains virtuous by limiting himself to such a life. If he can afford it he keeps a mistress. In strong contrast to China he does not add to his family this woman who has caught his fancy. If he did that, it would confuse the two areas of life which should be kept separate. The girl may be a geisha, highly trained in music and dance and massage and the arts of entertainment, or she may be a prostitute. In any case he signs a contract with the house where she is employed and this contract protects the girl from abandonment and ensures her a financial return. He sets her up in an establishment of her own. Only in highly exceptional cases when the girl has a child whom the man wishes to bring up with his own children does he bring her into his home, and then she is designated as one of the servants, not as a concubine. The child calls the legal wife 'mother,' and ties between the real mother and her child are not acknowledged. The whole Oriental arrangement of polygamy, which is so pronounced a traditional pattern in China, is thus quite un-Japanese. The Japanese keep family obligations and 'human feelings' even spatially apart.

Only the upper class can afford to keep mistresses, but most men have at some time visited geishas or prostitutes. Such visits are not in the least surreptitious. A man's wife may dress and prepare him for his evening of relaxation. The house he visits may send the bill to his wife and she pays it as a matter of course. She may be unhappy about it but that is her own affair. A visit to the geisha house is more expensive than a visit to a prostitute but the payment a man makes for the privilege of such an evening does not include the right to make her a sexual partner. What he gets is the pleasure of being entertained by beautifully dressed and punctiliously mannered girls who have been meticulously trained for their rôle. To gain access to a particular geisha, the man would have to become her patron and sign a contract according to which she would become his mistress, or he would have to captivate her by his charms so that she gave herself to him of her own free will. An evening with geisha girls, however, is no asexual affair. Their dances, their repartee, their songs, their gestures are traditionally suggestive and carefully calculated to express all that an upper-class wife's may not. They are 'in the circle of human feelings' and give relief from 'the circle of *ko*.' There is no reason not to indulge oneself but the two spheres belong apart.

Prostitutes live in licensed houses, and after an evening with a geisha a man may visit a prostitute if he wishes. The fee is low and men with little money have to content themselves with this form of relaxation and forego geishas. The pictures of the girls of the house are displayed outside and men commonly spend a long time quite publicly studying the pictures and making their choices. These girls have a low status and they are not put on a pinnacle as the geishas are. They are most of them daughters of the poor who have been sold to the establishment by their families when they were hard-pressed for money, and they are not trained in geisha arts of entertainment. In earlier days, before Japan realized Western disapproval of the custom and ended it, the girls themselves used to sit in public showing their impassive faces to customers choosing their human wares. Their photographs are a substitution.

One of these girls may be chosen by a man who becomes her exclusive patron and sets her up as a mistress after making a contract with the house. Such girls are protected by the terms of the agreement. A man may, however, take a servant girl or salesgirl as a mistress without signing a contract and these 'voluntary mistresses' are the ones who are most defenseless. They are precisely those girls who are most likely to have been in love with their partners, but they are outside all the recognized circles of obligation. When the Japanese read our tales and poems of young mourning women 'with my baby on my knee' abandoned by their lovers, they identify these mothers of illegitimate children with their 'voluntary mistresses.'

Homosexual indulgences are also part of traditional 'human feelings.' In Old Japan these were the sanctioned pleasures of men of high status such as the samurai and the priests. In the Meiji period when Japan made so many of her customs illegal in her effort to win the approval of Westerners, she ruled that this custom should be punishable by law. It still falls, however, among those 'human feelings' about which moralistic attitudes are inappropriate. It must be kept in its proper place and must not interfere with carrying on the family. Therefore the danger of a man or a woman's 'becoming' a homosexual, as the Western phrase has it, is hardly conceived, though a man can choose to become a male geisha professionally. The Japanese are especially shocked at adult passive homosexuals in the United States. Adult men in Japan would seek out boy partners, for adults consider the passive rôle to be beneath their dignity. The Japanese draw their own lines as to what a man can do and retain his self-respect, but they are not the ones we draw.

The Japanese are not moralistic about autoerotic pleasures, either. No people have ever had such paraphernalia for the purpose. In this field, too, the Japanese tried to forestall foreign condemnation by eliminating some of the more obvious publicity these objects received, but they do not themselves feel that they are instruments of evil. The strong Western attitude against masturbation, even stronger in most of Europe than in the United States, is deeply imprinted on our consciousness before we are grown up. A boy hears the whispered words that it makes a man crazy or that it makes him bald. His mother has been watchful when he was a baby, and perhaps she has made a great issue of it and physically punished him. Perhaps she tied his hands. Perhaps she told him God would punish him. Japanese babies and Japanese children do not have these experiences and as adults they cannot therefore reproduce our attitudes. Autoeroticism is a pleasure about which they feel no guilt and they think it is sufficiently controlled by assigning it to its minor place in a decorous life.

Intoxication is another of the permissible 'human feelings.' The Japanese consider our American total abstinence pledges as one of the strange vagaries of the Occident. So too they regard our local agitations to vote our home area dry. Drinking *sake* is a pleasure no man in his right mind would deny himself. But alcohol belongs among the minor relaxations and no man in his right mind, either, would become obsessed by it. According to their way of thinking one does not fear to 'become' a drunkard any more than one fears to 'become' a homosexual, and it is true that the compulsive drunkard is not a social problem in Japan. Alcohol is a pleasant relaxation and one's family and even the public does not consider a man repulsive when he is under the influence of liquor. He is not likely to be violent and certainly nobody thinks he is going to beat up his children. A crying jag is quite common and relaxation of the strict rules of Japanese posture and gestures is universal. At urban *sake* parties men like to sit in each other's laps.

Conventional Japanese strictly separate drinking from eating. As soon as a man tastes rice at a village party where *sake* is served it means that he has stopped drinking. He has stepped over into another 'circle' and he keeps them separate. At home he may have *sake* after his meal but he does not eat and drink at the same time. He gives himself up in turn to one or the other enjoyment.

These Japanese views on 'human feelings' have several consequences. It cuts the ground out from under the Occidental philosophy of two powers, the flesh and the spirit, continually fighting for supremacy in each human life. In Japanese philosophy the flesh is not evil. Enjoying its possible pleasures is no sin. The spirit and the body are not opposing forces in the universe and the Japanese carry this tenet to a logical conclusion: the world is not a battlefield between good and evil. Sir George Sansom writes: 'Throughout their history the Japanese seem to have retained in some measure this incapacity to discern, or this reluctance to grapple with, the problem of evil.'* They have in fact constantly repudiated it as a view of life. They believe that man has two souls, but they are not his good impulses fighting with his bad. They are the 'gentle' soul and the 'rough' soul and there are occasions in every man's—and every nation's—life when he should be 'gentle' and when he should be 'rough.' One soul is not destined for hell and one for heaven. They are both necessary and good on different occasions.

Even their gods are conspicuously good-evil in this same fashion. Their most popular god is Susanowo, 'His Swift Impetuous Male Augustness,' brother of the Sun Goddess, whose outrageous behavior toward his sister would in Western mythology identify him as a devil. His sister tries to throw him out of her rooms because she suspects his motives in coming to her. He behaves wantonly, scattering excrement over her dining hall where she and her followers are celebrating the ceremony of the First-fruits. He breaks down the divisions of the rice fields—a terrible offense. As worst offense of all—and most enigmatic to a Westerner—he flings into her chamber through a hole he makes in the roof a piebald horse which he 'had flayed with a backward flaying.' Susanowo, for all these outrages, is tried by the gods, heavily fined and banished from heaven to the Land

* Sansom, *op. cit.*, 1931, p. 51.

of Darkness. But he remains a favorite god of the Japanese pantheon and he duly receives his worship. Such god-characters are common in world mythologies. In the higher ethical religions, however, they have been excluded because a philosophy of cosmic conflict between good and evil makes it more congenial to separate supernatural beings into groups as different as black and white.

The Japanese have always been extremely explicit in denying that virtue consists in fighting evil. As their philosophers and religious teachers have constantly said for centuries such a moral code is alien to Japan. They are loud in proclaiming that this proves the moral superiority of their own people. The Chinese, they say, had to have a moral code which raised jen, just and benevolent behavior, to an absolute standard, by applying which all men and acts could be found wanting if they fell short. 'A moral code was good for the Chinese whose inferior natures required such artificial means of restraint.' So wrote the great eighteenth-century Shintoist, Motoöri, and modern Buddhist teachers and modern nationalistic leaders have written and spoken on the same theme. Human nature in Japan, they say, is naturally good and to be trusted. It does not need to fight an evil half of itself. It needs to cleanse the windows of its soul and act with appropriateness on every different occasion. If it has allowed itself to become 'dirty,' impurities are readily removed and man's essential goodness shines forth again. Buddhist philosophy has gone farther in Japan than in any other nation in teaching that every man is a potential Buddha and that rules of virtue are not in the sacred writings but in what one uncovers within one's own enlightened and innocent soul. Why should one distrust what one finds there? No evil is inherent in man's soul. They have no theology which cries with the Psalmist, 'Behold, I was shapen in iniquity, and in sin did my mother conceive me.' They teach no doctrine of the Fall of Man. 'Human feelings' are blessings which a man should not condemn. Neither the philosopher nor the peasant does condemn them.

To American ears such doctrines seem to lead to a philosophy of self-indulgence and license. The Japanese, however, as we have seen, define the supreme task of life as fulfilling one's obligations. They fully accept the fact that repaying *on* means sacrificing one's personal desires and pleasures. The idea that the pursuit of happiness is a serious goal of life is to them an amazing and immoral doctrine. Happiness is a relaxation in which one indulges when one can, but to dignify it as something by which the State and family should be judged is quite unthinkable. The fact that a man often suffers intensely in living up to his obligations of chu and ko and giri is no more than they expect. It makes life hard but they are prepared for that. They constantly give up pleasures which they consider in no way evil. That requires strength of will. But such strength is the most admired virtue in Japan.

It is consistent with this Japanese position that the 'happy ending' is so rare in their novels and plays. American popular audiences crave solutions. They want to believe that people live happily ever after. They want to know that people are rewarded for their virtue. If they must weep at the end of a play, it must be because there was a flaw in the hero's character or because he was victimized by a bad social order.

But it is far pleasanter to have everything come out happily for the hero. Japanese popular audiences sit dissolved in tears watching the hero come to his tragic end and the lovely heroine slain because of a turn of the wheel of fortune. Such plots are the high points of an evening's entertainment. They are what people go to the theater to see. Even their modern movies are built on the theme of the sufferings of the hero and the heroine. They are in love and give up their lovers. They are happily married and one or the other commits suicide in the proper performance of his duty. The wife who has devoted herself to rescuing her husband's career and arousing him to cultivate his great gifts as an actor hides herself in the great city on the eve of his success to free him for his new life and dies uncomplainingly in poverty on the day of his great triumph. There need be no happy ending. Pity and sympathy for the self-sacrificing hero and heroine has full right of way. Their suffering is no judgment of God upon them. It shows that they fulfilled their duty at all costs and allowed nothing—not abandonment or sickness or death—to divert them from the true path.

Their modern war films are in the same tradition. Americans who see these movies often say that they are the best pacifist propaganda they ever saw. This is a characteristic American reaction because the movies are wholly concerned with the sacrifice and suffering of war. They do not play up military parades and bands and prideful showings of fleet maneuvers or big guns. Whether they deal with the Russo-Japanese War or the China Incident, they starkly insist upon the monotonous routine of mud and marching, the sufferings of lowly fighting, the inconclusiveness of campaigns.

Their curtain scenes are not victory or even banzai charges. They are overnight halts in some featureless Chinese town deep in mud. Or they show maimed, halt and blind representatives of three generations of a Japanese family, survivors of three wars. Or they show the family at home, after the death of the soldier, mourning the loss of husband and father and breadwinner and gathering themselves together to go on without him. The stirring background of Anglo-American 'Cavalcade' movies is all absent. They do not even dramatize the theme of rehabilitation of wounded veterans. Not even the purposes for which the war was fought are mentioned. It is enough for the Japanese audience that all the people on the screen have repaid *on* with everything that was in them, and these movies therefore in Japan were propaganda of the militarists. Their sponsors knew that Japanese audiences were not stirred by them to pacifism.

10

The Dilemma of Virtue

THE JAPANESE VIEW of life is just what their formulas of chu and ko and giri and jin and human feelings say it is. They see the 'whole duty of man' as if it were parceled out into separate provinces on a map. In their phrase, one's life consists of 'the circle of chu' and 'the circle of ko' and 'the circle of giri' and 'the circle of jin' and 'the circle of human feelings' and many more. Each circle has its special detailed code and a man judges his fellows, not by ascribing to them integrated personalities, but by saying of them that 'they do not know ko' or 'they do not know giri.' Instead of accusing a man of being unjust, as an American would, they specify the circle of behavior he has not lived up to. Instead of accusing a man of being selfish or unkind, the Japanese specify the particular province within which he violated the code. They do not invoke a categorical imperative or a golden rule. Approved behavior is relative to the circle within which it appears. When a man acts 'for ko,' he is acting in one way; when he acts 'merely for giri' or 'in the circle of jin,' he is acting—so Westerners would judge—in quite different character. The codes, even for each 'circle,' are set up in such a way that, when conditions change within it, the most different behavior may be properly called for. Giri to one's lord demanded utmost loyalty until the lord insulted his retainer; afterward no treachery was too great. Until August, 1945, chu demanded of the Japanese people that they fight to the last man against the enemy. When the Emperor changed the requirements of chu by broadcasting Japan's capitulation, the Japanese outdid themselves in expressing their co-operation with the visitors.

This is baffling to Westerners. According to our experience, people act 'in character.' We separate the sheep from the goats by whether they are loyal or whether they are treacherous, whether they are co-operative or whether they are stiff-necked. We label people and expect their next behavior to be like their last. They are generous or stingy, willing or suspicious, conservative or liberal. We expect them to believe in one particular political ideology and consistently to fight the opposite ideology. In our war experience in Europe there were collaborationists and there were resistance people, and we doubted, quite rightly, that after VE-Day collaborationists would have changed their spots. In domestic controversies in the United States, we recognize, for instance, New Dealers and anti-New Dealers, and we judge that as new situations arise these two camps will continue to act in character. If individuals move from one side of the fence to the other—as when an unbeliever becomes a Catholic or a 'red' becomes a conservative—such a change has to be duly labeled as a conversion and a new personality built up to fit.

This Western faith in integrated behavior is of course not always justified, but it is no illusion. In most cultures, primitive or civilized, men and women picture themselves as acting as particular kinds of persons. If they are interested in power, they reckon their failures and successes in terms of others' submission to their will. If they are interested in being loved, they are frustrated in impersonal situations. They fancy themselves as sternly just or as having an 'artistic temperament' or as being a good homebody. They generally achieve a *Gestalt* in their own characters. It brings order into human existence.

Occidentals cannot easily credit the ability of the Japanese to swing from one behavior to another without psychic cost. Such extreme possibilities are not included in our experience. Yet in Japanese life the contradictions, as they seem to us, are as deeply based in their view of life as our uniformities are in ours. It is especially important for Occidentals to recognize that the 'circles' into which the Japanese divide life do not include any 'circle of evil.' This is not to say that the Japanese do not recognize bad behavior, but they do not see human life as a stage on which forces of good contend with forces of evil. They see existence as a drama which calls for careful balancing of the claims of one 'circle' against another and of one course of procedure against another, each circle and each course of procedure being in itself good. If everyone followed his true instincts, everyone would be good. As we saw, they regard even Chinese moral precepts as proving that the Chinese need that kind of thing. It proves the inferiority of the Chinese. Japanese, they say, have no need of over-all ethical commandments. In Sir George Sansom's phrase which we have already quoted, they 'do not grapple with the problem of evil.' According to their view, they adequately account for bad behavior by less cosmic means. Though every soul originally shines with virtue like a new sword, nevertheless, if it is not kept polished, it gets tarnished. This 'rust of my body,' as they phrase it, is as bad as it is on a sword. A man must give his character the same care that he would give a sword. But his bright and gleaming soul is still there under the rust and all that is necessary is to polish it up again.

This Japanese view of life makes their folk tales and novels and plays seem particularly inconclusive to Westerners—unless we are able, as often happens, to recast the plot to fit our demands for consistency of character and for conflict of good and evil. But that is not the way the Japanese look at these plots. Their comment is that the hero is caught in a conflict of 'giri against human feelings,' 'chu against ko,' 'giri against gimu.' A hero fails because he is allowing his human feelings to obscure his obligations of giri, or he cannot pay both the debt he owes as chu and the debt he owes as ko. He cannot do right (gi) because of giri. He is cornered by giri and sacrifices his family. The conflicts so portrayed are still between obligations both of which are in themselves binding. They are both 'good.' The choice between them is like the choice that faces a debtor who owes too many debts. He must pay some and ignore others for the time being, but the fact that he pays one debt does not free him of the rest of his debts.

This way of viewing the hero's life is in great contrast to the Western view. Our heroes are good precisely in that they have 'chosen the better part,' and are pitted against opponents who are bad. 'Virtue triumphs,' as we say. There should be a happy ending. The good should be rewarded. The Japanese, however, have an insatiable appetite for the story of the 'flagrant case' of the hero who finally settles incompatible debts to the world and to his name by choosing death as a solution. Such tales would in many cultures be stories teaching resignation to a bitter fate. But in Japan that is exactly what they are not. They are tales of initiative and ruthless determination. The heroes put forth every effort to pay some one obligation incumbent upon them, and, in so doing, they flout another obligation. But in the end they settle with the 'circle' they flouted.

The true national epic of Japan is the *Tale of the Forty-Seven Ronin.* It is not a tale that rates high in the world's literature but the hold it has on the Japanese is incomparable. Every Japanese boy knows not only the main story but the subordinate plots of the tale. Its stories are constantly told and printed and they are retold in a popular modern movie series. The graves of the forty-seven have been for generations a favorite pilgrimage where thousands went to pay tribute. They left their visiting cards, too, and the ground around the graves was often white with them.

The theme of the *Forty-Seven Ronin* centers around giri to one's lord. As the Japanese see it, it portrays the conflicts of giri with chu, of giri with righteousness—in which giri is of course virtuously triumphant,—and of 'merely giri' with limitless giri. It is an historical tale of 1703, the great days of feudalism when men were men, according to the modern Japanese daydream, and there was no 'unwillingness' in giri. The forty-seven heroes offer up everything to it, their reputations, their fathers, their wives, their sisters, their righteousness (gi). Finally they offer up to chu their own lives, dying by their own hands.

The Lord Asano was appointed by the Shogunate as one of two daimyo in charge of the ceremony at which all the daimyo made their periodical obeisance to the Shogun. The two masters of ceremonies were provincial lords and therefore they had to apply for instructions in required etiquette to a very great daimyo of the Court, the Lord Kira. Unfortunately Lord Asano's wisest retainer, Oishi—the hero of the tale—who would have counseled him prudently, was away in the home province and Asano was naïve enough not to arrange to pay a sufficient 'gift' to his great instructor. The retainers of the other daimyo who was being instructed by Kira were men of the world and showered the teacher with rich gifts. The Lord Kira therefore instructed Lord Asano with bad grace and purposely described to him an entirely wrong costume for his wear at the ceremony. The Lord Asano appeared thus clad on the great day and when he realized the insult put upon him he drew his sword and wounded Kira on the forehead before they could be separated. It was his virtue as a man of honor—his giri to his name—to avenge Kira's insult but it was against his chu to draw his sword in the Shogun's palace. The Lord Asano had conducted himself virtuously in giri to his name but he could only come to terms with chu by killing himself according to the rules of seppuku. He retired to his house and dressed himself for the ordeal, waiting only for the return of his wisest and most faithful retainer Oishi. When they had exchanged a long look of farewell, Lord Asano, having seated himself in required fashion, thrust his sword into his belly and died by his own hand. No relative being willing to succeed to the place of the dead lord who had violated chu and incurred the displeasure of the Shogunate, Asano's fief was confiscated and his retainers became masterless ronin.

According to the obligations of giri, Asano's samurai retainers owed it to their dead master to commit seppuku as he had done. If in giri to their lord they did what he had done in giri to his name, this would voice their protest against Kira's insult to their lord. But Oishi was secretly determined that seppuku was too small an act by which to express their giri. They must complete the vengeance their own lord had been unable to carry through when retainers separated him from his high-placed enemy. They must kill Lord Kira. But this could only be accomplished by violating chu. Lord Kira was too near to the Shogunate to make it possible for the ronin to get official permission from the State to carry out their revenge. In more usual cases, any group contemplating vengeance registered their plan with the Shogunate, stating the final date before which they would complete the act or abandon the enterprise. This arrangement allowed certain fortunate people to reconcile chu and giri. Oishi knew that this course was not open to him and his fellows. He therefore called together the ronin who had been Asano's samurai retainers but he spoke no word of his plan of killing Kira. There were more than three hundred of these ronin and, as the story was taught in Japanese schools in 1940, they all agreed to commit seppuku. Oishi knew, however, that not all of them had unlimited giri—in the Japanese phrase, 'giri plus sincerity'—and could therefore be trusted in the dangerous exploit of a vendetta against Kira. To separate those with 'merely' giri from those with giri plus sincerity he used the test of how they were to divide their lord's personal income. In Japanese eyes this was as much of a test as if they had not already agreed to commit suicide; their families would benefit. There was violent disagreement among the ronin about the basis of the division of property. The chief steward was the highest paid of the retainers and he led the faction which wanted the income divided according to previous salary. Oishi led the faction which wanted it divided equally among them all. As soon as it was well established which ones of the ronin had 'merely' giri, Oishi agreed to the chief steward's plan for partition of the estate and allowed those who had won to leave the company. The chief steward left and has earned thereby the fame of being a 'dog samurai,' a 'man who did not know giri,' and a reprobate. Oishi judged only forty-seven to be strong enough in giri to be made privy to his plan of vendetta. These forty-seven who joined him pledged by that act that no good faith, no affection, no gimu should stand in the way of the completion of their vow. Giri was to be their supreme law. The forty-seven cut their fingers and joined in a blood compact.

Their first task was to throw Kira off the scent. They disbanded and pretended to be lost to all honor. Oishi frequented the lowest public-houses and engaged in undignified brawls. Under cover of this abandoned life he divorced his wife—a usual and thoroughly justified step for any Japanese who was about to run foul of the law since it kept his wife and children from being held accountable along with him in the final act. Oishi's wife parted from him in great grief, but his son joined the ronin.

All Tokyo was speculating on the vendetta. All who respected the ronin were of course convinced that they would attempt to kill Lord Kira. But the forty-seven disclaimed any such intention. They pretended to be men who 'did not know giri.' Their fathers-in-law, outraged at such dishonorable conduct, turned them out of their homes and dissolved their marriages. Their friends ridiculed them. One day a close friend met Oishi drunk and reveling with women, and even to him Oishi denied his giri to his lord. 'Revenge?' he said. 'It is silly. One should enjoy life. Nothing is better than to drink and play around.' His friend disbelieved him, and pulled Oishi's sword out of its sheath, expecting its shining brilliance to disprove what its owner had said. But the sword was rusted. He was forced to believe and in the open street he kicked and spat upon the drunken Oishi.

One of the ronin, needing money to cover his part in the vendetta, had his wife sold as a prostitute. Her brother, also one of the ronin, discovered that knowledge of the vendetta had come into her hands and proposed to kill her with his own sword, arguing that with this proof of his loyalty Oishi would enroll him among the avengers. Another ronin killed his father-in-law. Another sent his sister to serve as maid and concubine to Lord Kira himself so that the ronin might have advice from inside the palace telling them when to attack; this act made it inevitable that she should commit suicide when vengeance was accomplished, for she had to clear herself by death of the fault of having appeared to be on the side of Lord Kira.

On a snowy night, December fourteenth, Kira held a *sake* party and the guards were drunk. The ronin raided the stronghold, overcame the guards, and went straight to Lord Kira's bedroom. He was not there, but his bed was still warm. The ronin knew he was hiding somewhere in the enclosure. At last they discovered a man crouched in an outhouse used for storing charcoal. One of the ronin drove his spear through a wall of the hut, but when he withdrew it there was no blood upon it. The spear had indeed pierced Kira, but as it was withdrawn he had wiped off the blood with his kimono sleeve. His trick was of no avail. The ronin forced him to come out. He claimed, however, that he was not Kira; he was only the chief steward. At this point one of the forty-seven remembered the wound their Lord Asano had given Kira in the Shogun's palace. By this scar they identified him and demanded his immediate seppuku. He refused—which proved of course that he was a coward. With the sword their own Lord Asano had used in his seppuku, they cut off his head, ceremonially washed it, and having finished their work, set off in procession to carry the doubly bloodied sword and the severed head to Asano's grave.

All Tokyo was filled with enthusiasm for the deed of the ronin. Their families and fathers-in-law who had doubted them rushed to embrace them and to do obeisance. Great lords urged hospitality upon them along the way. They proceeded to the grave and placed there not only the head and the sword but a written address to their lord which is still preserved.

> We have come this day to do homage here. . . . We could not have dared to present ourselves before you unless we

> had carried out the vengeance which you began. Every day that we waited seemed three autumns to us. . . . We have escorted my Lord Kira hither to your tomb. This sword you valued so greatly last year and entrusted to us we now bring back. We pray you to take it and strike the head of your enemy a second time and dispel your hatred forever. This is the respectful statement of forty-seven men.

Their giri was paid. They had still to pay their chu. Only in their death could the two coincide. They had broken the State rule against undeclared vendetta but they were not in revolt against chu. Whatever was demanded of them in the name of chu they must fulfill. The Shogunate ruled that the forty-seven should commit seppuku. As fifth-grade children's Japanese Readers say:

> Since they acted to avenge their lord, their unswerving giri had to be regarded as an example for ages eternal. . . . Therefore the Shogunate after deliberation commanded seppuku, a plan which killed two birds with one stone.

That is, in killing themselves with their own hands the ronin paid the supreme debt both to giri and to gimu.

This national epic of Japan varies somewhat in different versions. In the modern movie version, the bribery theme at the outset is changed to a sex theme: Lord Kira is discovered making advances to Asano's wife, and because of his attraction to her he humiliates Asano by giving him false instructions. Bribery is thus eliminated. But all the obligations of giri are told in blood-curdling detail. 'For giri they forsook their wives, parted with their children and lost (killed) their parents.'

The theme of the conflict between gimu and giri is the basis of many other tales and movies. One of the best historical movies is placed in the time of the third Tokugawa Shogun. This Shogun had been named to his office when he was a young and untried man, and his courtiers were divided among themselves about the succession, some of them supporting a near relative of the same age. One of the defeated daimyo nursed this 'insult' in his bosom in spite of the capable administration of the Third Shogun. He bided his time. At last the Shogun and his entourage notified him that they were to make a tour of certain fiefs. It was incumbent upon this daimyo to entertain the party and he seized the opportunity to even all scores and fulfill his giri to his name. His home was already a stronghold and he prepared it for the coming event so that all egress could be blocked and the stronghold sealed. Then he provided means by which the walls and ceilings could be knocked down on the heads of the Shogun and his party. His plot was staged in the grand style. His entertainment was meticulous. For the enjoyment of the Shogun he had one of his samurai dance before him and this samurai was under instructions to plunge his sword into the Shogun at the climax of the dance. In giri to his daimyo the samurai could in no wise refuse his lord's order. His chu, however, forbade him to lift his hand against the Shogun. The dance on the screen fully portrays the conflict. He must and he must not. He almost brings himself to strike the blow but he cannot. In spite of giri, chu is too strong. The dance degenerates and the Shogun's party becomes suspicious. They rise from their seats just as the desperate daimyo orders the demolition of the house. There is danger that the Shogun, though he has escaped the dancer's sword, will be killed in the ruins of the stronghold. At this point the sword dancer comes forward and guides the Shogun's party through underground passages so that they escape safely into the open. Chu has conquered giri. The Shogun's spokesman in gratitude urges their guide to go with them in honor to Tokyo. The guide, however, looks back into the falling house. 'It is impossible,' he says. 'I stay. It is my gimu and my giri.' He turns from them and dies in the ruins. 'In his death he satisfied both chu and giri. In death they coincided.'

The tales of olden times do not give central place to the conflict between obligations and 'human feelings.' In recent years it has become a principal theme. Modern novels tell of love and human kindness which have to be discarded because of gimu or giri, and this theme is played up instead of being minimized. Like their war movies, which readily seem to Westerners to be good pacifist propaganda, these novels often seem to us a plea for greater latitude to live according to the dictates of one's own heart. They are certainly testimony to this impulse. But over and over Japanese who discuss the plot of novels or movies see a different meaning. The hero we sympathize with because he is in love or cherishes some personal ambition, they condemn as weak because he has allowed these feelings to come between him and his gimu or his giri. Westerners are likely to feel it is a sign of strength to rebel against conventions and seize happiness in spite of obstacles. But the strong, according to Japanese verdict, are those who disregard personal happiness and fulfill their obligations. Strength of character, they think, is shown in conforming not in rebelling. The plots of their novels and movies, consequently, often have quite a different meaning in Japan from that which we give to them when we see them through Western eyes.

Japanese make the same kind of appraisal when they pass judgment on their own lives or on those of people they have known. They judge that a man is weak if he pays attention to his personal desires when they conflict with the code of obligations. All kinds of situations are judged in this way, but the one which is most opposite to Western ethics concerns a man's attitude toward his wife. His wife is only tangential to 'the circle of ko' but his parents are central. Therefore his duty is clear. A man of strong moral character obeys ko and accepts his mother's decision to divorce his wife. It only makes the man 'stronger' if he loves his wife and if she has borne him a child. In the Japanese phrase, 'ko may make you put your wife and children in the category of strangers.' Then your treatment of them belongs at best in 'the circle of jin.' At worst they become people who have no claims upon you. Even when a marriage is happy, a wife is not centrally placed in the circles of obligations. A man should therefore not elevate his relation to her so that it seems to be on a level with his feelings toward his parents or his country. It was a popular scandal in the nineteen-thirties when a prominent liberal spoke publicly about how happy he was in returning to Japan, and mentioned reunion with his wife as one of the reasons for his pleasure. He should have spoken of his parents, of Fujiyama, of his dedication to the national mission of Japan. His wife did not belong on this level.

The Japanese themselves have shown in the modern era that they were not satisfied to leave their code of morals so heavy with emphasis on keeping different levels separate and different 'circles' distinct. A great part of Japanese indoctrination has been devoted to making chu supreme. Just as statesmen simplified the hierarchy by putting the Emperor at the apex and eliminating the Shogun and the feudal lords, so in the moral realm they worked to simplify the system of obligations by bringing all lower virtues under the category of chu. By this means they sought not only to unify the country under 'Emperor worship,' but to lessen the atomism of Japanese morals. They sought to teach that in fulfilling chu one fulfilled all other duties. They sought to make it, not one circle on a chart, but the keystone of a moral arch.

The best and most authoritative statement of this program is the Imperial Rescript to Soldiers and Sailors given by the Emperor Meiji in 1882. This Rescript and the one on Education are the true Holy Writ of Japan. Neither of the Japanese religions makes a place for holy books. Shinto has none and the cults of Japanese Buddhism either make a dogma out of disillusion with textual scriptures or substitute for them the repetition of phrases like 'Glory to Amida' or 'Glory to the Lotus of the Book.' The Meiji Rescripts of admonition, however, are true Holy Writ. They are read as sacred rituals before hushed audiences formally bowed in reverence. They are treated as *torah*, taken from a shrine for reading and returned with obeisance before the audience is dismissed. Men appointed to read them have killed themselves because they misread a sentence. The Rescript to Soldiers and Sailors was primarily for men in the service. They were the ones who learned it verbatim and meditated upon it quietly for ten minutes each morning. It was read to them ritually on important national holidays, when the new conscripts entered the barracks, when those left who had finished their period of training and on similar occasions. It was also taught to all boys in middle schools and continuation classes.

The Rescript for Soldiers and Sailors is a document of several pages. It is carefully arranged under headings and is clear and specific. Nevertheless, it is a strange puzzle to a Westerner. Its precepts seem to him contradictory. Goodness and virtue are held up as true goals and described in ways Westerners can appreciate. And then the Rescript warns its hearers not to be like heroes of old who died in dishonor because, 'losing sight of the true path of public duty, *they kept faith in private relations.*' This is the official translation and though it is not literal it fairly represents the words of the original. 'You should, then,' the Rescript continues, 'take serious warning by these examples' of old-time heroes.

The 'warning' conveyed is not intelligible without a knowledge of the Japanese map of obligations. The whole Rescript shows an official attempt to minimize giri and to elevate chu. Not once in the whole text does the word giri appear in the sense in which it is a household word in Japan. Instead of naming giri, it emphasizes that there is a Higher Law, which is chu, and a Lower Law which is 'keeping faith in private relations.' The Higher Law, the Rescript is at pains to prove, is sufficient to validate all the virtues. 'Righteousness,' it says, 'is the fulfillment of gimu.' A soldier filled with chu inevitably has 'true valor' which means 'in daily intercourse to set gentleness first and to aim to win the love and esteem of others.' Such precepts, if followed, the Rescript argues by implication, will suffice without invoking giri. Obligations other than gimu are Lesser Law and a man should not acknowledge them without the most careful consideration.

> If you wish . . . to keep your word (in private relations) and (also) to fulfill your gimu . . . you must carefully consider at the outset whether you can accomplish it or not. If you . . . tie yourself to unwise obligations, you may find yourself in a position where you can neither go forwards nor backwards. If you are convinced that you cannot possibly keep your word and maintain righteousness (which the Rescript has just defined as the fulfillment of gimu), you had better abandon your (private) engagement at once. Ever since the ancient times there have been repeated instances of great men and heroes who, overwhelmed by misfortune, have perished and left a tarnished name to posterity, simply because in their effort to be faithful in small matters they failed to discern right and wrong with reference to fundamental principles, or because, losing sight of the true path of public duty, they kept faith in private relations.

All this instruction about the superiority of chu to giri is written, as we have said, without mentioning giri, but every Japanese knows the phrase, 'I could not do righteousness (gi) because of giri,' and the Rescript paraphrases it in the words, 'If you are convinced you cannot keep your word (your personal obligations) and fulfill righteousness . . .' With Imperial authority it says that in such a situation a man should abandon giri, remembering that it is a Lesser Law. The Higher Law, if he obeys its precepts, will still keep him virtuous.

This Holy Writ exalting chu is a basic document in Japan. It is difficult to say, however, whether its oblique detraction of giri weakened the popular hold of this obligation. Japanese frequently quote other parts of the Rescript—'Righteousness is the fulfillment of gimu,' 'If only the heart be sincere, anything can be accomplished'—to explain and justify their own and others' acts. But, though they would often be appropriate, the admonitions against keeping faith in private relations seem seldom to come to their lips. Giri remains today a virtue with great authority and to say of a man that 'he does not know giri' is one of the most drastic condemnations in Japan.

Japanese ethics are not easily simplified by introducing a Higher Law. As they have so often boasted, the Japanese do not have at hand a generalized virtue to use as a touchstone of good behavior. In most cultures individuals respect themselves in proportion as they attain some virtue like good will or good husbandry or success in their enterprises. They set up as a goal some life objective like happiness or power over others or liberty or social mobility. The Japanese follow more particularistic codes. Even when they talk about Higher Law, *tai setsu*, whether in feudal times or in the Rescript to Soldiers and Sailors, it is only in the sense that obligations to someone high in the hierarchy should overrule obligations to someone who is lower down. They are still particularistic. To them Higher Law is not, as it has generally been to Westerners, a loyalty to loyalty, as against a loyalty to a particular person or a particular cause.

When modern Japanese have attempted to make some one moral virtue supreme over all the 'circles,' they have usually selected 'sincerity.' Count Okuma, in discussing Japanese ethics, said that sincerity (*makoto*) 'is the precept of all precepts; the foundation of moral teachings can be implied in that one word. Our ancient vocabulary is void of ethical terms except for one solitary word, makoto.'* Modern novelists, too, who in the early years of this century celebrated the new Western individualism, became dissatisfied with the Occidental formulas and tried to celebrate sincerity (usually *magokoro*) as the only true 'doctrine.'

This moral stress on sincerity has the backing of the Rescript for Soldiers and Sailors itself. The Rescript begins with an historical prologue, a Japanese equivalent to American prologues which name Washington, Jefferson, and the Founding Fathers. In Japan this section reaches a climax by invoking *on* and chu:

> We (the Emperor) are the head and you are the body. We depend on you as our arms and legs. Whether we shall be able to protect our country, and repay the *on* of our ancestors, depends upon your fulfilling your obligations.

Then follow the precepts: (1) The supreme virtue is to fulfill the obligations of chu. A soldier or sailor, however skilled, in whom chu is not strong, is a mere puppet; a body of soldiers wanting in chu is in crisis a mere rabble. 'Therefore, neither be led astray by current opinions *nor meddle in politics*, but with singleness do chu, remembering that *gi* (righteousness) is weightier than a mountain while death is lighter than a feather.' (2) The second injunction is to observe outward appearance and behavior, i.e., in reference to rank in

* Count Shinenobu Okuma, *Fifty Years of New Japan*. English version edited by Marcus B. Huish, London, 1909, II:37.

the Army. 'Regard the orders of superiors as issuing directly from Us' and treat inferiors with consideration. (3) The third is valor. True valor is contrasted with 'burn-blood barbaric acts' and is defined as 'never despising an inferior or fearing a superior. Those who thus appreciate true valor should in their daily intercourse set gentleness first and aim to win the love and esteem of others.' (4) The fourth injunction is the warning against 'keeping faith in private relations,' and (5) the fifth is an admonition to be frugal. 'If you do not make simplicity your aim, you will become effeminate and frivolous and acquire fondness for luxurious and extravagant ways; you will finally grow selfish and sordid and sink to the last degree of baseness, so that neither loyalty nor valour will avail to save you from the contempt of the world.... Being harassed with anxiety lest it should break out, We hereby reiterate Our warning.'

The final paragraph of the Rescript calls these five precepts 'the Grand Way of Heaven and Earth and the universal law of humanity.' They are 'the soul of Our soldiers and sailors.' And, in turn, 'the soul' of these five precepts 'is sincerity. If the heart be not sincere, words and deeds, however good, are all mere outward show and all avail nothing. If only the heart be sincere, anything can be accomplished.' The five precepts will thus be 'easy to observe and practice.' It is characteristically Japanese that sincerity should be tacked on at the end after all the virtues and obligations have been spelled out. The Japanese do not, as the Chinese do, base all virtues on the promptings of the benevolent heart; they first set up the code of duties and then add, at the end, the requirement that one carry these out with all one's heart and with all one's soul and with all one's strength and with all one's mind.

Sincerity has the same kind of meaning in the teachings of the great Buddhist sect of Zen. In Suzuki's great compendium of Zen he gives a dialogue between the pupil and the Master:

> *Monk:* I understand that when a lion seizes upon his opponent, whether it is a hare or an elephant, he makes an exhaustive use of his power; pray tell me what is this power?
>
> *Master:* The spirit of sincerity (literally, the power of not-deceiving).
>
> Sincerity, that is, not-deceiving, means 'putting forth one's whole being,' technically known as 'the whole being in action' . . . in which nothing is kept in reserve, nothing is expressed under disguise, nothing goes into waste. When a person lives like this, he is said to be a golden-haired lion; he is the symbol of virility, sincerity, whole-heartedness; he is divinely human.

Special Japanese meanings of this word 'sincerity' have already been referred to in passing. *Makoto* does not mean what sincerity does in English usage. It means both far less and far more. Westerners have always been quick to see that it means far less than it does in their language, and they have often said that when a Japanese says anyone is insincere, he means only that the other person doesn't agree with him. There is a certain truth in this, for calling a man 'sincere' in Japan has no reference to whether he is acting 'genuinely' according to the love or hate, determination or amazement which is uppermost in his soul. The kind of approval Americans express by saying, 'He was sincerely glad to see me,' 'He was sincerely pleased,' is alien in Japan. They have a whole series of proverbial expressions casting scorn on such a 'sincerity.' They say derisively, 'Behold the frog who when he opens his mouth displays his whole inside'; 'Like a pomegranate who when it gapes its mouth shows all that's in its heart'; it is a shame to any man to 'blurt out his feelings'; it 'exposes' him. These associations with 'sincerity' which are so important in the United States have no place in the meaning of the word 'sincerity' in Japan. When the Japanese boy accused the American missionary of insincerity, it never occurred to him to consider whether the American 'genuinely' felt amazement at the poor lad's plan to go to America without even a shoestring. When Japanese statesmen in the last decade accused the United States and England of insincerity—as they constantly did—they did not even think whether the Western nations were acting in ways they did not in reality feel. They were not even accusing them of being hypocrites—which would have been a minor accusation. Similarly when the Rescript for Soldiers and Sailors says 'sincerity is the soul of these precepts,' it does not mean that the virtue that will put all other virtues into effect is a genuineness in the soul which will make a man act and speak in conformity to his own inner promptings. It certainly does not mean that he is enjoined to be genuine, no matter how much his convictions may differ from others'

Nevertheless makoto has its positive meanings in Japan, and since the Japanese so strongly stress the ethical rôle of this concept it is urgently necessary for Westerners to grasp the sense in which they use it. The basic Japanese sense of makoto is well illustrated in the *Tale of the Forty-Seven Ronin*. 'Sincerity' in that story is a plus sign added on to giri. 'Giri plus makoto' is contrasted with 'merely giri,' and means 'giri as an example for ages eternal.' In the contemporary Japanese phrase, 'makoto is what makes it stick.' The 'it' in this phrase refers, according to context, to any precept of the Japanese code or any attitude stipulated in the Japanese Spirit.

Usage in the Japanese Relocation Camps during the war was exactly parallel to that in *The Forty-Seven Ronin*, and it shows clearly how far the logic is extended and how opposite to American usage the meaning can become. The stock accusation of the pro-Japan Issei (American immigrants born in Japan) against the pro-United States Nisei (second-generation immigrants) was that they lacked makoto. What the Issei were saying was that these Nisei did not have that quality of the soul which made the Japanese Spirit—as officially defined in Japan during the war—'stick.' The Issei did not mean at all that their children's pro-Americanism was hypocritical. Far from it, for their accusations of insincerity were only the more convinced when the Nisei volunteered for the United States Army and it was quite apparent to anybody that their support of their adopted country was prompted by a genuine enthusiasm.

A basic meaning of 'sincerity' as the Japanese use it, is that it is the zeal to follow the 'road' mapped out by the Japanese code and the Japanese Spirit. Whatever special meanings *makoto* has in particular contexts can always be read off as praise of some agreed-on aspects of Japanese

Spirit and well-accepted guide posts on the map of virtues. Once one has accepted the fact that 'sincerity' does not have the American meaning it is a most useful word to note in all Japanese texts. For it almost unfailingly identifies those positive virtues the Japanese actually stress. Makoto is constantly used to praise a person who is not self-seeking. This is a reflection of the great condemnation Japanese ethics pronounces on profit-making. Profit—when it is not a natural consequence of hierarchy—is judged to be the result of exploitation, and the go-between who has turned aside to make a profit out of his job becomes the hated moneylender. He is always declared to 'lack sincerity.' Makoto, too, is constantly used as a term of praise for the man who is free of passion, and this mirrors Japanese ideas of self-discipline. A Japanese worthy of being called sincere, too, never verges on the danger of insulting a person he does not mean to provoke to aggression, and this mirrors their dogma that a man is responsible for the marginal consequences of his acts as well as for the act itself. Finally, only one who is makoto can 'lead his people,' put his skills to effective use and be free of psychic conflict. These three meanings, and a host of others, state quite simply the homogeneity of Japanese ethics; they reflect the fact that a man can be effective and unconflicted in Japan only when he is carrying out the code.

Since these are the meanings of Japanese 'sincerity,' this virtue, in spite of the Rescript and of Count Okuma, does not simplify Japanese ethics. It does not put a 'foundation' under their morality, nor give it a 'soul.' It is an exponent which, properly placed after any number, raises it to a higher power. A^2 will square 9 or 159 or *b* or *x*, quite indifferently. And likewise *makoto* raises to a higher power any article in the Japanese code. It is not, as it were, a separate virtue but the enthusiasm of the zealot for his creed.

Whatever the Japanese have tried to do to their code, it remains atomistic, and the principle of virtue remains that of balancing one play, in itself good, against another play which is also in itself good. It is as if they had set up their ethics like a bridge game. The good player is the one who accepts the rules and plays within them. He distinguishes himself from the bad player because of the fact that he is disciplined in his calculations and can follow other players' leads with full knowledge of what they mean under the rules of the game. He plays, as we say, according to Hoyle, and there are endless minutiae of which he must take account at every move. Contingencies that may come up are covered in the rules of the game and the score is agreed upon in advance. Good intentions, in the American sense, become irrelevancies.

In any language the contexts in which people speak of losing or gaining self-respect throw a flood of light on their view of life. In Japan 'respecting yourself' is always to show yourself the careful player. It does not mean, as it does in English usage, consciously conforming to a worthy standard of conduct—not truckling to another, not lying, not giving false testimony. In Japan self-respect (*jicho*) is literally 'a self that is weighty,' and its opposite is 'a self that is light and floating.' When a man says 'You must respect yourself,' it means, 'You must be shrewd in estimating all the factors involved in the situation and do nothing that will arouse criticism or lessen your chances of success.' 'Respecting yourself' often implies exactly the opposite behavior from that which it means in the United States. An employee says, 'I must respect myself (jicho),' and it means, not that he must stand on his rights, but that he must say nothing to his employers that will get him into trouble. 'You must respect yourself' had this same meaning, too, in political usage. It meant that a 'person of weight' could not respect himself if he indulged in anything so rash as 'dangerous thoughts.' It had no implication, as it would in the United States, that even if thoughts are dangerous a man's self-respect requires that he think according to his own lights and his own conscience.

'You must respect yourself' is constantly on parents' lips in admonishing their adolescent children, and it refers to observing proprieties and living up to other people's expectation. A girl is thus admonished to sit without moving, her legs properly placed, and a boy to train himself and learn to watch for cues from others 'because now is the time that will decide your future.' When a parent says to them, 'You did not behave as a self-respecting person should,' it means that they are accused of an impropriety rather than of lack of courage to stand up for the right as they saw it.

A farmer who cannot meet his debt to the moneylender says of himself 'I should have had self-respect,' but that does not mean that he accuses himself of laziness or of fawning upon his creditor. It means that he should have foreseen the emergency and been more circumspect. A man of standing in the community says, 'My self-respect requires this,' and he does not mean that he must live up to certain principles of truthfulness and probity but that he must manipulate the affair with full consideration for the position of his family; he must throw the whole weight of his status into the matter.

A business executive who says of his firm 'We must show self-respect' means that prudence and watchfulness must be redoubled. A man discussing a necessity to avenge himself speaks of 'revenging with self-respect,' and this has no reference to heaping coals of fire upon the head of his enemy or to any moral rules he intends to follow; it is equivalent to saying 'I shall exact a perfect revenge,' i.e., one meticulously planned and taking into account every factor in the situation. Strongest phrase of all in Japanese is 'to double self-respect with self-respect' and that means to be circumspect to the *n*th degree. It means never to jump to a hasty conclusion. It means to calculate ways and means so that no more and no less effort is used than is strictly necessary to attain the goal.

All these meanings of self-respect fit the Japanese view of life as a world in which you move with great care 'according to Hoyle.' This way of defining self-respect does not allow a man to claim an alibi for his failure on the ground of good intentions. Each move has its consequences and one should not act without estimating them. It is quite proper to be generous, but you must foresee that the recipient of your favors will feel that he has been made 'to wear an *on*.' You must be wary. It is quite allowable to criticize another, but you must do so only if you intend to take on all the consequences of his resentment. A sneer such as the American missionary was accused of by the young artist is out of the question precisely because the missionary's intentions were good; he did not take account of the full meaning of his move on the chessboard. It was in the Japanese view completely undisciplined.

The strong identification of circumspection with self-respect includes, therefore, watchfulness of all the cues one observes in other people's acts, and a strong sense that other people are sitting in judgment. 'One cultivates self-respect (one must jicho),' they say, 'because of society.' 'If there were no society one would not need to respect oneself (cultivate jicho).' These are extreme statements of an external sanction for self-respect. They are statements which take no account of internal sanctions for proper behavior. Like the popular sayings of many nations, they exaggerate the case, for Japanese sometimes react as strongly as any Puritan to a private accumulation of guilt. But their extreme statements nevertheless point out correctly where the emphasis falls in Japan. It falls on the importance of shame rather than on the importance of guilt.

In anthropological studies of different cultures the distinction between those which rely heavily on shame and those that rely heavily on guilt is an important one. A society that inculcates absolute standards of morality and relies on men's developing a conscience is a guilt culture by definition, but a man in such a society may, as in the United States, suffer in addition from shame when he accuses himself of gaucheries which are in no way sins. He may be exceedingly chagrined about not dressing appropriately for the occasion or about a slip of the tongue. In a culture where shame is a major sanction, people are chagrined about acts which we expect people to feel guilty about. This chagrin can be very intense and it cannot be relieved, as guilt can be, by confession and atonement. A man who has sinned can get relief by unburdening himself. This device of confession is used in our secular therapy and by many religious groups which have otherwise little in common. We know it brings relief. Where shame is the major sanction, a man does not experience relief when he makes his fault public even to a confessor. So long as his bad behavior does not 'get out into the world' he need not be troubled and confession appears to him merely a way of courting trouble. Shame cultures therefore do not provide for confessions, even to the gods. They have ceremonies for good luck rather than for expiation.

True shame cultures rely on external sanctions for good behavior, not, as true guilt cultures do, on an internalized conviction of sin. Shame is a reaction to other people's criticism. A man is shamed either by being openly ridiculed and rejected or by fantasying to himself that he has been made ridiculous. In either case it is a potent sanction. But it requires an audience or at least a man's fantasy of an audience. Guilt does not. In a nation where honor means living up to one's own picture of oneself, a man may suffer from guilt though no man knows of his misdeed and a man's feeling of guilt may actually be relieved by confessing his sin.

The early Puritans who settled in the United States tried to base their whole morality on guilt and all psychiatrists know what trouble contemporary Americans have with their consciences. But shame is an increasingly heavy burden in the United States and guilt is less extremely felt than in earlier generations. In the United States this is interpreted as a relaxation of morals. There is much truth in this, but that is because we do not expect shame to do the heavy work of morality. We do not harness the acute personal chagrin which accompanies shame to our fundamental system of morality.

The Japanese do. A failure to follow their explicit sign-posts of good behavior, a failure to balance obligations or to foresee contingencies is a shame (*haji*). Shame, they say, is the root of virtue. A man who is sensitive to it will carry out all the rules of good behavior. 'A man who knows shame' is sometimes translated 'virtuous man,' sometimes 'man of honor.' Shame has the same place of authority in Japanese ethics that 'a clear conscience,' 'being right with God,' and the avoidance of sin have in Western ethics. Logically enough, therefore, a man will not be punished in the afterlife. The Japanese—except for priests who know the Indian sutras—are quite unacquainted with the idea of reincarnation dependent upon one's merit in this life, and —except for some well-instructed Christian converts—they do not recognize post-death reward and punishment or a heaven and a hell.

The primacy of shame in Japanese life means, as it does in any tribe or nation where shame is deeply felt, that any man watches the judgment of the public upon his deeds. He need only fantasy what their verdict will be, but he orients himself toward the verdict of others. When everybody is playing the game by the same rules and mutually supporting each other, the Japanese can be light-hearted and easy. They can play the game with fanaticism when they feel it is one which carries out the 'mission' of Japan. They are most vulnerable when they attempt to export their virtues into foreign lands where their own formal signposts of good behavior do not hold. They failed in their 'good will' mission to Greater East Asia, and the resentment many of them felt at the attitudes of Chinese and Filipinos toward them was genuine enough.

Individual Japanese, too, who have come to the United States for study or business and have not been motivated by nationalistic sentiments have often felt deeply the 'failure' of their careful education when they tried to live in a less rigidly charted world. Their virtues, they felt, did not export well. The point they try to make is not the universal one that it is hard for any man to change cultures. They try to say something more and they sometimes contrast the difficulties of their own adjustment to American life with the lesser difficulties of Chinese or Siamese they have known. The specific Japanese problem, as they see it, is that they have been brought up to trust in a security which depends on others' recognition of the nuances of their observance of a code. When foreigners are oblivious of all these proprieties, the Japanese are at a loss. They cast about to find similar meticulous proprieties according to which Westerners live and when they do not find them, some speak of the anger they feel and some of how frightened they are.

No one has described these experiences in a less exacting culture better than Miss Mishima in her autobiography, *My Narrow Isle.** She had sought eagerly to come to an American college and she had fought down her conservative family's unwillingness to accept the *on* of an American

* Mishima, Sumie Seo, *My Narrow Isle*, 1941, p. 107.

fellowship. She went to Wellesley. The teachers and the girls, she says, were wonderfully kind, but that made it, so she felt, all the more difficult. 'My pride in perfect manneredness, a universal characteristic of the Japanese, was bitterly wounded. I was angry at myself for not knowing how to behave properly here and also at the surroundings which seemed to mock at my past training. Except for this vague but deep-rooted feeling of anger there was no emotion left in me.' She felt herself 'a being fallen from some other planet with senses and feelings that have no use in this other world. My Japanese training, requiring every physical movement to be elegant and every word uttered to be according to etiquette, made me extremely sensitive and self-conscious in this environment, where I was completely blind, socially speaking.' It was two or three years before she relaxed and began to accept the kindness offered her. Americans, she decided, lived with what she calls 'refined familiarity.' But 'familiarity had been killed in me as sauciness when I was three.'

Miss Mishima contrasts the Japanese girls she knew in America with the Chinese girls and her comments show how differently the United States affected them. The Chinese girls had 'self-composure and sociableness quite absent in most Japanese girls. These upper-class Chinese girls seemed to me the most urbane creatures on earth, every one of them having a graciousness nearing regal dignity and looking as if they were the true mistresses of the world. Their fearlessness and superb self-composure, not at all disturbed even in this great civilization of machinery and speed, made a great contrast with the timidity and oversensitiveness of us Japanese girls, showing some fundamental difference in social background.'

Miss Mishima, like many other Japanese, felt as if she were an expert tennis player entered in a croquet tournament. Her own expertness just didn't count. She felt that what she had learned did not carry over into the new environment. The discipline to which she had submitted was useless. Americans got along without it.

Once Japanese have accepted, to however small a degree, the less codified rules that govern behavior in the United States they find it difficult to imagine their being able to manage again the restrictions of their old life in Japan. Sometimes they refer to it as a lost paradise, sometimes as a 'harness,' sometimes as a 'prison,' sometimes as a 'little pot' that holds a dwarfed tree. As long as the roots of the miniature pine were kept to the confines of the flower pot, the result was a work of art that graced a charming garden. But once planted out in open soil, the dwarfed pine could never be put back again. They feel that they themselves are no longer possible ornaments in that Japanese garden. They could not again meet the requirements. They have experienced in its most acute form the Japanese dilemma of virtue.

II

Self-Discipline

THE SELF-DISCIPLINES of one culture are always likely to seem irrelevancies to observers from another country. The disciplinary techniques themselves are clear enough, but why go to all the trouble? Why voluntarily hang yourself from hooks, or concentrate on your navel, or never spend your capital? Why concentrate on one of these austerities and demand no control at all over some impulses which to the outsider are truly important and in need of training? When the observer belongs to a country which does not teach technical methods of self-discipline and is set down in the midst of a people who place great reliance upon them, the possibility of misunderstanding is at its height.

In the United States technical and traditional methods of self-discipline are relatively undeveloped. The American assumption is that a man, having sized up what is possible in his personal life, will discipline himself, if that is necessary, to attain a chosen goal. Whether he does or not, depends on his ambition, or his conscience, or his 'instinct of workmanship,' as Veblen called it. He may accept a Stoic regime in order to play on a football team, or give up all relaxations to train himself as a musician, or to make a success of his business. He may eschew evil and frivolity because of his conscience. But in the United States self-discipline itself, as a technical training, is not a thing to learn like arithmetic quite apart from its application in a particular instance. Such techniques, when they do occur in the United States, are taught by certain European cult-leaders or by Swamis who teach inventions made in India. Even the religious self-disciplines of meditation and prayer, as they were taught and practiced by Saint Theresa or Saint John of the Cross, have barely survived in the United States.

The Japanese assumption, however, is that a boy taking his middle-school examinations, or a man playing in a fencing match, or a person merely living the life of an aristocrat, needs a self-training quite apart from learning the specific things that will be required of him when he is tested. No matter what facts he has crammed for his examination, no matter how expert his sword thrusts, no matter how meticulous his punctilio, he needs to lay aside his books and his sword and his public appearances and undergo a special kind of training. Not all Japanese submit to esoteric training, of course, but, even for those who do not, the phraseology and the practice of self-discipline have a recognized place in life. Japanese of all classes judge themselves and others in terms of a whole set of concepts which depend upon their notion of generalized technical self-control and self-governance.

Their concepts of self-discipline can be schematically divided into those which give competence and those which give something more. This something more I shall call expertness. The two are divided in Japan and aim at accomplishing a different result in the human psyche and have a different rationale and are recognized by different signs. Many instances of the first type, self-disciplinary competence, have already been described. The Army officer who said of his men who had been engaged in peacetime maneuvers for sixty hours with only ten-minute opportunities for sleep, that 'they know how to sleep; they need training in how to stay awake,' was, in spite of what seem to us extreme demands, aiming only at competent behavior. He was stating a well-accepted principle of Japanese psychic economy that the will should be supreme over the almost infinitely teachable body and that the body itself does not have laws of well-being which a man ignores at his own cost. The whole Japanese theory of 'human feelings' rests on this assumption. When it is a matter of the really serious affairs of life, the demands of the body, no matter how essential to health, no matter how approved and cultivated as things apart, should be drastically subordinated. No matter at what price of self-discipline, a man should manifest the Japanese Spirit.

It does violence, however, to Japanese assumptions to phrase their position in this way. For 'at the price of whatever self-discipline' means in ordinary American usage almost the same thing as 'at the price of whatever self-sacrifice.' Often too it means 'at the price of whatever personal frustration.' The American theory of discipline—whether imposed from the outside or introjected as a censoring conscience—is that from childhood men and women have to be socialized by discipline, either freely accepted or imposed by authority. This is a frustration. The individual resents this curtailment of his wishes. He has to sacrifice, and inevitable aggressive emotions are awakened within him. This view is not only that of many professional psychologists in America. It is also the philosophy within which each generation is brought up by parents in the home, and the psychologists' analysis has therefore a great deal of truth in our own society. A child 'has to' be put to bed at a certain hour, and he learns from his parents' attitude that going to bed is a frustration. In countless homes he shows his resentment in a nightly battle royal. He is already a young indoctrinated American who regards sleeping as something a person 'has to' do and he kicks against the pricks. His mother rules, too, that there are certain things he 'has to' eat. It may be oatmeal or spinach or bread or orange juice, but the American child learns to raise a protest against foods he 'has to' eat. Food that is 'good for' him he concludes is not food that tastes good. This is an American convention that is foreign in Japan, as it is also in some Western nations like Greece. In the United States, becoming adult means emancipation from food frustrations. A grown-up person can eat the food that tastes good instead of the food that is good for him.

These ideas about sleep and food, however, are small in comparison with the whole Occidental concept of self-sacrifice. It is standard Western doctrine that parents make great sacrifices for their children, wives sacrifice their careers for their husbands, husbands sacrifice their freedom to become breadwinners. It is hard for Americans to conceive that in some societies men and women do not recognize the necessity of self-sacrifice. It is nevertheless true. In such societies people say that parents naturally find their children delightful, that women prefer marriage to any other course, and that a man earning his family's support is pursuing his favorite occupation as a hunter or a gardener. Why talk of self-sacrifice? When society stresses these interpretations and allows people to live according to them, the notion of self-sacrifice may hardly be recognized.

In other cultures all those things a person does for other people at such 'sacrifice' in the United States are considered as reciprocal exchanges. They are either investments which will later be repaid or they are returns for value already received. In such countries even the relations between father and son may be treated in this way, and what the father does for the son during the boy's early life, the son will do for the father during the old man's later life and after his death. Every business relation too is a folk contract, which, while it often ensures equivalence in kind, just as commonly binds one party to protect and the other to serve. If the benefits on both sides are regarded as advantages, neither party regards his duties as a sacrifice.

The sanction behind services to others in Japan is of course reciprocity, both in kind and in hierarchal exchange of complementary responsibilities. The moral position of self-sacrifice is therefore very different from that in the United States. The Japanese have always objected specifically to the teachings of Christian missionaries about sacrifice. They argue that a good man should not think of what he does for others as frustrating to himself. 'When we do the things you call self-sacrifice,' a Japanese said to me, 'it is because we wish to give or because it is good to give. We are not sorry for ourselves. No matter how many things we actually give up for others, we do not think that this giving elevates us spiritually or that we should be "rewarded" for it.' A people who have organized their lives around such elaborate reciprocal obligations as the Japanese naturally find self-sacrifice irrelevant. They push themselves to the limit to fulfil extreme obligations, but the traditional sanction of reciprocity prevents them from feeling the self-pity and self-righteousness that arises so easily in more individualistic and competitive countries.

Americans, in order to understand ordinary self-disciplinary practices in Japan, therefore, have to do a kind of surgical operation on our idea of 'self-discipline.' We have to cut away the accretions of 'self-sacrifice' and 'frustration' that have clustered around the concept in our culture. In Japan one disciplines oneself to be a good player, and the Japanese attitude is that one undergoes the training with no more consciousness of sacrifice than a man who plays bridge. Of course the training is strict, but that is inherent in the nature of things. The young child is born happy but without the capacity to 'savor life.' Only through mental training (or self-discipline; *shuyo*) can a man or woman gain the power to live fully and to 'get the taste' of life. The phrase is usually translated 'only so can he enjoy life.' Self-discipline 'builds up the belly (the seat of control)'; it enlarges life.

'Competent' self-discipline in Japan has this rationale that it improves a man's conduct of his own life. Any impatience he may feel while he is new in the training will pass, they say, for eventually he will enjoy it—or give it up. An apprentice tends properly to his business, a boy learns *judo* (jujitsu), a young wife adjusts to the demands of her mother-in-law; it is quite understood that in the first stages of training, the man or woman unused to the new requirements may wish to be free of this shuyo. Their fathers may talk to them and say, 'What do you wish? Some training is necessary to savor life. If you give this up and do not train yourself at all, you will be unhappy as a natural consequence. And if these natural consequences should occur, I should not be inclined to protect you against public opinion.' Shuyo, in the phrase they use so often, polishes away 'the rust of the body.' It makes a man a bright sharp sword, which is, of course, what he desires to be.

All this stress on how self-discipline leads to one's own advantage does not mean that the extreme acts the Japanese code often requires are not truly serious frustrations, and that such frustrations do not lead to aggressive impulses. This distinction is one which Americans understand in games and sports. The bridge champion does not complain of the self-sacrifice that has been required of him to learn to play well; he does not label as 'frustrations' the hours he has had to put in in order to become an expert. Nevertheless, physicians say that in some cases the great attention necessary when a man is playing either for high stakes or for a championship, is not unrelated to stomach ulcers and excessive bodily tensions. The same thing happens to people in Japan. But the sanction of reciprocity, and the Japanese conviction that self-discipline is to one's own advantage, make many acts seem easy to them which seem insupportable to Americans. They pay much closer attention to behaving competently and they allow themselves fewer alibis than Americans. They do not so often project their dissatisfactions with life upon scapegoats, and they do not so often indulge in self-pity because they have somehow or other not got what Americans call average happiness. They have been trained to pay much closer attention to the 'rust of the body' than is common among Americans.

Beyond and above 'competent' self-discipline, there is also the plane of 'expertness.' Japanese techniques of this latter sort have not been made very intelligible to Western readers by Japanese authors who have written about them, and Occidental scholars who have made a specialty of this subject have often been very cavalier about them. Sometimes they have called them 'eccentricities.' One French scholar writes that they are all 'in defiance of common sense,' and that the greatest of all disciplinary sects, the Zen cult, is 'a tissue of solemn nonsense.' The purposes their techniques are intended to accomplish, however, are not impenetrable, and the whole subject throws a considerable light on Japanese psychic economy.

A long series of Japanese words name the state of mind the expert in self-discipline is supposed to achieve. Some of these terms are used for actors, some for religious devotees, some for fencers, some for public speakers, some for painters, some for masters of the tea ceremony. They all have the same general meaning, and I shall use only the word *muga*, which is the word used in the flourishing upper-class cult of Zen Buddhism. The description of this state of expertness is that it denotes those experiences, whether secular or religious, when 'there is no break, not even the thickness of a hair' between a man's will and his act. A discharge of electricity passes directly from the positive to the negative pole. In people who have not attained expertness, there is, as it were, a non-conducting screen which stands between the will and the act. They call this the 'observing self,' the 'interfering self,' and when this has been removed by special kinds of training the expert loses all sense that 'I am doing it.' The circuit runs free. The act is effortless. It is 'one-pointed.' The deed completely reproduces the picture the actor had drawn of it in his mind.

The most ordinary people seek this kind of 'expertness' in Japan. Sir Charles Eliot, the great English authority on Buddhism, tells of a schoolgirl who applied

> to a well-known missionary in Tokyo and said that she wished to become a Christian. When questioned as to her reasons she replied that her great desire was to go up in an aeroplane. On being invited to explain the connection between aeroplanes and Christianity, she replied that she had been told that before she went up in an aeroplane she must have a very calm and well-regulated mind and that this kind of mind was only acquired by religious training. She thought that among the religions Christianity was probably the best and so she came to ask for teaching.*

The Japanese not only connect Christianity and airplanes; they connect training for 'a calm and well-regulated mind' with an examination in pedagogy or with speech-making or with a statesman's career. Technical training for one-pointedness seems to them an unquestioned advantage in almost any undertaking.

Many civilizations have developed techniques of this kind, but the Japanese goals and methods have a marked

* Eliot, Sir Charles, *Japanese Buddhism*, p. 286.

character all their own. This is especially interesting because many of the techniques are derived from India where they are known as Yoga. Japanese techniques of self-hypnotism, concentration, and control of the senses still show kinship with Indian practices. There is similar emphasis on emptying the mind, on immobility of the body, on ten thousands of repetitions of the same phrase, on fixing the attention on a chosen symbol. Even the terminology used in India is still recognizable. Beyond these bare bones of the cult, however, the Japanese version has little in common with the Hindu.

Yoga in India is an extreme cult of asceticism. It is a way of obtaining release from the round of reincarnation. Man has no salvation except this release, *nirvana*, and the obstacle in his path is human desire. These desires can be eliminated by starving them out, by insulting them, and by courting self-torture. Through these means a man may reach sainthood and achieve spirituality and union with the divine. Yoga is a way of renouncing the world of the flesh and of escaping the treadmill of human futility. It is also a way of laying hold of spiritual powers. The journey toward one's goal is the faster the more extreme the asceticism.

Such philosophy is alien in Japan. Even though Japan is a great Buddhist nation, ideas of transmigration and of nirvana have never been a part of the Buddhist faith of the people. These doctrines are personally accepted by some Buddhist priests, but they have never affected folkways or popular thought. No animal or insect is spared in Japan because killing it would kill a transmigrated human soul, and Japanese funeral ceremonies and birth rituals are innocent of any notions of a round of reincarnations. Transmigration is not a Japanese pattern of thought. The idea of nirvana, too, not only means nothing to the general public but the priesthoods themselves modify it out of existence. Priestly scholars declare that a man who has been 'enlightened' (*satori*) is already in nirvana; nirvana is here and now in the midst of time, and a man 'sees nirvana' in a pine tree and a wild bird. The Japanese have always been uninterested in fantasies of a world of the hereafter. Their mythology tells of gods but not of the life of the dead. They have even rejected Buddhist ideas of differential rewards and punishments after death. Any man, the least farmer, becomes a Buddha when he dies; the very word for the family memorial tablets in the household shrine is 'the Buddhas.' No other Buddhist country uses such language, and when a nation speaks so boldly of its ordinary dead, it is quite understandable that it does not picture any such difficult goal as attainment of nirvana. A man who becomes a Buddha anyway need not set himself to attain the goal of absolute surcease by lifelong mortification of the flesh.

Just as alien in Japan is the doctrine that the flesh and the spirit are irreconciliable. Yoga is a technique to eliminate desire, and desire has its seat in the flesh. But the Japanese do not have this dogma. 'Human feelings' are not of the Evil One, and it is a part of wisdom to enjoy the pleasures of the senses. The one condition is that they be sacrificed to the serious duties of life. This tenet is carried to its logical extreme in the Japanese handling of the Yoga cult: not only are all self-tortures eliminated but the cult in

Japan is not even one of asceticism. Even the 'Enlightened' in their retreats, though they were called hermits, commonly established themselves in comfort with their wives and children in charming spots in the country. The companionship of their wives and even the birth of subsequent children were regarded as entirely compatible with their sanctity. In the most popular of all Buddhist sects priests marry anyway and raise families; Japan has never found it easy to accept the theory that the spirit and the flesh are incompatible. The saintliness of the 'enlightened' consisted in their self-disciplinary meditations and in their simplification of life. It did not consist in wearing unclean clothing or shutting one's eyes to the beauties of nature or one's ears to the beauty of stringed instruments. Their saints might fill their days with the composition of elegant verses, the ritual of tea ceremony and 'viewings' of the moon and the cherry blossoms. The Zen cult even directs its devotees to avoid 'the three insufficiencies: insufficiency of clothing, of food, and of sleep.'

The final tenet of Yoga philosophy is also alien in Japan: that the techniques of mysticism which it teaches transport the practitioner to ecstatic union with the Universe. Wherever the techniques of mysticism have been practiced in the world, whether by primitive peoples or by Mohammedan dervishes or by Indian Yogis or by medieval Christians, those who practice them have almost universally agreed, whatever their creed, that they become 'one with the divine,' that they experience ecstasy 'not of this world.' The Japanese have the techniques of mysticism without the mysticism. This does not mean that they do not achieve trance. They do. But they regard even trance as a technique which trains a man in 'one-pointedness.' They do not describe it as ecstasy. The Zen cult does not even say, as mystics in other countries do, that the five senses are in abeyance in trance; they say that the 'six' senses are brought by this technique to a condition of extraordinary acuteness. The sixth sense is located in the mind, and training makes it supreme over the ordinary five, but taste, touch, sight, smell, and hearing are given their own special training during trance. It is one of the exercises of group Zen to perceive soundless footsteps and be able to follow them accurately as they pass from one place to another or to discriminate tempting odors of food—purposely introduced—without breaking trance. Smelling, seeing, hearing, touching, and tasting 'help the sixth sense,' and one learns in this state to make 'every sense alert.'

This is very unusual training in any cult of extra-sensory experience. Even in trance such a Zen practitioner does not try to get outside of himself, but in the phrase Nietzsche uses of the ancient Greeks, 'to remain what he is and retain his civic name.' There are many vivid statements of this view of the matter among the sayings of the great Japanese Buddhist teachers. One of the best is that of Dogen, the great thirteenth-century founder of the Soto cult of Zen, which is still the largest and most influential of the Zen cults. Speaking of his own enlightenment (satori), he said, 'I recognized only that my eyes were horizontal above my perpendicular nose. . . . There is nothing mysterious (in Zen experience). Time passes as it is natural, the sun rising in the east and the moon setting in the west.'* Nor do Zen writings allow that trance experience gives power other than self-disciplined human power; 'Yoga claims that various supernatural powers can be acquired by meditation,' a Japanese Buddhist writes, 'but Zen does not make any such absurd claims.'†

The Japanese thus wipe the slate clean of the assumptions on which Yoga practices are based in India. Japan, with a vital love of finitude which reminds one of the ancient Greeks, understands the technical practices of Yoga as being a self-training in perfection, a means whereby a man may obtain that 'expertness' in which there is not the thickness of a hair between a man and his deed. It is a training in efficiency. It is a training in self-reliance. Its rewards are here and now, for it enables a man to meet any situation with exactly the right expenditure of effort, neither too much nor too little, and it gives him control of his otherwise wayward mind so that neither physical danger from outside nor passion from within can dislodge him.

Such training is of course just as valuable for a warrior as for a priest, and it was precisely the warriors of Japan who made the Zen cult their own. One can hardly find elsewhere than in Japan techniques of mysticism pursued without the reward of the consummating mystic experience and appropriated by warriors to train them for hand-to-hand combat. Yet this has been true from the earliest period of Zen influence in Japan. The great book by the Japanese founder, Ei-sai, in the twelfth century was called *The Protection of the State by the Propagation of Zen*, and Zen has

* Nukariya, Kaiten, *The Religion of the Samurai*. London, 1913, p. 197.
† *Ibid.*, p. 194.

trained warriors, statesmen, fencers, and university students to achieve quite mundane goals. As Sir Charles Eliot says, nothing in the history of the Zen cult in China gave any indication of the future that awaited it as a military discipline in Japan. 'Zen has become as decidedly Japanese as tea ceremonies or No plays. It might have been supposed that in a troubled period like the twelfth and thirteenth centuries this contemplative and mystic doctrine, which finds truth not in scripture but in the immediate experience of the human mind, would have flourished in monastic harbours of refuge among those who had left the storms of the world, but not that it would have been accepted as the favourite rule of life for the military class. Yet such it became.'*

Many Japanese sects, both Buddhist and Shintoist, have laid great emphasis on mystic techniques of contemplation, self-hypnotism, and trance. Some of them, however, claim the result of this training as evidences of the grace of God and base their philosophy on *tariki*, 'help of another,' i.e., of a gracious god. Some of them, of which Zen is the paramount example, rely only on 'self-help,' *jiriki*. The potential strength, they teach, lies only within oneself, and only by one's own efforts can one increase it. Japanese samurai found this entirely congenial, and whether as monks, statesmen, or educators—for they served in all these rôles—they used the Zen techniques to buttress a rugged individualism. Zen teachings were excessively explicit. 'Zen seeks only the light man can find in himself. It tolerates no hindrance to this seeking. Clear every obstacle out of your way. . . . If

* Eliot, Sir Charles, *Japanese Buddhism*, p. 186.

on your way you meet Buddha, kill him! If you meet the Patriarchs, kill them! If you meet the Saints, kill them all. That is the only way of reaching salvation.'*

He who seeks after truth must take nothing at second-hand, no teaching of the Buddha, no scriptures, no theology. 'The twelve chapters of the Buddhist canon are a scrap of paper.' One may with profit study them, but they have nothing to do with the lightning flash in one's own soul which is all that gives Enlightenment. In a Zen book of dialogues a novice asks a Zen priest to expound the Sutra of the Lotus of the Good Law. The priest gave him a brilliant exposition, and the listener said witheringly, 'Why, I thought Zen priests disdained texts, theories, and systems of logical explanations.' 'Zen,' returned the priest, 'does not consist in knowing nothing, but in the belief that *to know* is outside of all texts, of all documents. You did not tell me you wanted *to know*, but only that you wished an explanation of the text.'†

The traditional training given by Zen teachers was intended to teach novices how 'to know.' The training might be physical or it might be mental, but it must be finally validated in the inner consciousness of the learner. Zen training of the fencer illustrates this well. The fencer, of course, has to learn and constantly practice the proper sword thrusts, but his proficiency in these belongs in the field of mere 'competence.' In addition he must learn to be *muga.* He is made to stand first on the level floor, concentrating on the few inches of surface which support his body. This

* Quoted by E. Steinilber-Oberlin, *The Buddhist Sects of Japan.* London, 1938, p. 143.

† *Ibid.*, p. 175.

tiny surface of standing room is gradually raised till he has learned to stand as easily on a four-foot pillar as in a court yard. When he is perfectly secure on that pillar, he 'knows.' His mind will no longer betray him by dizziness and fear of falling.

This Japanese use of pillar-standing transforms the familiar Western medieval austerity of Saint Simeon Stylites into a purposeful self-discipline. It is no longer an austerity. All kinds of physical exercises in Japan, whether of the Zen cult, or the common practices of the peasant villages, undergo this kind of transformation. In many places of the world diving into freezing water and standing under mountain waterfalls, are standard austerities, sometimes to mortify the flesh, sometimes to obtain pity from the gods, sometimes to induce trance. The favorite Japanese cold-austerity was standing or sitting in an ice-cold waterfall before dawn, or dousing oneself three times during a winter night with icy water. But the object was to train one's conscious self till one no longer noticed the discomfort. A devotee's purpose was to train himself to continue his meditation without interruption. When neither the cold shock of the water nor the shivering of the body in the cold dawn registered in his consciousness he was 'expert.' There was no other reward.

Mental training had to be equally self-appropriated. A man might associate himself with a teacher, but the teacher could not 'teach' in the Occidental sense, because nothing a novice learned from any source outside himself was of any importance. The teacher might hold discussions with the novice, but he did not lead him gently into a new intellectual realm. The teacher was considered to be most helpful when he was most rude. If, without warning, the master broke the tea bowl the novice was raising to his lips, or tripped him, or struck his knuckles with a brass rod, the shock might galvanize him into sudden insight. It broke through his complacency. The monkish books are filled with incidents of this kind.

The most favored technique for inducing the novice's desperate attempt 'to know' were the *koan*, literally 'the problems.' There are said to be seventeen hundred of these problems, and the anecdote books make nothing of a man's devoting seven years to the solution of one of them. They are not meant to have rational solutions. One is 'To conceive the clapping of one hand.' Another is 'To feel the yearning for one's mother before one's own conception.' Others are, 'Who is carrying one's lifeless body?' 'Who is it who is walking toward me?' 'All things return into One; where does this last return?' Such Zen problems as these were used in China before the twelfth or thirteenth century, and Japan adopted these techniques along with the cult. On the continent, however, they did not survive. In Japan they are a most important part of training in 'expertness.' Zen handbooks treat them with extreme seriousness. 'Koan enshrine the dilemma of life.' A man who is pondering one, they say, reaches an impasse like 'a pursued rat that has run up a blind tunnel,' he is like a man 'with a ball of red-hot iron stuck in his throat,' he is 'a mosquito trying to bite a lump of iron.' He is beside himself and redoubles his efforts. Finally the screen of his 'observing self' between his mind and his problem falls aside; with the swiftness of a flash of lightning the two—mind and problem—come to terms. He 'knows.'

After these descriptions of bow-string-taut mental effort it is an anticlimax to search the incident books for great truths gained with all this expenditure. Nangaku, for instance, spent eight years on the problem, 'Who is it who is walking toward me?' At last he understood. His words were: 'Even when one affirms that there is something here, one omits the whole.' Nevertheless, there is a general pattern in the revelations. It is suggested in the lines of dialogue:

Novice: How shall I escape from the Wheel of Birth and Death?

Master: Who puts you under restraint? (i.e., binds you to this Wheel.)

What they learn, they say, is, in the famous Chinese phrase, that they 'were looking for an ox when they were riding on one.' They learn that 'What is necessary is not the net and the trap but the fish or the animal these instruments were meant to catch.' They learn, that is, in Occidental phraseology, that both horns of the dilemma are irrelevant. They learn that goals may be attained with present means if the eyes of the spirit are opened. Anything is possible, and with no help from anyone but oneself.

The significance of the koan does not lie in the truths these seekers after truth discover, which are the world-wide truths of the mystics. It lies in the way the Japanese conceive the search for truth.

The koan are called 'bricks with which to knock upon the door.' 'The door' is in the wall built around unenlightened human nature, which worries about whether present means are sufficient and fantasies to itself a cloud of watchful witnesses who will allot praise or blame. It is the wall of *haji* (shame) which is so real to all Japanese. Once the brick has battered down the door and it has fallen open, one is in free air and one throws away the brick. One does not go on solving more koan. The lesson has been learned and the Japanese dilemma of virtue has been solved. They have thrown themselves with desperate intensity against an impasse; for 'the sake of the training' they have become as 'mosquitoes biting a lump of iron.' In the end they have learned that there is no impasse—no impasse between gimu and giri, either, or between giri and human feelings, between righteousness and giri. They have found a way out. They are free and for the first time they can fully 'taste' life. They are muga. Their training in 'expertness' has been successfully achieved.

Suzuki, the great authority on Zen Buddhism, describes muga as 'ecstasy with no sense of *I am doing it*,' 'effortlessness.'* The 'observing self' is eliminated; a man 'loses himself,' that is, he ceases to be a spectator of his acts. Suzuki says: 'With the awaking of consciousness, the will is split into two: . . . actor and observer. Conflict is inevitable, for the actor(-self) wants to be free from the limitations' of the observer-self. Therefore in Enlightenment the disciple discovers that there is no observer-self, 'no soul entity as an unknown or unknowable quantity.'† Nothing remains but

* Suzuki, Professor Daisetz Teitaro, *Essays in Zen Buddhism*, vol. 3, p. 318 (Kyoto, 1927, 1933, 1934).

† Quoted by Sir Charles Eliot, *Japanese Buddhism*, p. 401.

the goal and the act that accomplishes it. The student of human behavior could rephrase this statement to refer more particularly to Japanese culture. As a child a person is drastically trained to observe his own acts and to judge them in the light of what people will say; his observer-self is terribly vulnerable. To deliver himself up to the ecstasy of his soul, he eliminates this vulnerable self. He ceases to feel that '*he* is doing it.' He then feels himself trained in his soul in the same way that the novice in fencing feels himself trained to stand without fear of falling on the four-foot pillar.

The painter, the poet, the public speaker and the warrior use this training in muga similarly. They acquire, not Infinitude, but a clear undisturbed perception of finite beauty or adjustment of means and ends so that they can use just the right amount of effort, 'no more and no less,' to achieve their goal.

Even a person who has undergone no training at all may have a sort of muga experience. When a man watching Noh or Kabuki plays completely loses himself in the spectacle, he too is said to lose his observing self. The palms of his hands become wet. He feels 'the sweat of muga.' A bombing pilot approaching his goal has 'the sweat of muga' before he releases his bombs. '*He* is not doing it.' There is no observer-self left in his consciousness. An anti-aircraft gunner, lost to all the world beside, is said similarly to have 'the sweat of muga' and to have eliminated the observer-self. The idea is that in all such cases people in this condition are at the top of their form.

Such concepts are eloquent testimony to the heavy burden the Japanese make out of self-watchfulness and self-surveillance. They are free and efficient, they say, when these restraints are gone. Whereas Americans identify their observer-selves with the rational principle within them and pride themselves in crises on 'keeping their wits about them,' the Japanese feel that a millstone has fallen from around their necks when they deliver themselves up to the ecstasy of their souls and forget the restraints self-watchfulness imposes. As we have seen, their culture dins the need for circumspection into their souls, and the Japanese have countered by declaring that there is a more efficient plane of human consciousness where this burden falls away.

The most extreme form in which the Japanese state this tenet, at least to the ears of an Occidental, is the way they supremely approve of the man 'who lives as already dead.' The literal Western translation would be 'the living corpse,' and in all Occidental languages 'the living corpse' is an expression of horror. It is the phrase by which we say that a man's self has died and left his body encumbering the earth. No vital principle is left in him. The Japanese use 'living as one already dead' to mean that one lives on the plane of 'expertness.' It is used in common everyday exhortation. To encourage a boy who is worrying about his final examinations from middle school, a man will say, 'Take them as one already dead and you will pass them easily.' To encourage someone who is undertaking an important business deal, a friend will say, 'Be as one already dead.' When a man goes through a great soul crisis and cannot see his way ahead, he quite commonly emerges with the resolve to live 'as one already dead.' The great Christian leader Kagawa, since VJ-Day made a member of the House of Lords, says in his fictionalized autobiography: 'Like a man bewitched by an evil spirit he spent every day in his room weeping. His fits of sobbing verged on hysteria. His agony lasted for a month and a half but life finally gained the victory. . . . He would live endued with the strength of death. . . . He would enter into the conflict as one already dead. . . . He decided to become a Christian.'* During the war Japanese soldiers said, 'I resolve to live as one already dead and thus repay *ko-on* to the Emperor,' and this covered such behavior as conducting one's own funeral before embarking, pledging one's body 'to the dust of Iwo Jima,' and resolving 'to fall with the flowers of Burma.'

The philosophy which underlies muga underlies also 'living as already dead.' In this state a man eliminates all self-watchfulness and thus all fear and circumspection. He becomes as the dead, who have passed beyond the necessity of taking thought about the proper course of action. The dead are no longer returning *on*; they are free. Therefore to say, 'I will live as one already dead' means a supreme release from conflict. It means, 'My energy and attention are free to pass directly to the fulfillment of my purpose. My observer-self with all its burden of fears is no longer between me and my goal. With it have gone the sense of tenseness and strain and the tendency toward depression that troubled my earlier strivings. Now all things are possible to me.'

In Western phraseology, the Japanese in the practice of muga and of 'living as one already dead' eliminate the conscience. What they call 'the observing-self,' 'the interfering

* Kagawa, Toyohiko, *Before the Dawn*, p. 240.

self,' is a censor judging one's acts. It points up vividly the difference between Western and Eastern psychology that when we speak of a conscienceless American we mean a man who no longer feels the sense of sin which should accompany wrongdoing, but that when a Japanese uses the equivalent phrase he means a man who is no longer tense and hindered. The American means a bad man; the Japanese means a good man, a trained man, a man able to use his abilities to the utmost. He means a man who can perform the most difficult and devoted deeds of unselfishness. The great American sanction for good behavior is guilt; a man who because of a calloused conscience can no longer feel this has become antisocial. The Japanese diagram the problem differently. According to their philosophy man in his inmost soul is good. If his impulse can be directly embodied in his deed, he acts virtuously and easily. Therefore he undergoes, in 'expertness,' self-training to eliminate the self-censorship of shame (haji). Only then is his 'sixth sense' free of hindrance. It is his supreme release from self-consciousness and conflict.

This Japanese philosophy of self-discipline is abracadabra only so long as it is separated from their individual life experiences in Japanese culture. We have already seen how heavily this shame (haji) which they assign to 'the observing self' weighs upon the Japanese, but the true meaning of their philosophy in their psychic economy is still obscure without a description of Japanese child-rearing. In any culture traditional moral sanctions are transmitted to each new generation, not merely in words, but in all the elders' attitudes toward their children, and an outsider can hardly understand any nation's major stakes in life without studying the way children are brought up there. Japanese child-rearing makes clearer many of their national assumptions about life which we have so far described only at the adult level.

12

The Child Learns

JAPANESE BABIES are not brought up in the fashion that a thoughtful Westerner might suppose. American parents, training their children for a life so much less circumspect and stoical than life in Japan, nevertheless begin immediately to prove to the baby that his own little wishes are not supreme in this world. We put him immediately on a feeding schedule and a sleeping schedule, and no matter how he fusses before bottle time or bed time, he has to wait. A little later his mother strikes his hand to make him take his finger out of his mouth or away from other parts of his body. His mother is frequently out of sight and when she goes out he has to stay behind. He has to be weaned before he prefers other foods, or if he is bottle fed, he has to give up his bottle. There are certain foods that are good for him and he must eat them. He is punished when he does not do what is right. What is more natural for an American to suppose than that these disciplines are redoubled for the little Japanese baby who, when he is a finished product, will have to subordinate his own wishes and be so careful and punctilious an observer of such a demanding code?

The Japanese, however, do not follow this course. The

arc of life in Japan is plotted in opposite fashion to that in the United States. It is a great shallow U-curve with maximum freedom and indulgence allowed to babies and to the old. Restrictions are slowly increased after babyhood till having one's own way reaches a low just before and after marriage. This low line continues many years during the prime of life, but the arc gradually ascends again until after the age of sixty men and women are almost as unhampered by shame as little children are. In the United States we stand this curve upside down. Firm disciplines are directed toward the infant and these are gradually relaxed as the child grows in strength until a man runs his own life when he gets a self-supporting job and when he sets up a household of his own. The prime of life is with us the high point of freedom and initiative. Restrictions begin to appear as men lose their grip or their energy or become dependent. It is difficult for Americans even to fantasy a life arranged according to the Japanese pattern. It seems to us to fly in the face of reality.

Both the American and the Japanese arrangement of the arc of life, however, have in point of fact secured in each country the individual's energetic participation in his culture during the prime of life. To secure this end in the United States, we rely on increasing his freedom of choice during this period. The Japanese rely on maximizing the restraints upon him. The fact that a man is at this time at the peak of his physical strength and at the peak of his earning powers does not make him master of his own life. They have great confidence that restraint is good mental training (*shuyo*) and produces results not attained by freedom. But the Japanese increase of restraints upon the man or woman during their most active producing periods by no means indicates that these restraints cover the whole of life. Childhood and old age are 'free areas.'

A people so truly permissive to their children very likely want babies. The Japanese do. They want them, first of all, as parents do in the United States, because it is a pleasure to love a child. But they want them, too, for reasons which have much less weight in America. Japanese parents need children, not alone for emotional satisfaction, but because they have failed in life if they have not carried on the family line. Every Japanese man must have a son. He needs him to do daily homage to his memory after his death at the living-room shrine before the miniature gravestone. He needs him to perpetuate the family line down the generations and to preserve the family honor and possessions. For traditional social reasons the father needs his son almost as much as the young son needs his father. The son will take his father's place in the on-going future and this is not felt as supplanting but as insuring the father. For a few years the father is trustee of the 'house.' Later it will be his son. If the father could not pass trusteeship to his son, his own rôle would have been played in vain. This deep sense of continuity prevents the dependency of the fully grown son on his father, even when it is continued so much longer than it is in the United States, from having the aura of shame and humiliation which it so generally has in Western nations.

A woman too wants children not only for her emotional satisfaction in them but because it is only as a mother that she gains status. A childless wife has a most insecure position in the family, and even if she is not discarded she can never look forward to being a mother-in-law and exercising authority over her son's marriage and over her son's wife. Her husband will adopt a son to carry on his line but according to Japanese ideas the childless woman is still the loser. Japanese women are expected to be good childbearers. The average annual birth-rate during the first half of the nineteen-thirties was 31.7 per 1000 which is high even when compared to prolific countries of Eastern Europe. In the United States in 1940 the rate was 17.6 per 1000. Japanese mothers, too, begin their childbearing early, and girls of nineteen bear more children than women of any other age.

Childbirth is as private in Japan as sexual intercourse and women may not cry out in labor because this would publicize it. A little pallet bed has been prepared for the baby with its own new mattress and bedcover. It would be a bad omen for the child not to have its own new bed, even if the family can do no more than have the quilt covers and the stuffing cleaned and renovated to make them 'new.' The little bed quilt is not as stiff as grown-ups' covers and it is lighter. The baby is therefore said to be more comfortable in its own bed, but the deeply felt reason for its separate bed is still felt to be based on a kind of sympathetic magic: a new human being must have its own new bed. The baby's pallet is drawn up close to the mother's, but the baby does not sleep with its mother until it is old enough to show initiative. When it is perhaps a year old, they say the baby stretches out its arms and makes its demand known. Then the baby sleeps in its mother's arms under her covers.

For three days after its birth the baby is not fed, for the Japanese wait until the true milk comes. After this the baby may have the breast at any time either for food or comfort. The mother enjoys nursing too. The Japanese are convinced that nursing is one of a woman's greatest physiological pleasures and the baby easily learns to share her pleasure. The breast is not only nourishment: it is delight and comfort. For a month the baby lies on his little bed or is held in his mother's arms. It is only after the baby has been taken to the local shrine and presented there at the age of about thirty days that his life is thought to be firmly anchored in his body so that it is safe to carry him around freely in public. After he is a month old, he is carried on his mother's back. A double sash holds him under his arms and under his behind and is passed around the mother's shoulders and tied in front at the waist. In cold weather the mother's padded jacket is worn right over the baby. The older children of the family, both boys and girls, carry the baby, too, even at play when they are running for base or playing hopscotch. The villagers and the poorer families especially depend on child nurses, and 'living in public, as the Japanese babies do, they soon acquire an intelligent, interested look, and seem to enjoy the games of the older children upon whose backs they are carried as much as the players themselves.'* The spread-eagle strapping of the baby on the back in Japan has much in common with the shawl-carrying common in the Pacific Islands and elsewhere. It makes for passivity and babies carried in these ways tend to grow up, as the Japanese do too, with a capacity for sleeping any-

* Bacon, Alice Mabel, *Japanese Women and Girls,* p. 6.

where, anyhow. But the Japanese strapping does not encourage as complete passivity as shawl and bag carrying. The baby 'learns to cling like a kitten to the back of whoever carries it. . . . The straps that tie it to the back are sufficient for safety; but the baby . . . is dependent on its own exertions to secure a comfortable position and it soon learns to ride its bearer with considerable skill instead of being merely a bundle tied to the shoulders.'*

The mother lays the baby on its bed whenever she is working and carries it with her wherever she goes on the streets. She talks to it. She hums to it. She puts it through the etiquette motions. If she returns a greeting herself, she moves the baby's head and shoulders forward so that it too makes salutation. The baby is always counted in. Every afternoon she takes it with her into the hot bath and plays with it as she holds it on her knees.

For three or four months the baby wears diapers, very heavy cloth pads upon which Japanese sometimes blame their bow-leggedness. When the baby is three or four months old, the mother begins his nursery training. She anticipates his needs, holding him in her hands outside the door. She waits for him, usually whistling low and monotonously, and the child learns to know the purpose of this auditory stimulus. Everyone agrees that a baby in Japan, as in China too, is trained very early. If there are slips, some mothers pinch the baby but generally they only change the tone of their voices and hold the hard-to-train baby outside the door at more frequent intervals. If there is withholding, the mother gives the baby an enema or a purge.

* *Op. cit.*, p. 10.

Mothers say that they are making the baby more comfortable; when he is trained he will no longer have to wear the thick uncomfortable diapers. It is true that a Japanese baby must find diapers unpleasant, not only because they are heavy but because custom does not decree that they be changed whenever he wets them. The baby is nevertheless too young to perceive the connection between nursery training and getting rid of uncomfortable diapers. He experiences only an inescapable routine implacably insisted upon. Besides, the mother has to hold the baby away from her body, and her grip must be firm. What the baby learns from the implacable training prepares him to accept in adulthood the subtler compulsions of Japanese culture.*

The Japanese baby usually talks before it walks. Creeping has always been discouraged. Traditionally there was a feeling that the baby ought not to stand or take steps till it was a year old and the mother used to prevent any such attempts. The government in its cheap, widely circulated *Mother's Magazine* has for a decade or two taught that walking should be encouraged and this has become much more general. Mothers loop a sash under the baby's arms or support it with their hands. But babies still tend to talk even earlier. When they begin to use words the stream of baby talk with which adults like to amuse a baby becomes more purposive. They do not leave the baby's acquiring of language to chance imitation; they teach the baby words and grammar and respect language, and both the baby and the grown-ups enjoy the game.

* Geoffrey Gorer has also emphasized the rôle of Japanese toilet training in *Themes in Japanese Culture*, Transactions of the New York Academy of Science, vol. 5, pp. 106–124, 1943.

When children can walk they can do a lot of mischief in a Japanese home. They can poke their fingers through paper walls, and they can fall into the open fire pit in the middle of the floor. Not content with this, the Japanese even exaggerate the dangers of the house. It is 'dangerous' and completely taboo to step on the threshold. The Japanese house has, of course, no cellar and is raised off the ground on joists. It is seriously felt that the whole house can be thrown out of shape even by a child's step upon the threshold. Not only that, but the child must learn not to step or to sit where the floor mats join one another. Floor mats are of standard size and rooms are known as 'three-mat rooms' or 'twelve-mat rooms.' Where these mats join, children are often told, the samurai of old times used to thrust their swords up from below the house and pierce the occupants of the room. Only the thick soft floor mats provide safety; even the cracks where they meet are dangerous. The mother puts feelings of this sort into the constant admonitions she uses to the baby: 'Dangerous' and 'Bad.' The third usual admonition is 'Dirty.' The neatness and cleanness of the Japanese house is proverbial and the baby is admonished to respect it.

Most Japanese children are not weaned till shortly before a new baby is born, but the government's *Mother's Magazine* has in late years approved of weaning the baby at eight months. Middle-class mothers often do this, but it is far from being the common custom in Japan. True to the Japanese feeling that nursing is a great pleasure to the mother, those circles which are gradually adopting the custom regard the shorter nursing period as a mother's sacrifice to the welfare of her child. When they accept the new dictum that 'the child who nurses long is weak,' they blame the mother for her self-indulgence if she has not weaned her baby. 'She says she can't wean her baby. It's only that she hasn't made up her own mind. She wants to go on. She is getting the better part.' With such an attitude, it is quite understandable that eight-month weaning has not become widespread. There is a practical reason also for late weaning. The Japanese do not have a tradition of special foods for a just-weaned baby. If he is weaned young, he is fed the water in which rice has been boiled, but ordinarily he passes directly from his mother's milk to the usual adult fare. Cow's milk is not included in Japanese diet and they do not prepare special vegetables for children. Under the circumstances there is a reasonable doubt whether the government is correct in teaching that 'the child who nurses long is weak.'

Children are usually weaned after they can understand what is said to them. They have sat in their mother's lap at the family table during meals and been fed bits of the food; now they eat more of it. Some children are feeding problems at this time, and this is easy to understand when they are weaned because of the birth of a new baby. Mothers often offer them sweets to buy them off from begging to nurse. Sometimes a mother will put pepper on her nipples. But all mothers tease them by telling them they are proving that they are mere babies if they want to nurse. 'Look at your little cousin. He's a man. He's little like you and he doesn't ask to nurse.' 'That little boy is laughing at you because you're a boy and you still want to nurse.' Two-, three-, and four-year-old children who are still demanding their mother's breast will often drop it and feign indifference when an older child is heard approaching.

This teasing, this urging a child toward adulthood, is not confined to weaning. From the time the child can understand what is said to it, these techniques are common in any situation. A mother will say to her boy baby when he cries, 'You're not a girl,' or 'You're a man.' Or she will say, 'Look at that baby. He doesn't cry.' When another baby is brought to visit, she will fondle the visitor in her own child's presence and say, 'I'm going to adopt this baby. I want such a nice, good child. You don't act your age.' Her own child throws itself upon her, often pommeling her with its fists, and cries, 'No, no, we don't want any other baby. I'll do what you say.' When the child of one or two has been noisy or has failed to be prompt about something, the mother will say to a man visitor, 'Will you take this child away? We don't want it.' The visitor acts out his rôle. He starts to take the child out of the house. The baby screams and calls upon its mother to rescue it. He has a full-sized tantrum. When she thinks the teasing has worked, she relents and takes back the child, exacting its frenzied promise to be good. The little play is acted out sometimes with children who are as old as five and six.

Teasing takes another form too. The mother will turn to her husband and say to the child, 'I like your father better than you. He is a nice man.' The child gives full expression to his jealousy and tries to break in between his father and mother. His mother says, 'Your father doesn't shout around the house and run around the rooms.' 'No, no,' the child protests, 'I won't either. I am good. *Now* do you love me?'

When the play has gone on long enough, the father and mother look at one another and smile. They may tease a young daughter in this way as well as a young son.

Such experiences are rich soil for the fear of ridicule and of ostracism which is so marked in the Japanese grown-up. It is impossible to say how soon little children understand that they are being made game of by this teasing, but understand it they do sooner or later, and when they do, the sense of being laughed at fuses with the panic of the child threatened with loss of all that is safe and familiar. When he is a grown man, being laughed at retains this childhood aura.

The panic such teasing occasions in the two- to five-year-old child is the greater because home is really a haven of safety and indulgence. Division of labor, both physical and emotional, is so complete between his father and mother that they are seldom presented to him as competitors. His mother or his grandmother runs the household and admonishes the child. They both serve his father on their knees and put him in the position of honor. The order of precedence in the home hierarchy is clear-cut. The child has learned the prerogatives of elder generations, of a male as compared with a female, of elder brother as compared with younger brother. But at this period of his life a child is indulged in all these relationships. This is strikingly true if he is a boy. For both girls and boys alike the mother is the source of constant and extreme gratifications, but in the case of a three-year-old boy he can gratify against her even his furious anger. He may never manifest any aggression toward his father, but all that he felt when he was teased by his parents and his resentments against being 'given away' can be expressed in tantrums directed against his mother and his grandmother. Not all little boys, of course, have these tantrums, but in both villages and upper-class homes they are looked upon as an ordinary part of child life between three and six. The baby pommels his mother, screams, and, as his final violence, tears down her precious hair-do. His mother is a woman and even at three years old he is securely male. He can gratify even his aggressions.

To his father he may show only respect. His father is the great exemplar to the child of high hierarchal position, and, in the constantly used Japanese phrase, the child must learn to express the proper respect to him 'for training.' He is less of a disciplinarian than in almost any Western nation. Discipline of the children is in the woman's hands. A simple silent stare or a short admonition is usually all the indication of his wishes he gives to his little children, and these are rare enough to be quickly complied with. He may make toys for his children in his free hours. He carries them about on occasion long after they can walk—as the mother does too—and for his children of this age he casually assumes nursery duties which an American father ordinarily leaves to his wife.

Children have great freedom with their grandparents, though they are also objects of respect. Grandparents are not cast in the rôle of disciplinarians. They may take that rôle when they object to the laxness of the children's upbringing, and this is the occasion of a good deal of friction. The child's grandmother is usually at hand twenty-four hours of the day, and the rivalry for the children between father's mother and mother is proverbial in Japanese homes.

From the child's point of view he is courted by both of them. From the grandmother's point of view, she often uses him in her domination of her daughter-in-law. The young mother has no greater obligation in life than satisfying her mother-in-law and she cannot protest, however much the grandparents may spoil her children. Grandmother gives them candies after Mother has said they should not have any more, and says pointedly, '*My* candies aren't poison.' Grandmother in many households can make the children presents which Mother cannot manage to get them and has more leisure to devote to the children's amusements.

The older brothers and sisters are also taught to indulge the younger children. The Japanese are quite aware of the danger of what we call the baby's 'nose being put out of joint' when the next baby is born. The dispossessed child can easily associate with the new baby the fact that he has had to give up his mother's breast and his mother's bed to the newcomer. Before the new baby is born the mother tells the child that now he will have a real live doll and not just a 'pretend' baby. He is told that he can sleep now with his father instead of his mother, and this is pictured as a privilege. The children are drawn into preparations for the new baby. The children are usually genuinely excited and pleased by the new baby but lapses occur and are regarded as thoroughly expectable and not as particularly threatening. The dispossessed child may pick up the baby and start off with it, saying to his mother, 'We'll give this baby away.' 'No,' she answers, 'it's our baby. See, we'll be good to it. It likes you. We need you to help with the baby.' The little scene sometimes recurs over a considerable time but mothers seem to worry little about it. One provision for the situation occurs automatically in large families: the alternate children are united by closer ties. The oldest child will be favored nurse and protector of the third child and the second child of the fourth. The younger children reciprocate. Until children are seven or eight, what sex the children are generally makes little difference in this arrangement.

All Japanese children have toys. Fathers and mothers and all the circle of friends and relatives make or buy dolls and all their appurtenances for the children, and among poorer people they cost practically nothing. Little children play housekeeping, weddings, and festivals with them, after arguing out just what the 'right' grown-up procedures are, and sometimes submitting to mother a disputed point. When there are quarrels, it is likely that the mother will invoke *noblesse oblige* and ask the older child to give in to the younger one. The common phrase is, 'Why not lose to win?' She means, and the three-year-old quickly comes to understand her, that if the older child gives up his toy to the younger one the baby will soon be satisfied and turn to something else; then the admonished child will have won his toy back even though he relinquished it. Or she means that by accepting an unpopular rôle in the master-servants game the children are proposing, he will nevertheless 'win' the fun they can have. 'To lose to win' becomes a sequence greatly respected in Japanese life even when people are grown-up.

Besides the techniques of admonition and teasing, distracting the child and turning his mind away from its object has an honored place in child-rearing. Even the constant giving of candies is generally thought of as part of the technique of distraction. As the child gets nearer to school age techniques of 'curing' are used. If a little boy has tantrums or is disobedient or noisy his mother may take him to a Shinto or Buddhist shrine. The mother's attitude is, '*We* will go to get help.' It is often quite a jaunt and the curing priest talks seriously with the boy, asking his day of birth and his troubles. He retires to pray and comes back to pronounce the cure, sometimes removing the naughtiness in the form of a worm or an insect. He purifies him and sends him home freed. 'It lasts for a while,' Japanese say. Even the most severe punishment Japanese children ever get is regarded as 'medicine.' This is the burning of a little cone of powder, the *moxa*, upon the child's skin. It leaves a lifelong scar. Cauterization by *moxa* is an old, widespread Eastern Asiatic medicine, and it was traditionally used to cure many aches and pains in Japan too. It can also cure tantrums and obstinacy. A little boy of six or seven may be 'cured' in this way by his mother or his grandmother. It may even be used twice in a difficult case but very seldom indeed is a child given the *moxa* treatment for naughtiness a third time. It is not a punishment in the sense that 'I'll spank you if you do that' is a punishment. But it hurts far worse than spanking, and the child learns that he cannot be naughty with impunity.

Besides these means of dealing with obstreperous children, there are conventions for teaching necessary physical skills. There is great emphasis on the instructor's putting children with his own hands physically through the motions. The child should be passive. Before the child is two

years old, the father folds its legs for it in the correct sitting position, legs folded back and instep to the floor. The child finds it difficult at first not to fall over backward, especially since an indispensable part of the sitting training is the emphasis on immobility. He must not fidget or shift position. The way to learn, they say, is to relax and be passive, and this passivity is underscored by the father's placing of his legs. Sitting is not the only physical position to be learned. There is also sleeping. Modesty in a woman's sleeping position is as strong in Japan as modesty about being seen naked is in the United States. Though the Japanese did not feel shame in nudity in the bath until the government tried to introduce it during their campaign to win the approval of foreigners, their feeling about sleeping positions is very strong. The girl child must learn to sleep straight with her legs together, though the boy has greater freedom. It is one of the first rules which separate the training of boys and girls. Like almost all other requirements in Japan, it is stricter in upper classes than in lower, and Mrs. Sugimoto says of her own samurai upbringing: 'From the time I can remember I was always careful about lying quiet on my little wooden pillow at night. . . Samurai daughters were taught never to lose control of mind or body—even in sleep. Boys might stretch themselves into the character *dai*, carelessly outspread; but girls must curve into the modest, dignified character *kinoji*, which means "spirit of control." '*
Women have told me how their mothers or nurses arranged their limbs for them when they put them to bed at night.

* Sugimoto, Etsu Inagaki, *A Daughter of the Samurai*. Doubleday Page and Company, 1926, pp. 15, 24.

In the traditional teaching of writing, too, the instructor took the child's hand and made the ideographs. It was 'to give him the feel.' The child learned to experience the controlled, rhythmic movements before he could recognize the characters, much less write them. In modern mass education this method of teaching is less pronounced but it still occurs. The bow, the handling of chopsticks, shooting an arrow, or tying a pillow on the back in lieu of a baby may all be taught by moving the child's hands and physically placing his body in the correct position.

Except among the upper classes children do not wait to go to school before they play freely with other children of the neighborhood. In the villages they form little play gangs before they are three and even in towns and cities they play with startling freedom in and out of vehicles in the crowded streets. They are privileged beings. They hang around the shops listening to grown-ups, or play hopscotch or handball. They gather for play at the village shrine, safe in the protection of its patron spirit. Girls and boys play together until they go to school, and for two or three years after, but closest ties are likely to be between children of the same sex and especially between children of the same chronological age. These age-groups (*donen*), especially in the villages, are lifelong and survive all others. In the village of Suye Mura, 'as sexual interests decrease parties of donen are the true pleasures left in life. Suye (the village) says, "Donen are closer than a wife." '*

These pre-school children's gangs are very free with each other. Many of their games are unabashedly obscene from

* Embree, John F., *Suye Mura*, p. 190.

a Western point of view. The children know the facts of life both because of the freedom of grown-ups' conversation and because of the close quarters in which a Japanese family lives. Besides, their mothers ordinarily call attention to their children's genitals when they play with them and bathe them, certainly to those of their boy children. The Japanese do not condemn childish sexuality except when it is indulged in the wrong places and in wrong company. Masturbation is not regarded as dangerous. The children's gangs are also very free in hurling criticisms at each other—criticisms which in later life would be insults—and in boasting—boasts which would later be occasions of deep shame. 'Children,' the Japanese say, their eyes smiling benignantly, 'know no shame (*haji*).' They add, 'That is why they are so happy.' It is the great gulf fixed between the little child and the adult, for to say of a grown person, 'He knows no shame' is to say that he is lost to decency.

Children of this age criticize each other's homes and possessions and they boast especially about their fathers. 'My father is stronger than yours,' 'My father is smarter than yours' is common coin. They come to blows over their respective fathers. This kind of behavior seems to Americans hardly worth noting, but in Japan it is in great contrast to the conversation children hear all about them. Every adult's reference to his own home is phrased as 'my wretched house' and to his neighbor's as 'your august house'; every reference to his family, as 'my miserable family,' and to his neighbor's as 'your honorable family.' Japanese agree that for many years of childhood—from the time the children's play gangs form till the third year of elementary school, when the children are nine—they occupy themselves constantly with these individualistic claims. Sometimes it is, 'I will play overlord and you'll be my retainers.' 'No, I won't be a servant. I will be overlord.' Sometimes it is personal boasts and derogation of the others. 'They are free to say whatever they want. As they get older they find that what they want isn't allowed, and then they wait till they're asked and they don't boast any more.'

The child learns in the home his attitudes toward the supernatural. The priest does not 'teach' him and generally a child's experiences with organized religion are on those occasions when he goes to a popular festival and, along with all others who attend, is sprinkled by the priest for purification. Some children are taken to Buddhist services, but usually this too occurs at festivals. The child's constant and most deep-seated experiences with religion are always the family observances that center around the Buddhist and the Shinto shrines in his own home. The more conspicuous is the Buddhist shrine with the family grave tablets before which are offered flowers, branches of a certain tree, and incense. Food offerings are placed there daily and the elders of the family announce all family events to the ancestors and bow daily before the shrine. In the evening little lamps are lighted there. It is quite common for people to say that they do not like to sleep away from home because they feel lost without these presences which preside over the house. The Shinto shrine is usually a simple shelf dominated by a charm from the temple of Ise. Other sorts of offerings may be presented here. Then too there is the Kitchen-god covered with soot in the kitchen, and a host of charms may be fastened on doors and walls. They are all protections and make home safe. In the villages the village shrine is similarly a safe place because benevolent gods protect it with their presence. Mothers like to have their children play there where it is safe. Nothing in the child's experience makes him fear the gods or shape his conduct to satisfy just or censorious gods. They should be graciously entertained in return for their benefits. They are not authoritarian.

The serious business of fitting a boy into the circumspect patterns of adult Japanese life does not really begin till after he has been in school for two or three years. Up to that time he has been taught physical control, and when he was obstreperous, his naughtiness has been 'cured' and his attention distracted. He has been unobtrusively admonished and he has been teased. But he has been allowed to be willful, even to the extent of using violence against his mother. His little ego has been fostered. Not much changes when he first goes to school. The first three grades are co-educational and the teacher, whether a man or a woman, pets the children and is one of them. More emphasis at home and in school, however, is laid on the dangers of getting into 'embarrassing' situations. Children are still too young for 'shame,' but they must be taught to avoid being 'embarrassed.' The boy in the story who cried 'Wolf, wolf' when there was no wolf, for instance, 'fooled people. If you do anything of this kind, people do not trust you and that is an embarrassing fact.' Many Japanese say that it was their schoolmates who laughed at them first when they made mistakes—not their teachers or their parents. The job of their elders, indeed, is not, at this point, themselves to use ridicule on the children, but gradually to integrate the fact of ridicule with the moral lesson of living up to giri-to-the-world. Obligations which were, when the children were six, the loving devotion of a faithful dog—the story of the good dog's *on*, quoted earlier, is from the six-year-olds' reader—now gradually become a whole series of restraints. 'If you do this, if you do that,' their elders say, 'the world will laugh at you.' The rules are particularistic and situational and a great many of them concern what we should call etiquette. They require subordinating one's own will to the ever-increasing duties to neighbors, to family and to country. The child must restrain himself, he must recognize his indebtedness. He passes gradually to the status of a debtor who must walk circumspectly if he is ever to pay back what he owes.

This change of status is communicated to the growing boy by a new and serious extension of the pattern of babyhood teasing. By the time he is eight or nine his family may in sober truth reject him. If his teacher reports that he has been disobedient or disrespectful and gives him a black mark in deportment, his family turn against him. If he is criticized for some mischief by the storekeeper, 'the family name has been disgraced.' His family are a solid phalanx of accusation. Two Japanese I have known were told by their fathers before they were ten not to come home again and were too shamed to go to relatives. They had been punished by their teachers in the schoolroom. In both cases they lived in outhouses, where their mothers found them and finally arranged for their return. Boys in later elementary school are sometimes confined to the house for *kinshin*, 'repentance,' and must occupy themselves with that Japanese obsession, the writing of diaries. In any case the family shows that now it looks upon the boy as their representative in the world and they proceed against him because he has incurred criticism. He has not lived up to his giri-to-the-world. He cannot look to his family for support. Nor can he look to his age group. His schoolmates ostracize him for offenses and he has to apologize and make promises before he is readmitted.

'It is worth emphasizing,' as Geoffrey Gorer says, 'that the degree to which this is carried is very uncommon sociologically. In most societies where the extended family or other fractional social group is operative, the group will usually rally to protect one of its members who is under criticism or attack from members of other groups. Provided that the approval of one's own group is maintained, one can face the rest of the world with the assurance of full support in case of need or attack. In Japan however it appears that the reverse is the case; one is only sure of support from one's own group as long as approval is given by other groups; if outsiders disapprove or criticize, one's own group will turn against one and act as the punishing agents, until or unless the individual can force the other group to withdraw its criticism. By this mechanism the approval of the "outside world" takes on an importance probably unparalleled in any other society.'*

The girl's training up to this point does not differ in kind from the boy's, however different in detail. She is more re-

* Gorer, Geoffrey, *Japanese Character Structure,* mimeographed, The Institute for International Studies, 1943, p. 27.

strained than her brother in the home. More duties are put upon her—though the little boy too may be nursemaid—and she always gets the little end of the horn in matters of presents and attention. She does not have the characteristic boys' tantrums, either. But she has been wonderfully free for an Asiatic little girl. Dressed in bright reds, she has played in the streets with the boys, she has fought with them and often held up her own end. She, too, as a child 'knew no shame.' Between six and nine she gradually learns her responsibilities to 'the world' much as her brother does and by much the same experiences. At nine the school classes are divided into girls' and boys' sections, and boys make a great deal of their new male solidarity. They exclude girls and object to having people see them talking to them. Girls, too, are warned by their mothers that such association is improper. Girls at this age are said to become sullen and withdrawn and hard to teach. Japanese women have said that it is the end of 'childish fun.' Childhood ends for girls in an exclusion. They have no path marked out for them now for many, many years but 'to double jicho with jicho.' The lesson will go on and on, both when they are betrothed and when they are married.

Boys, however, have not yet, when they have learned jicho and giri-to-the-world, acquired all that is incumbent upon an adult Japanese male. 'From the age of ten,' Japanese say, 'he learns giri-to-his-name.' They mean of course that he learns that it is a virtue to resent insult. He must learn the rules too: when to close with the adversary and when to take indirect means to clear his honor. I do not think they mean that the boy has to learn the aggressiveness that the insult behavior implies; boys who have been allowed in early childhood so much aggressiveness toward their mothers and who have fought out with their age mates so many kinds of slurs and counterclaims, hardly have to learn to be aggressive when they are ten. But the code of giri-to-one's-name, when boys are included under its provisions in their teens, channels their aggressiveness into accepted forms and provides them with specified ways of dealing with it. As we have seen, the Japanese often turn this aggressiveness against themselves instead of using violence against others. Even school boys are no exception.

For those boys who continue their schooling beyond the six-year elementary school—some 15 per cent of the population, though the proportion in the male population is larger—the time when they are becoming responsible for giri-to-their-name falls when they are suddenly exposed to the fierce competition of middle-school entrance examinations and the competitive ranking of every student in every subject. There is no gradual experience which leads up to this, for competition is minimized almost to the vanishing point in elementary school and at home. The sudden new experience helps to make rivalry bitter and preoccupying. Competition for place and suspicion of favoritism are rife. This competition, however, does not figure so largely in the life stories as does the middle-school convention of older boys tormenting the lower classmen. The upper classes of middle-school order the younger classes about and put them through various kinds of hazing. They make them do silly and humiliating stunts. Resentments are extremely common, for Japanese boys do not take such things in a spirit of fun.

A younger boy who has been made to grovel before an upper-classman and run servile errands hates his tormentor and plans revenge. The fact that the revenge has to be postponed makes it all the more absorbing. It is giri-to-his-name and he regards it as a virtue. Sometimes he is able, through family pull, to get the tormentor discharged from a job years later. Sometimes he perfects himself in jujitsu or sword play and publicly humiliates him on a city street after they have both left school. But unless he sometime evens the score he has that 'feeling of something left undone' which is the core of the Japanese insult contest.

For those boys who do not go on to middle school, the same kind of experience may come in their Army training. In peacetime one boy in four was drafted, and the hazing of first-year recruits by second-year recruits was even more extreme than in the middle and upper schools. It had nothing to do with officers in the Army, and only exceptionally even with non-commissioned officers. The first article of the Japanese code was that any appeal to officers caused one to lose face. It was fought out among the recruits. The officers accepted it as a method of 'hardening' troops but they were not involved. Second-year men passed on to the first-years the resentments they had accumulated the year before and proved their 'hardness' by their ingenuity in devising humiliations. The draftees have often been described as coming out of their Army training with changed personalities, as 'true jingo nationalists,' but the change is not so much because they are taught any theory of the totalitarian state and certainly not because of any inculcation of chu to the Emperor. The experience of being put through humiliating stunts is much more important. Young men trained in family life in the Japanese manner and deadly serious about their *amour-propre* may easily become brutalized in such a situation. They cannot stand ridicule. What they interpret as rejection may make them good torturers in their turn.

These modern Japanese situations in middle school and in the Army take their character, of course, from old Japanese customs about ridicule and insult. The middle and upper schools and the Army did not create the Japanese reaction to them. It is easy to see that the traditional code of giri-to-one's-name makes hazing practices rankle more bitterly in Japan than they do in America. It is also consistent with old patterns that the fact that each hazed group will pass on the punishment in time to a victim group does not prevent a boy's preoccupation with settling scores with his actual tormentor. Scapegoating is not the constantly recurring folkway in Japan that it is in many Western nations. In Poland, for instance, where new apprentices and even young harvesters are severely hazed, resentment is not vented against the hazers, but upon the next crop of apprentices and harvesters. Japanese boys will also have this satisfaction, of course, but they are primarily concerned with the immediate insult contest. The tormented 'feel good' when they are able to settle scores with the tormentors.

In the reconstruction of Japan those leaders who have their country's future at heart would do well to pay particular attention to hazing and the custom of making boys do silly stunts in the post-adolescent schools and in the Army. They would do well to emphasize school spirit, even the 'old school tie,' in order to break down the upper-under classmen distinctions. In the Army they would do well to forbid hazing. Even though the second-year recruits should insist on Spartan discipline in their relations with the first-years, as Japanese officers of all ranks did, such insistence is no insult in Japan. The hazing behavior is. If no older boy in school or Army could with impunity make a younger one wag his tail like a dog or perform like a cicada or stand on his head while the others ate, it would be a change more effective in the re-education of Japan than denials of the Emperor's divinity or elimination of nationalistic material from textbooks.

Women do not learn the code of giri-to-one's-name and they do not have the modern experiences of boys' middle schools and Army training. Nor do they go through analogous experiences. Their life cycle is much more consistent than their brothers'. From their earliest memories they have been trained to accept the fact that boys get the precedence and the attention and the presents which are denied to them. The rule of life which they must honor denies them the privilege of overt self-assertion. Nevertheless, as babies and as little children, they have shared with their brothers the privileged life of little children in Japan. They have been specially dressed in bright reds as little girls, a color they will give up as adults until they are allowed it again when they reach their second privileged period at the age of sixty. In the home they may be courted like their brothers in the contest between mother and grandmother. Their brothers and sisters, too, demand that a sister, like any other member of the family, like them 'best.' The children ask her to show her preference by letting them sleep with her, and she can often distribute her favors from the grandmothers to the two-year-old baby. Japanese do not like to sleep alone, and a child's pallet can be laid at night close up beside that of a chosen elder's. The proof that 'you like me best' that day is very often that the beds of the two are pulled up close together. Girls are allowed compensations even at the period when they are excluded from boys' play groups at nine or ten. They are flattered by new kinds of hair-do, and at the age of fourteen to eighteen their coiffure is the most elaborate in Japan. They reach the age when they may wear silk instead of cotton and when every effort is made to provide them with clothes that enhance their charms. In these ways girls are given certain gratifications.

The responsibility for the restraints that are required of them, too, is placed squarely upon them, and not vested in an arbitrarily authoritarian parent. Parents exercise their prerogatives not by corporal punishments but by their calm, unswerving expectation that the girl will live up to what is required of her. It is worthwhile quoting an extreme example of such training because it gives so well the kind of non-authoritarian pressure which is also characteristic of less strict and privileged upbringing. From the age of six little Etsu Inagaki was taught to memorize the Chinese classics by a learned Confucian scholar.

> Throughout my two-hour lesson he never moved the slightest fraction of an inch except for his hands and his lips. And I sat before him on the matting in an equally correct and unchanging position. Once I moved. It was in the midst of a lesson. For some reason I was restless and swayed my body slightly, allowing my folded knee to slip a trifle from the proper angle. The faintest shade of surprise crossed my

> instructor's face; then very quietly he closed his book, saying gently but with a stern air: 'Little Miss, it is evident that your mental attitude today is not suited for study. You should retire to your room and meditate.' My little heart was almost killed with shame. There was nothing I could do. I humbly bowed to the picture of Confucius and then to my teacher, and, backing respectfully from the room, I slowly went to my father to report as I always did, at the close of my lesson. Father was surprised, as the time was not yet up, and his unconscious remark, 'How quickly you have done your work!' was like a death knell. The memory of that moment hurts like a bruise to this very day.*

And Mrs. Sugimoto summarizes one of the most characteristic parental attitudes in Japan when she describes a grandmother in another context:

> Serenely she expected everyone to do as she approved; there was no scolding nor arguing, but her expectation, soft as silk floss and quite as strong, held her little family to the paths that seemed right to her.

One of the reasons why this 'expectation, soft as silk floss and quite as strong,' can be so effective is that training is so explicit for every art and skill. It is the *habit* that is taught, not just the rules. Whether it is proper use of chopsticks in childhood or proper ways of entering a room, or is the tea ceremony or massage later in life, the movements are performed over and over literally under the hands of grown-ups till they are automatic. Adults do not consider that children will 'pick up' the proper habits when the time to employ them comes around. Mrs. Sugimoto describes how she set her husband's table after she was betrothed at four-

* Sugimoto, Etsu Inagaki, *A Daughter of the Samurai.* Doubleday Page and Company, 1926, p. 20.

teen. She had never seen her future husband. He was in America and she was in Echigo, but over and over, under her mother's and her grandmother's eyes, 'I myself cooked the food which Brother told us Matsuo especially liked. His table was placed next to mine and I arranged for it to be always served before my own. Thus I learned to be watchful for the comfort of my prospective husband. Grandmother and Mother always spoke as if Matsuo were present, and I was as careful of my dress and conduct as if he had really been in the room. Thus I grew to respect him and to respect my own position as his wife.'*

A boy too receives careful habit training by example and imitation, though it is less intensive than the girl's. When he has 'learned,' no alibi is accepted. After adolescence, however, he is left, in one important field of his life, largely to his own initiative. His elders do not teach him habits of courting. The home is a circle from which all overt amorous behavior is excluded, and the segregation of unrelated boys and girls has been extreme since he was nine or ten. The Japanese ideal is that his parents will arrange a marriage for him before he has really been interested in sex, and it is therefore desirable that a boy should be 'shy' in his behavior with girls. In the villages there is a vast amount of teasing on the subject which often does keep boys 'shy.' But boys try to learn. In the old days, and even recently in more isolated villages of Japan, many girls, sometimes the great majority, were pregnant before marriage. Such pre-marital experience was a 'free area' not involved in the serious business of life. The parents were expected to arrange the mar-

* *A Daughter of the Samurai*, p. 92.

riages without reference to these affairs. But nowadays, as a Japanese said to Doctor Embree in Suye Mura, 'Even a servant girl has enough education to know that she must keep her virginity.' Discipline for those boys who go to middle school, too, is sternly directed against any kind of association with the opposite sex. Japanese education and public opinion tries to prevent pre-marital familiarity between the sexes. In their movies, they reckon as 'bad' those young men who show some signs of being at ease with a young woman; the 'good' ones are those who, to American eyes, are brusque and even uncivil to an attractive girl. Being at ease with a girl means that these boys have 'played around,' or have sought out geishas or prostitutes or café girls. The geisha house is the 'best' way to learn because 'she teaches you. A man can relax and just watch.' He need not be afraid of exhibiting clumsiness, and sex relations with the geisha girl are not expected of him. But not many Japanese boys can afford the geisha house. They can go to cafés and watch how men treat the girls familiarly, but such observation is not the kind of training they have learned to expect in other fields. Boys keep their fear of gaucherie for a long time. Sex is one of the few areas of their lives where they have to learn some new kind of behavior without the personal tutelage of accredited elders. Families of standing provide 'bride books' and screens with many detailed pictures for the young couple when they marry, and, as one Japanese said, 'You can learn from books, the way you learn the rules for making a garden. Your father doesn't teach you how to make a Japanese garden; it's a hobby you learn when you're older.' The juxtaposition of sex and gardening as two things you learn from books is interesting, even though most Japanese young men learn sex behavior in other ways. In any case, they do not learn through meticulous adult tutelage. This difference in training underscores for the young man the Japanese tenet that sex is an area removed from that serious business of life over which his elders preside and in which they painstakingly train his habits. It is an area of self-gratification which he masters with much fear of embarrassment. The two areas have their different rules. After his marriage he may have sexual pleasures elsewhere without being in the least surreptitious about it, and in so doing he does not infringe upon his wife's rights nor threaten the stability of his marriage.

His wife has not the same privilege. Her duty is faithfulness to her husband. She would have to be surreptitious. Even when she might be tempted, comparatively few women in Japan live their lives in sufficient privacy to carry off a love affair. Women who are regarded as nervous or unstable are said to have *hysteri*. 'The most frequent difficulty of women involves not their social but their sexual lives. Many cases of insanity and most of *hysteri* (nervousness, instability) are clearly due to sexual maladjustments. A girl must take whatever her husband may give her of sexual satisfaction.'* Most women's diseases, the farmers say in Suye Mura, 'begin in the womb' and then go to the head. When her husband looks elsewhere, she may have recourse to the accepted Japanese customs of masturbation, and, from the peasant villages to the homes of the great, women

* Embree, J. F., *Suye Mura*, p. 175.

treasure traditional implements for this purpose. She is granted in the villages, moreover, certain exuberances in erotic behavior when she has borne a child. Before she is a mother, she would not make a sex joke, but afterward, and as she grows older, her conversation at a mixed party is full of them. She entertains the party, too, with very free sexual dances, jerking her hips back and forth to the accompaniment of ribald songs. 'These performances invariably bring roars of laughter.' In Suye Mura, too, when recruits were welcomed back at the outskirts of the village after their Army training, women dressed as men and made obscene jokes and pretended to rape young girls.

Japanese women are therefore allowed certain kinds of freedom about sexual matters, the more, too, the lower-born they are. They must observe many taboos during most of their lives but there is no taboo which requires them to deny that they know the facts of life. When it gratifies the men, they are obscene. Likewise, when it gratifies the men, they are asexual. When they are of ripe age, they may throw off taboos, and if they are low-born, be as ribald as any man. The Japanese aim at proper behavior for various ages and occasions rather than at consistent characters like the Occidental 'pure woman' and the 'hussy.'

The man also has his exuberances, as well as his areas where great restraint is required. Drinking in male company, especially with geisha attendants, is a gratification which he makes the most of. Japanese men enjoy being tipsy and there is no rule which bids a man carry his liquor well. They relax their formal postures when they have had a few thimblefuls of *sake*, and they like to lean against each other and be very familiar. They are seldom violent or aggressive when they are drunk, though a few 'hard-to-get-along-with men' may get quarrelsome. Apart from such 'free areas' as drinking, men should never be, as they say, unexpected. To speak of anyone, in the serious conduct of his life, as unexpected, is the nearest the Japanese come to a curse word except for the word 'fool.'

The contradictions which all Westerners have described in Japanese character are intelligible from their child rearing. It produces a duality in their outlook on life, neither side of which can be ignored. From their experience of privilege and psychological ease in babyhood they retain through all the disciplines of later life the memory of an easier life when they 'did not know shame.' They do not have to paint a Heaven in the future; they have it in their past. They rephrase their childhood in their doctrine of the innate goodness of man, of the benevolence of their gods, and of the incomparable desirability of being a Japanese. It makes it easy for them to base their ethics on extreme interpretations of the 'Buddha-seed' in every man and of every man's becoming a kami on death. It gives them assertiveness and a certain self-confidence. It underlies their frequent willingness to tackle any job, no matter how far above their ability it may seem to be. It underlies their readiness to pit their judgment even against their own Government, and to testify to it by suicide. On occasion, it gives them a capacity for mass megalomania.

Gradually, after they are six or seven, responsibility for circumspection and 'knowing shame' is put upon them and upheld by the most drastic of sanctions: that their own family will turn against them if they default. The pressure is not that of a Prussian discipline, but it is inescapable. In their early privileged period the ground has been prepared for this development both by the persistent inescapable training in nursery habits and posture, and by the parents' teasing which threatens the child with rejection. These early experiences prepare the child to accept great restraints upon himself when he is told that 'the world' will laugh at him and reject him. He clamps down upon the impulses he expressed so freely in earlier life, not because they are evil but because they are now inappropriate. He is now entering upon serious life. As he is progressively denied the privileges of childhood he is granted the gratifications of greater and greater adulthood, but the experiences of that earlier period never truly fade out. In his philosophy of life he draws freely upon them. He goes back to them in his permissiveness about 'human feelings.' He re-experiences them all through his adulthood in his 'free areas' of life.

One striking continuity connects the earlier and the later period of the child's life: the great importance of being accepted by his fellows. This, and not an absolute standard of virtue, is what is inculcated in him. In early childhood, his mother took him into her bed when he was old enough to ask, he counted the candies he and his brothers and sisters were given as a sign of how he ranked in his mother's affection, he was quick to notice when he was passed over and he asked even his older sister, 'Do you love me *best*?' In the later period he is asked to forego more and more personal satisfactions, but the promised reward is that he will be approved and accepted by 'the world.' The punishment is that 'the world' will laugh at him. This is of course a sanction invoked in child training in most cultures, but it is exceptionally heavy in Japan. Rejection by 'the world' has been dramatized for the child by his parents' teasing when they threatened to get rid of him. All his life ostracism is more dreaded than violence. He is allergic to threats of ridicule and rejection, even when he merely conjures them up in his own mind. Because there is little privacy in a Japanese community, too, it is no fantasy that 'the world' knows practically everything he does and can reject him if it disapproves. Even the construction of the Japanese house—the thin walls that permit the passage of sounds and which are pushed open during the day—makes private life extremely public for those who cannot afford a wall and garden.

Certain symbols the Japanese use help to make clear the two sides of their character which are based on the discontinuity of their child rearing. That side which is built up in the earliest period is the 'self without shame,' and they test how far they have kept it when they look at their own faces in the mirror. The mirror, they say, 'reflects eternal purity.' It does not foster vanity nor reflect the 'interfering self.' It reflects the depths of the soul. A person should see there his 'self without shame.' In the mirror he sees his own eyes as the 'door' of his soul, and this helps him to live as a 'self without shame.' He sees there the idealized parental image. There are descriptions of men who always carry a mirror with them for this purpose, and even of one who set up a special mirror in his household shrine in which to contemplate himself and examine his soul; he 'enshrined himself'; he 'worshipped himself.' It was unusual, but it was only a small step to take, for all household Shinto shrines have mirrors on them as sacred objects. During the war the Japanese radio carried a special paean of approval for a classroom of girls who had bought themselves a mirror. There was no thought of its being a sign of vanity. It was described as a renewed dedication to calm purposes in the depths of their souls. Looking into it was an external observance which would testify to the virtue of their spirit.

Japanese feelings about the mirror are derived from the time before the 'observing self' was inculcated in the child. They do not see the 'observing self' in the looking glass. There their selves are spontaneously good as they were in childhood, without the mentor of 'shame.' The same symbolism they attribute to the mirror is the basis too of their ideas of 'expert' self-discipline, in which they train themselves with such persistence to eliminate the 'observing self' and get back the directness of early childhood.

In spite of all the influences their privileged early childhood has upon the Japanese, the restraints of the succeeding period when shame becomes the basis of virtue are not felt solely as deprivations. Self-sacrifice, as we have seen, is one of the Christian concepts they have often challenged; they repudiate the idea that they are sacrificing themselves. Even in extreme cases, the Japanese speak, instead, of 'voluntary' death in payment of chu or ko or giri, and this does not seem to them to fall in the category of self-sacrifice. Such a voluntary death, they say, achieves an object you yourself desire. Otherwise it would be a 'dog's death,' which means to them a worthless death; it does not mean, as in English, death in the gutter. Less extreme courses of conduct, too, which in English are called self-sacrificing, in Japanese belong rather in the category of self-respect. Self-respect (jicho) always means restraint, and restraint is valuable just as self-respect is. Great things can only be achieved through self-restraint, and the American emphasis on freedom as a prerequisite for achievement has never seemed to them, with their different experiences, to be adequate. They accept as a principal tenet in their code the idea that through self-restraint they make their selves more valuable. How else could they control their dangerous selves, full of impulses that might break out and confound a proper life? As one Japanese expresses it:

> The more coats of varnish that are laid on the foundation by laborious work throughout the years, the more valuable becomes the lacquer work as a finished product. So it is with a people . . . It is said of the Russians: 'Scratch a Russian and you find a Tartar.' One might with equal justice say of the Japanese: 'Scratch a Japanese, scrape off the varnish, and you find a pirate.' Yet it should not be forgotten that in Japan varnish is a valuable product and an aid to handicraft. There is nothing spurious about it; it is not a daub to cover defects. It is at least as valuable as the substance it adorns.*

The contradictions in Japanese male behavior which are so conspicuous to Westerners are made possible by the discontinuity of their upbringing, which leaves in their consciousness, even after all the 'lacquering' they undergo, the deep imprint of a time when they were like little gods in their little world, when they were free to gratify even their aggressions, and when all satisfactions seemed possible. Be-

* Nohara, Komakichi, *The True Face of Japan*. London, 1936, p. 50.

cause of this deeply implanted dualism, they can swing as adults from excesses of romantic love to utter submission to the family. They can indulge in pleasure and ease, no matter to what lengths they go in accepting extreme obligations. Their training in circumspection makes them in action an often timid people, but they are brave even to foolhardiness. They can prove themselves remarkably submissive in hierarchal situations and yet not be easily amenable to control from above. In spite of all their politeness, they can retain arrogance. They can accept fanatic discipline in the Army and yet be insubordinate. They can be passionately conservative and yet be attracted by new ways, as they have successively demonstrated in their adoption of Chinese customs and of Western learning.

The dualism in their characters creates tensions to which different Japanese respond in different ways, though each is making his own solution of the same essential problem of reconciling the spontaneity and acceptance he experienced in early childhood with the restraints which promise security in later life. A good many have difficulty in resolving this problem. Some stake everything on ruling their lives like pedants and are deeply fearful of any spontaneous encounter with life. The fear is the greater because spontaneity is no fantasy but something they once experienced. They remain aloof, and, by adhering to the rules they have made their own, feel that they have identified themselves with all that speaks with authority. Some are more dissociated. They are afraid of their own aggressiveness which they dam up in their souls and cover with a bland surface behavior. They often keep their thoughts busy with trivial minutiae in order to stave off awareness of their real feelings. They are mechanical in the performance of a disciplined routine which is fundamentally meaningless to them. Others, who have been more caught by their early childhood, feel a consuming anxiety in the face of all that is demanded of them as adults and try to increase their dependence when it is no longer appropriate. They feel that any failure is an aggression against authority and any striving therefore throws them into great agitation. Unforeseen situations which cannot be handled by rote are frightening to them.*

These are characteristic dangers to which the Japanese are exposed when their anxiety about rejection and censure are too much for them. When they are not overpressed, they show in their lives both the capacity for enjoying life and the carefulness not to step on others' toes which has been bred into them in their upbringing. It is a very considerable achievement. Their early childhood has given them assertiveness. It has not awakened a burdening sense of guilt. The later restraints have been imposed in the name of solidarity with their fellows, and the obligations are reciprocal. There are designated 'free areas' where impulse life can still be gratified, no matter how much other people may interfere with their wishes in certain matters. The Japanese have always been famous for the pleasure they get from innocent things: viewing the cherry blossoms, the moon, chrysanthemums, or new fallen snow; keeping insects caged in the house for their 'song'; writing little verses;

* Cases based on Rorschach tests given to Japanese in War Relocation Camp by Doctor Dorothea Leighton, and analyzed by Frances Holter.

making gardens; arranging flowers, and drinking ceremonial tea. These are not activities of a deeply troubled and aggressive people. They do not take their pleasures sadly either. A Japanese rural community, in those happier days before Japan embarked on its disastrous Mission, could be in its leisure time as cheerful and sanguine as any living people. In its hours of work it could be as diligent.

But the Japanese ask a great deal of themselves. To avoid the great threats of ostracism and detraction, they must give up personal gratifications they have learned to savor. They must put these impulses under lock and key in the important affairs of life. The few who violate this pattern run the risk of losing even their respect for themselves. Those who do respect themselves (jicho) chart their course, not between 'good' and 'evil,' but between 'expected man' and 'unexpected man,' and sink their own personal demands in the collective 'expectation.' These are the good men who 'know shame (haji)' and are endlessly circumspect. They are the men who bring honor to their families, their villages, and their nation. The tensions that are thus generated are enormous, and they express themselves in a high level of aspiration which has made Japan a leader in the Orient and a great power in the world. But these tensions are a heavy strain upon the individual. Men must be watchful lest they fail, or lest anyone belittle their performances in a course of action which has cost them so much abnegation. Sometimes people explode in the most aggressive acts. They are roused to these aggressions, not when their principles or their freedom is challenged, as Americans are, but when they detect an insult or a detraction. Then their dangerous selves erupt, against the detractor if that is possible, otherwise against themselves.

The Japanese have paid a high price for their way of life. They have denied themselves simple freedoms which Americans count upon as unquestioningly as the air they breathe. We must remember, now that the Japanese are looking to de-mok-ra-sie since their defeat, how intoxicating it can be to them to act quite simply and innocently as one pleases. No one has expressed this better than Mrs. Sugimoto in describing the plant as-you-please garden she was given at the mission school in Tokyo where she was sent to learn English. The teachers let each girl have a plot of wild ground and any seeds she asked for.

> This plant-as-you-please garden gave me a wholly new feeling of personal right. . . . The very fact that such happiness could exist in the human heart was a surprise to me. . . . I, with no violation of tradition, no stain on the family name, no shock to parent, teacher or townspeople, no harm to anything in the world was free to act.*

All the other girls planted flowers. She arranged to plant—potatoes.

> No one knows the sense of reckless freedom which this absurd act gave me. . . . The spirit of freedom came knocking at my door.

It was a new world.

> At my home there was one part of the garden that was supposed to be wild. . . . But someone was always busy trimming the pines or cutting the hedge, and every morning Jiya wiped off the stepping stones, and, after sweeping beneath the pine trees, carefully scattered fresh pine needles gathered from the forest.

* *A Daughter of the Samurai*, pp. 135–136.

This simulated wildness stood to her for the simulated freedom of will in which she had been trained. And all Japan was full of it. Every great half-sunken rock in Japanese gardens has been carefully chosen and transported and laid on a hidden platform of small stones. Its placing is carefully calculated in relation to the stream, the house, the shrubs, and the trees. So, too, chrysanthemums are grown in pots and arranged for the annual flower shows all over Japan with each perfect petal separately disposed by the grower's hand and often held in place by a tiny invisible wire rack inserted in the living flower.

Mrs. Sugimoto's intoxication when she was offered a chance to put aside the wire rack was happy and innocent. The chrysanthemum which had been grown in the little pot and which had submitted to the meticulous disposition of its petals discovered pure joy in being natural. But today among the Japanese, the freedom to be 'unexpected,' to question the sanctions of haji (shame), can upset the delicate balance of their way of life. Under a new dispensation they will have to learn new sanctions. And change is costly. It is not easy to work out new assumptions and new virtues. The Western world can neither suppose that the Japanese can take these on sight and make them truly their own, nor must it imagine that Japan cannot ultimately work out a freer, less rigorous ethics. The Nisei in the United States have already lost the knowledge and the practice of the Japanese code, and nothing in their ancestry holds them rigidly to the conventions of the country from which their parents came. So too the Japanese in Japan can, in a new era, set up a way of life which does not demand the old requirements of individual restraint. Chrysanthemums can be beautiful without wire racks and such drastic pruning.

In this transition to a greater psychic freedom, the Japanese have certain old traditional virtues which can help to keep them on an even keel. One of these is that self-responsibility which they phrase as their accountability for 'the rust of my body,'—that figure of speech which identifies one's body with a sword. As the wearer of a sword is responsible for its shining brilliancy, so each man must accept responsibility for the outcome of his acts. He must acknowledge and accept all natural consequences of his weakness, his lack of persistence, his ineffectualness. Self-responsibility is far more drastically interpreted in Japan than in free America. In this Japanese sense the sword becomes, not a symbol of aggression, but a simile of ideal and self-responsible man. No balance wheel can be better than this virtue in a dispensation which honors individual freedom, and Japanese child-rearing and philosophy of conduct have inculcated it as a part of the Japanese Spirit. Today the Japanese have proposed 'to lay aside the sword' in the Western sense. In their Japanese sense, they have an abiding strength in their concern with keeping an inner sword free from the rust which always threatens it. In their phraseology of virtue the sword is a symbol they can keep in a freer and more peaceful world.

13

The Japanese Since VJ-Day

AMERICANS have good reason to be proud of their part in the administration of Japan since VJ-Day. The policy of the United States was laid down in the State-War-Navy directive which was transmitted by radio on August 29, and it has been administered with skill by General MacArthur. The excellent grounds for such pride have often been obscured by partisan praise and criticism in the American press and on the radio, and few people have known enough about Japanese culture to be sure whether a given policy was desirable or undesirable.

The great issue at the time of Japan's surrender was the nature of the occupation. Were the victors to use the existing government, even the Emperor, or was it to be liquidated? Was there to be a town-by-town, province-by-province administration, with Military Government officers of the United States in command? The pattern in Italy and Germany had been to set up local A.M.G. headquarters as integral parts of the combat forces, and to place authority for local domestic matters in the hands of the Allied administrators. On VJ-Day, those in charge of A.M.G. in the Pacific still expected to institute such a rule in Japan. The

Japanese also did not know what responsibility for their own affairs they would be allowed to retain. The Potsdam Proclamation had stated only that 'points in Japanese territory to be designated by the Allies shall be occupied to secure the basic objectives we are here setting forth,' and that there must be eliminated for all time 'the authority and influence of those who have deceived and misled the people of Japan into embarking on world conquest.'

The State-War-Navy directive to General MacArthur embodied a great decision on these matters, a decision which General MacArthur's Headquarters fully supported. The Japanese were to be responsible for the administration and reconstruction of their country. 'The Supreme Commander will exercise his authority through Japanese governmental machinery and agencies, including the Emperor, to the extent that this satisfactorily furthers United States objectives. The Japanese government will be permitted, under his instructions (General MacArthur's), to exercise the normal powers of government in matters of domestic administration.' General MacArthur's administration of Japan is, therefore, quite unlike that of Germany or Italy. It is exclusively a headquarters organization, utilizing Japanese officialdom from top to bottom. It addresses its communications to the Imperial Japanese Government, not to the Japanese people or to the residents of some town or province. Its business is to state goals for the Japanese government to work toward. If a Japanese Minister believes them impossible, he can offer to resign, but, if his case is good, he may get the directive modified.

This kind of administration was a bold move. The advantages of this policy from the point of view of the United States are clear enough. As General Hilldring said at the time:

> The advantages which are gained through the utilization of the national government are enormous. If there were no Japanese Government available for our use, we would have to operate directly the whole complicated machine required for the administration of a country of seventy million people. These people differ from us in language, customs, and attitudes. By cleaning up and using the Japanese Government machinery as a tool we are saving our time and our manpower and our resources. In other words, we are requiring the Japanese to do their own house-cleaning, but we are providing the specifications.

When this directive was being drawn up in Washington, however, there were still many Americans who feared that the Japanese would be sullen and hostile, a nation of watchful avengers who might sabotage any peaceful program. These fears did not prove to be justified. And the reasons lay in the curious culture of Japan more than in any universal truths about defeated nations or politics or economics. Probably among no other peoples would a policy of good faith have paid off as well as it did in Japan. In Japanese eyes it removed from the stark fact of defeat the symbols of humiliation and challenged them to put into effect a new national policy, acceptance of which was possible precisely because of the culturally conditioned character of the Japanese.

In the United States we have argued endlessly about hard and soft peace terms. The real issue is not between hard and soft. The problem is to use that amount of hardness, no more and no less, which will break up old and dangerous patterns of aggressiveness and set new goals. The means to be chosen depend on the character of the people and upon the traditional social order of the nation in question. Prussian authoritarianism, embedded as it is in the family and in the daily civic life, makes necessary certain kinds of peace terms for Germany. Wise peace directives would differ from those for Japan. Germans do not regard themselves, like the Japanese, as debtors to the world and to the ages. They strive, not to repay an incalculable debt, but to avoid being victims. The father is an authoritarian figure, and, like any other person who has superior status, it is he who, as the phrase is, 'enforces respect.' It is he who feels himself threatened if he does not get it. In German life each generation of sons revolt in adolescence against their authoritarian fathers and then regard themselves as surrendering finally at adulthood to a drab and unexciting life which they identify as that of their parents. The high point of existence remains, for life, those years of the *Sturm und Drang* of adolescent rebellion.

The problem in Japanese culture is not crass authoritarianism. The father is a person who treats his young children with a respect and fondness which has seemed to almost all Western observers to be exceptional in Occidental experience. Because the Japanese child takes for granted certain kinds of real comradeship with his father and is overtly proud of him, the father's simple change of voice can make the child carry out his wishes. But the father is no martinet to his young children, and adolescence is not a period of revolt against parental authority. Rather it is a period when children become the responsible and obedient representatives of their family before the judging eyes of the world. They show respect to their fathers, as the Japanese say, 'for the practice,' 'for the training,' that is, as a respect-object he is a depersonalized symbol of hierarchy and of the proper conduct of life.

This attitude which is learned by the child in his earliest experiences with his father becomes a pattern throughout Japanese society. Men who are accorded the highest marks of respect because of their hierarchal position do not characteristically themselves wield arbitrary power. The officials who head the hierarchy do not typically exercise the actual authority. From the Emperor down, advisers and hidden forces work in the background. One of the most accurate descriptions of this aspect of Japanese society was given by the leader of one of the super-patriotic societies of the type of the Black Dragon to a Tokyo English-newspaper reporter in the early 1930s. 'Society,' he said, meaning of course Japan, 'is a triangle controlled by a pin in one corner.'* The triangle, in other words, lies on the table for all to see. The pin is invisible. Sometimes the triangle lies to the right, sometimes to the left. It swings on a pivot which never avows itself. Everything is done, as Westerners so often say, 'with mirrors.' Every effort is made to minimize the appearance of arbitrary authority, and to make every act appear to be a gesture of loyalty to the status-symbol who is so constantly divorced from real exercise of power. When the Japanese do identify a source of unmasked power, they regard it, as they have always regarded the moneylender

* Quoted by Upton Close, *Behind the Face of Japan*, 1942, p. 136.

and the *narikin*, as exploitive and as unworthy of their system.

The Japanese, viewing their world in this way, can stage revolts against exploitation and injustice without ever becoming revolutionists. They do not offer to tear the fabric of their world in pieces. They can institute the most thoroughgoing changes, as they did in the Meiji era, without casting any aspersion upon the system. They called it a Restoration, a 'dipping back' into the past. They are not revolutionists, and Western writers who have based their hopes upon ideological mass movements in Japan, who during the war magnified the Japanese underground and looked to it for leadership in capitulation, and who since VJ-Day have prophesied the triumph of radical policies at the polls, have gravely misunderstood the situation. They have been wrong in the prophecies they have made. The conservative Premier, Baron Shidehara, spoke more accurately for the Japanese when he formed his cabinet in October, 1945:

> The Government of the new Japan has a democratic form which respects the will of the people. . . . In our country from olden days the Emperor made his will the will of the people. This is the spirit of Emperor Meiji's Constitution, and the democratic government I am speaking of can be considered truly a manifestation of this spirit.

Such a phrasing of democracy seems less than nothing to American readers, but there is no doubt that Japan can more readily extend the area of civil liberties and build up the welfare of her people on the basis of such an identification than on the basis of Occidental ideology.

Japan will, of course, experiment with Western political

mechanics of democracy, but the Western arrangements will not be trusted tools with which to fashion a better world, as they are in the United States. Popular elections and the legislative authority of elected persons will create as many difficulties as they solve. When such difficulties develop, Japan will modify the methods upon which we rely to achieve democracy. Then American voices will be raised to say that the war has been fought in vain. We believe in the rightness of our tools. At best, however, popular elections will be peripheral to Japanese reconstruction as a peaceful nation for a long time to come. Japan has not changed so fundamentally since the 1890s, when she first experimented with elections, that some of the old difficulties Lafcadio Hearn described then will not be likely to recur:

> There was really no personal animosity in those furious election contests which cost so many lives; there was scarcely any personal antagonism in those parliamentary debates of which the violence astonished strangers. The political struggles were not really between individuals but between clan interests or party interests; and the devoted followers of each clan or party understood the new politics only as a new kind of war—a war of loyalty to be fought for the leader's sake.*

In more recent elections in the nineteen-twenties, villagers used to say before they cast their ballots, 'My neck is washed clean for the sword,' a phrase which identified the contest with the old attacks of the privileged samurai upon the common people. All the connotations of elections in Japan will

* *Japan: An Interpretation,* 1904, p. 453.

differ even today from those in the United States, and this will be true quite apart from whether Japan is or is not pursuing dangerous aggressive policies.

Japan's real strength which she can use in remaking herself into a peaceful nation lies in her ability to say of a course of action, 'That failed,' and then to throw her energies into other channels. The Japanese have an ethic of alternatives. They tried to achieve their 'proper place' in war, and they lost. That course, now, they can discard, because their whole training has conditioned them to possible changes of direction. Nations with a more absolutist ethic must convince themselves that they are fighting for principles. When they surrender to the victors, they say, 'Right was lost when we were defeated,' and their self-respect demands that they work to make this 'right' win next time. Or they can beat their breasts and confess their guilt. The Japanese need do neither. Five days after VJ-Day, before an American had landed on Japan, the great Tokyo paper, the *Mainichi Shimbun*, could speak of defeat and of the political changes it would bring, and say, 'But it was all to the good for the ultimate salvation of Japan.' The editorial stressed that no one should forget for a moment that they had been completely defeated. Because their effort to build up a Japan based on sheer might had met with utter failure, they must henceforth tread the path of a peaceful nation. The *Asahi*, another great Tokyo newspaper, that same week characterized Japan's late 'excessive faith in military force' as 'a serious error' in its national and international policy. 'The old attitude, from which we could gain so little and suffered so much, should be discarded for a new one which is rooted in international co-operation and love of peace.'

The Westerner observes this shift in what he regards as principles and suspects it. It is, however, an integral part of the conduct of life in Japan, whether in personal or in international relations. The Japanese sees that he has made an 'error' in embarking on a course of action which does not achieve its goal. When it fails, he discards it as a lost cause, for he is not conditioned to pursue lost causes. 'It is no use,' he says, 'biting one's navel.' Militarism was in the nineteen-thirties the accepted means by which they thought to gain the admiration of the world—an admiration to be based on their armed might—and they accepted all the sacrifices such a program required. On August 14, 1945, the Emperor, the sanctioned voice of Japan, told them that they had lost. They accepted all that such a fact implied. It meant the presence of American troops, so they welcomed them. It meant the failure of their dynastic enterprise, so they were willing to consider a Constitution which outlawed war. Ten days after VJ-Day, their newspaper, the *Yomiuri-Hochi*, could write about the 'Beginning of a New Art and New Culture,' and could say, 'There must be a firm conviction in our hearts that military defeat has nothing to do with the value of a nation's culture. Military defeat should serve as an impetus . . . (for) it has taken no less than national defeat for the Japanese people to lift their minds truly to the world, to see things objectively as they really are. Every irrationality that has warped Japanese thinking must be eliminated by frank analysis. . . . It takes courage to look this defeat in the face as a stark fact, (but we must) put our faith in Nippon's culture of tomorrow.' They had tried one course of action and been defeated. Today they would try the peaceful arts of life. 'Japan,' their editorials repeated, 'must be respected among the nations of the world,' and it was the duty of the Japanese to deserve this respect on a new basis.

These newspaper editorials were not just the voice of a few intellectuals; the common people on a Tokyo street and in a remote village make the same right-about-face. It has been incredible to American occupying troops that these friendly people are the ones who had vowed to fight to the death with bamboo spears. The Japanese ethic contains much which Americans repudiate, but American experiences during the occupation of Japan have been an excellent demonstration of how many favorable aspects a strange ethic can have.

American administration of Japan under General MacArthur has accepted this Japanese ability to sail a new course. It has not impeded that course by insisting on using techniques of humiliation. It would have been culturally acceptable according to Western ethics if we had done so. For it is a tenet of Occidental ethics that humiliation and punishment are socially effective means to bring about a wrongdoer's conviction of sin. Such admission of sin is then a first step in his rehabilitation. The Japanese, as we have seen, state the issue in another way. Their ethic makes a man responsible for all the implications of his acts, and the natural consequences of an error should convince him of its undesirability. These natural consequences may even be defeat in an all-out war. But these are not situations which the Japanese must resent as humiliating. In the Japanese lexicon, a person or a nation humiliates another by detraction, ridicule, contempt, belittling, and insisting on symbols of dishonor. When the Japanese believe themselves humiliated, revenge is a virtue. No matter how strongly Western ethics condemn such a tenet, the effectiveness of American occupation of Japan depends on American self-restraint on this point. For the Japanese separate ridicule, which they terribly resent, from 'natural consequences,' which according to the terms of their surrender include such things as demilitarization and even Spartan imposition of indemnities.

Japan, in her one great victory over a major power, showed that even as a victor she could carefully avoid humiliating a defeated enemy when it finally capitulated and when she did not consider that that nation had sneered at her. There is a famous photograph of the surrender of the Russian Army at Port Arthur in 1905 which is known to every Japanese. It shows the Russians wearing their swords. The victors and the vanquished can be distinguished only by their uniforms for the Russians were not stripped of their arms. The well-known Japanese account of that surrender tells that when General Stoessel, the Russian commander, signified his willingness to receive Japanese propositions of surrender, a Japanese captain and interpreter went to his headquarters taking food. 'All the horses except General Stoessel's own had been killed and eaten so that the present of fifty chickens and a hundred fresh eggs which the Japanese brought with them was welcome indeed.' The meeting of General Stoessel and General Nogi was arranged for the following day. 'The two generals clasped hands. Stoessel expressed his admiration for the courage of the Japanese and . . . General Nogi praised the long and brave defense of the Russians. Stoessel expressed his sympathy with Nogi for the loss of his two sons in the campaign. . . . Stoessel presented his fine white Arab horse to General Nogi, but Nogi said that, much as he would like to receive it as his own from the General's hands, it must first be presented to the Emperor. He promised, however, that if it came back to him, as he had every reason to believe it would, he would take care of it as if it had always been his.'* Everyone in Japan knew the stable which General Nogi built for General Stoessel's horse in his front yard—a stable often described as more pretentious than Nogi's own house, and after General Nogi's death a part of the Nogi national shrine.

It has been said that the Japanese have changed between that day of the Russian surrender and the years of their occupation of the Philippines, for instance, when their wanton destructiveness and cruelty were known to all the world. To a people with the extreme situational ethics of the Japanese, however, this is not the necessary conclusion. In the first place, the enemy did not capitulate after Bataan; there was only a local surrender. Even when the Japanese, in their turn, surrendered in the Philippines, Japan was still fighting. In the second place, the Japanese never considered that the Russians had 'insulted' them in the early years of this century, whereas every Japanese was reared in the nineteen-twenties and -thirties to regard United States policy as 'taking Japan cheap,' or in their phrase, 'making her as faeces.' This had been Japan's reaction to the Exclusion Act, to the part the United States played in the Treaty of Ports-

* Quoted from a Japanese account, by Upton Close, *Behind the Face of Japan*, 1942, p. 294. This version of the Russian surrender does not have to be literally true to have cultural importance.

mouth and in the Naval Parity agreements. The Japanese had been encouraged to regard in the same way the growing economic rôle of the United States in the Far East and our racial attitudes toward the non-white peoples of the world. The victory over Russia and the victory over the United States in the Philippines, therefore, illustrate Japanese behavior in its two most opposed aspects: when insults are involved and when they are not.

The final victory of the United States again changed the situation for the Japanese. Their ultimate defeat brought about, as is usual in Japanese life, the abandonment of the course they had been pursuing. The peculiar ethic of the Japanese allowed them to wipe the slate clean. United States policy and General MacArthur's administration have avoided writing fresh symbols of humiliation upon that washed slate, and have held simply to insisting on those things which in Japanese eyes are 'natural consequences' of defeat. It has worked.

The retention of the Emperor has been of great importance. It has been handled well. It was the Emperor who called first upon General MacArthur, not MacArthur upon him, and this was an object lesson to the Japanese the force of which it is hard for Westerners to appreciate. It is said that when it was suggested to the Emperor that he disavow his divinity, he protested that it would be a personal embarrassment to strip himself of something he did not have. The Japanese, he said truthfully, did not consider him a god in the Western sense. MacArthur's Headquarters, however, urged upon him that the Occidental idea of his claim to divinity was bad for Japan's international repute, and the

Emperor agreed to accept the embarrassment the disavowal would cost him. He spoke on New Year's Day, and asked to have all comments on his message translated for him from the world press. When he had read them, he sent a message to General MacArthur's Headquarters saying that he was satisfied. Foreigners had obviously not understood before, and he was glad he had spoken.

The policy of the United States has also allowed the Japanese certain gratifications. The State-Army-Navy directive specifies that 'encouragement shall be given and favor shown to the development of organizations in labor, industry and agriculture, organized on a democratic basis.' Japanese labor has organized in many industries, and the old farmers' unions which were active in the 1920s and 1930s are asserting themselves again. To many Japanese this initiative which they can now take to better their condition is a proof that Japan has won something as a consequence of this war. One American correspondent tells of a striker in Tokyo who looked up at a G.I. and said, beaming broadly, 'Japan *win*, no?' Strikes in Japan today have many parallels to the old Peasants' Revolts where the farmers' plea was always that the taxes and corvées to which they were subject interfered with adequate production. They were not class warfare in the Western sense, and they were not an attempt to change the system itself. Throughout Japan today strikes do not slow up production. The favorite form is for the workers 'to occupy the plant, continue work and make management lose face by increasing production. Strikers at a Mitsui-owned coal mine barred all management personnel from the pits and stepped daily output up from 250 tons to 620. Workers at Ashio copper mines operated during a "strike," increased production, and doubled their own wages.'*

The administration of any defeated country is, of course, difficult, no matter how much good sense the accepted policy shows. In Japan the problems of food and shelter and reconversion are inevitably acute. They would be at least equally acute under an administration which did not make use of Japanese governmental personnel. The problem of demobilized soldiers, which was so much dreaded by American administrators before the war ended, is certainly less threatening than it would have been if Japanese officials had not been retained. But it is not easily solved. The Japanese are aware of the difficulty and their newspapers spoke feelingly last fall about how bitter the brew of defeat was to the soldiers who had suffered and lost, and it begged them not to let this interfere with their 'judgment.' The repatriated army has in general shown remarkable 'judgment,' but unemployment and defeat throw some soldiers into the old pattern of secret societies for nationalistic goals. They can easily resent their present status. The Japanese no longer accord them their old privileged position. The wounded soldier used to be clothed all in white and people bowed to him on the street. Even a peacetime Army recruit was given a send-off party and a welcome-home party by his hamlet. There were drinks and refreshments and dancing and costumes, and he sat in the place of honor. Now the repatriated soldier gets no such attentions. His family makes a place for him, but that is all. In many cities and towns he

* *Time*, February 18, 1946.

is cold-shouldered. It is easy, knowing how bitterly the Japanese take such a change of behavior, to imagine his satisfaction in joining up with his old comrades to bring back the old days when the glory of Japan was entrusted to soldiers' hands. Some of his war comrades will tell him, too, how luckier Japanese soldiers are already fighting with the Allies in Java and in Shansi and in Manchuria; why should he despair? He too will fight again, they will tell him. Nationalistic secret societies are old, old institutions in Japan; they 'cleared the name' of Japan. Men conditioned to feel that 'the world tips' so long as anything is left undone to even scores were always possible candidates for such undercover societies. The violence which these societies, such as the Black Dragon and the Black Ocean, espoused is the violence which Japanese ethics allows as giri to one's name, and the long effort of the Japanese Government to emphasize gimu at the expense of giri to one's name will have to be continued in the coming years if this violence is to be eliminated.

It will require more than an appeal to 'judgment.' It will require a reconstruction of Japanese economy which will give a livelihood and 'proper place' to men who are now in their twenties and thirties. It will require improvement in the lot of the farmer. The Japanese return, whenever there is economic distress, to their old farm villages, and the tiny farms, encumbered with debts and in many places with rents, cannot feed many more mouths. Industry too must be set going, for the strong feeling against dividing the inheritance with younger sons eventually sends all but the eldest out to seek their fortune in the city.

The Japanese have a long hard road before them, no doubt, but if rearmament is not provided for in the State budget they have an opportunity to raise their national standard of living. A nation like Japan which spent half its national income on armament and the armed forces for a decade before Pearl Harbor can lay the foundation of a healthy economy if it outlaws such expenditures and progressively reduces its requisitions from the farmers. As we have seen, the Japanese formula for division of farm products was 60 per cent for the cultivator; 40 per cent he paid out in taxes and rents. This is in great contrast to rice countries like Burma and Siam where 90 per cent was the traditional proportion left to the cultivator. This huge requisition upon the cultivator in Japan was what ultimately made possible the financing of the national war machine.

Any European or Asiatic country which is not arming during the next decade will have a potential advantage over the countries which are arming, for its wealth can be used to build a healthy and prosperous economy. In the United States we hardly take this situation into account in our Asiatic and European policies, for we know that we would not be impoverished in this country by expensive programs of national defense. Our country was not devastated. We are not primarily an agricultural country. Our crucial problem is industrial overproduction. We have perfected mass production and mechanical equipment until our population cannot find employment unless we set in motion great programs of armament or of luxury production or of welfare and research services. The need for profitable investment of capital is also acute. This situation is quite different outside the United States. It is different even in Western Europe. In spite of all demands for reparations, a Germany which is not allowed to rearm could in a decade or so have laid the foundations of a sound and prosperous economy which would be impossible in France if her policy is to build up great military power. Japan could make the most of a similar advantage over China. Militarization is a current goal in China and her ambitions are supported by the United States. Japan, if she does not include militarization in her budget, can, if she will, provide for her own prosperity before many years, and she could make herself indispensable in the commerce of the East. She could base her economy on the profits of peace and raise the standard of living of her people. Such a peaceful Japan could attain a place of honor among the nations of the world, and the United States could be of great assistance if it continued to use its influence in support of such a program.

What the United States cannot do—what no outside nation could do—is to create by fiat a free, democratic Japan. It has never worked in any dominated country. No foreigner can decree, for a people who have not his habits and assumptions, a manner of life after his own image. The Japanese cannot be legislated into accepting the authority of elected persons and ignoring 'proper station' as it is set up in their hierarchal system. They cannot be legislated into adopting the free and easy human contacts to which we are accustomed in the United States, the imperative demand to be independent, the passion each individual has to choose his own mate, his own job, the house he will live in and the obligations he will assume. The Japanese themselves, however, are quite articulate about changes in this direction which they regard as necessary. Their public men have said since VJ-Day that Japan must encourage its men and women to live their own lives and to trust their own consciences. They do not say so, of course, but any Japanese understands that they are questioning the rôle of 'shame' (haji) in Japan, and that they hope for a new growth of freedom among their countrymen: freedom from fear of the criticism and ostracism of 'the world.'

For social pressures in Japan, no matter how voluntarily embraced, ask too much of the individual. They require him to conceal his emotions, to give up his desires, and to stand as the exposed representative of a family, an organization or a nation. The Japanese have shown that they can take all the self-discipline such a course requires. But the weight upon them is extremely heavy. They have to repress too much for their own good. Fearing to venture upon a life which is less costly to their psyches, they have been led by militarists upon a course where the costs pile up interminably. Having paid so high a price, they became self-righteous and have been contemptuous of people with a less demanding ethic.

The Japanese have taken the first great step toward social change by identifying aggressive warfare as an 'error' and a lost cause. They hope to buy their passage back to a respected place among peaceful nations. It will have to be a peaceful world. If Russia and the United States spend the coming years in arming for attack, Japan will use her know-how to fight in that war. But to admit that certainty does not call in question the inherent possibility of a peaceful Japan. Japan's motivations are situational. She will seek her place within a world at peace if circumstances permit. If not, within a world organized as an armed camp.

At present the Japanese know militarism as a light that failed. They will watch to see whether it has also failed in other nations of the world. If it has not, Japan can relight her own warlike ardor and show how well she can contribute. If it has failed elsewhere, Japan can set herself to prove how well she has learned the lesson that imperialistic dynastic enterprises are no road to honor.

*Glossary**

ai, love; specifically a superior's love of a dependent.

arigato, thank you; 'this difficult thing.'

buraku, a hamlet of some fifteen houses; a district in a village.

bushido, 'the way of the samurai.' A term popularized during this century to designate traditional Japanese ideals of conduct. Doctor Inazo Nitobe in *Bushido, The Soul of Japan*, itemizes as Bushido: rectitude or justice, courage, benevolence, politeness, sincerity, honor, loyalty, and self-control.

chu, fealty to the Emperor.

daimyo, a feudal lord.

donen, age-mates.

eta, a pariah class in pre-Meiji times.

geisha, a courtesan especially trained and given high prestige.

gi, righteousness.

gimu, a category of Japanese obligations. *Vide* Chart, p. 116.

giri, a category of Japanese obligations. *Vide* Chart, p. 116.

go, a unit of measure of capacity; less than one cup.

haji, shame.

haraki'ri or ***seppuku***, suicide according to the samurai code. Seppuku is the more elegant term.

* Literal translations are in quotation marks.

When no accent is indicated, give all syllables equal value. The accents which are marked are rough approximations meant only to help English-speaking readers.

Vowels and diphthongs are sounded as follows:

a as in *art*	*i* as in *police*
ai as in *aisle*	*ĭ* as in *tin*
e as in *get*	*o* as in *pole*
ei as in *veil*	*u* as in *rude*

g is always hard, as in *go*.

hysteri, nervousness and instability. Generally used of women.

inkyo, the state of formal retirement from active life.

Issei, an American of Japanese ancestry born in Japan. *Vide* Nisei.

isshin, to restore, to dip back into the past. A slogan of the Meiji Restoration.

jen (Chinese), good human relations, benevolence.

jicho', self-respect; circumspection. 'To double jicho with jicho,' to be superlatively circumspect.

jin (written with the same character as Chinese *jen*), obligation which is outside the obligatory code. But *vide* 'knowing *jin*,' p. 119, footnote.

jingi (variant of jin), an obligation outside the obligatory code.

jiri'ki, 'self-help,' spiritual training dependent solely on one's own disciplined human powers. *Vide* tariki.

judo, a form of jujitsu. Japanese wrestling.

jujitsu, Japanese wrestling.

kabuki, popular drama. *Vide* noh.

kagura, traditional dances performed at Shinto shrines.

kami, head, source. Shinto term for deity.

kamika'ze, 'divine wind.' The hurricane which drove back and overturned Genghis Khan's invading fleet in the thirteenth century. The pilots of suicide planes in World War II were called the Kamikaze Corps.

katajikĕnai', thank you; 'I am insulted.'

kino do'ku, thank you; 'this poisonous feeling.'

kinshin, repentance. A period of withdrawal to remove 'the rust of the body.'

ko, filial piety.

koan (pronounce *ko-an*), problems having no rational answer, set by the Zen cult for those in training.

ko-on, obligation to the Emperor, the State.

magokoro, 'sincerity.'

makoto, 'sincerity.'

Glossary

Meiji Era, the period of the reign of the Emperor Meiji, 1868–1912. It designates the beginning of the modern era in Japan.

moxa, powdered leaves of a certain plant, which are burned in a cone on the surface of the body for curative purposes. It cures ailments and naughtiness.

muga, the elimination of the observer-self achieved by those who have taken training.

narikin', *nouveau riche.* 'A pawn promoted to queen' (chess).

nirva'na (Sanskrit), final emancipation of the soul from transmigration; state of not-being; absorption into the divine.

Nisei, an American of Japanese ancestry born in the United States. *Vide* Issei.

noh, classic drama. *Vide* kabuki.

nushi, master.

on (pronounce *own*), a category of incurred obligations. *Vide* Chart, p. 116.

oya, parents.

ronin, in feudal times samurai retainers who, because of disgrace or because of the death or dishonor of their overlord, had become masterless men.

sake (pronounce *sa-ke*), a rice-beer which is the principal alcoholic drink of the Japanese.

samurai, in feudal times the warriors, two-sword men. Below them were the common people: farmers, artisans, and merchants.

satori, Buddhist enlightenment.

seppu'ku or *haraki'ri,* suicide by piercing the abdomen. In feudal times it was the exclusive privilege of the nobles and samurai.

shogun, in pre-Meiji times the actual ruler of Japan; succession was hereditary as long as a family could remain in power. The Shogun was always invested by the Emperor.

shuyo, self-discipline; mental training.

sonno joi, 'Restore the Emperor and expel the barbarians (Westerners).' A slogan of the Meiji Restoration.

sumimasen', thank you; I'm sorry; 'this never ends.'

sutra (Sanskrit), short collections of dialogues and aphorisms. The disciples of Gautama Buddha wrote such sutras in the conversational idiom of their day (Pali).

tai setsu, Higher Law.

tari'ki, 'help of another.' Spiritual blessing which is an act of grace. *Vide* jiriki.

tonari gumi, small neighborhood groups of about five to ten families.

yoga (Sanskrit), a form of ascetic philosophy and practice prevalent in India from earliest historical times.

zaibatsu, big business; influential members of the economic hierarchy.

Zen, a Buddhist cult introduced from China and important in Japan since the twelfth century. It was an upper-class cult of the rulers and warriors and still contrasts with the great tariki Buddhist cults with their huge membership.

Index

Index

Index

To order use coupon on next page.